Blue-Collar Life

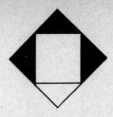

Blue-Collar Life

Arthur B. Shostak

Drexel Institute of Technology

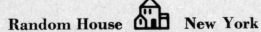

Random House **New York**

First Printing

Copyright © 1969 by Random House, Inc.
All rights reserved under International
and Pan-American Copyright Conventions. Published in the United States by
Random House, Inc., New York, and
simultaneously in Canada by Random
House of Canada Limited, Toronto.

Library of Congress Catalog Card Number: 72–79120

Manufactured in the United States of
America by Colonial Press, Clinton, Mass.

Designed by Saul Schnurman

For Scott, my oldest son, in the hope that this book may help his generation come together in new and enriching ways.

We are told in *The Origin of Species* that the greatest anomaly in nature is a bird that cannot fly. I should have thought it was a human spirit that cannot soar . . .

Attributed to Benjamin Disraeli by Theodore Bonnet, in *The Mudlark*, Doubleday, 1949.

Preface

America has a working class that is admired and even envied by people everywhere, but few of the admirers or envious really know very much about this country's blue-collarites. America is attempting to move millions of poverty dwellers into the ranks of its stable blue-collarites, but few decision makers are really acquainted with the life style they would have millions adopt. America anticipates the gradual disappearance of its blue-collarites into the lower middle-class, but few seers can really distinguish between the casual and the intransigent components of the blue-collar style of life. And America trusts in the power of incremental reforms to meet the deepest crisis of the times, but addresses few reforms to either the more casual or serious of underrecognized blue-collar problems.

Accordingly, my goal in this book is to help answer four related questions: Is the working class as well off as others believe? Is the life style of stable blue-collarites an unequivocal answer to the plight of the nation's poor? Is the American manual worker truly disappearing as a separate and distinct social, psychological, and political entity? And is there anything that social planning and deliberate social change can contribute to the blue-collar pursuit of the "good life"?

The American worker with whom I am concerned is the Caucasian male blue-collarite and his dependents, basically a group of 21 million men (including service workers not engaged in private household work). I do not discuss 5 million

Negro male blue-collarites for three reasons: There are not enough reliable research reports with which to work. Second, it appears that the Negro blue-collarite has much higher status within the black community than he has in the white, and, in other like ways, has significant social attributes that make his a special case. And finally, Negro and white blue-collarites are so differently distributed throughout the labor force as to strongly recommend separate consideration of each. In this volume I undertake an analysis exclusively of the situation of Caucasian workers; with a pilot interview study of 30 Negro blue-collar families completed in Spring 1968 I have already begun my own study and book on the black worker.

Similarly, in this volume I do not discuss nearly 9 million female blue-collarites of white and nonwhite races. Again, my reasons here are three: There are far too few reliable research reports with which to work. There is reason to believe the female worker has lower status within the larger community than does the male, and, in other like ways, has significant social attributes that make hers a special case. And finally, female and male blue-collarites are distributed so differently throughout the labor force, many more women than men being secondary wage-earners, as to strongly recommend the exclusion of female blue-collarites from this volume's concern. Separate treatment by another writer in another volume cannot come soon enough.

Two final refinements warrant review. I do not discuss the style of life of the nation's three million unemployed blue-collarites. Far too little is presently known in the matter to support more than speculation, although enough is known to suggest the appropriateness of discussion being set apart from that concerned with the situation of the steadily employed. Nor do I attempt generalizations about white male blue-collarites regardless of age. My research suggests to me that different age-cohorts, or generations, of blue-collarites have a life-experience peculiarly their own. Believing this, and anxious at the same time to illuminate the lives of the largest number of contemporary blue-collarites of my choice, I have elected to focus especially on one generation, that of the median-age forty-three-year-old Caucasian male worker.

With this book I hope to stimulate some of the vast amount of research that needs to be done on the life style of *all* blue-collar Americans. I am especially hopeful that others will join me hereafter in more explicit studies of the ultimate quality of a chosen style of life. New research, possibly stimulated in part by this book, must ask: How can the range of choice be maximized so that blue-collarites can choose freely from new alternatives to components of their style of life?

Should we soon replace cross-cultural and interclass envy with genuine insight, substitute for vague antipoverty goals a clearer notion of what really lies beyond poverty, and abandon gross cultural prophecy for far more refined prognosis, much will have been gained. Should we build on this foundation a new exploration of the overwhelming issue of the "good life"—directly where the blue-collarite is concerned, and of necessity, involving all our lives—so very much the better.

PHILADELPHIA   A.B.S.
AUGUST 1969

Acknowledgments

My task was made considerably easier by the generous cooperation of Professors Robert Blood, Jr., Charles H. Coates, N. J. Demerath, III, William Dobriner, Richard Hamilton, Sam Kaplan, Mirra Komarovsky, David Lockwood, Lee Rainwater, and Hyman J. Weiner, all of whom answered at length my inquiries concerning their original research on blue-collarites. General assistance was ably provided by undergraduates Bonnie Cosgrove, Veronica Krepol, and Thomas Land, while my graduate assistant for 1965–1967, Miss Phyllis Padow, handled the many difficult research tasks set her with skill and patience. Two good friends, Mrs. Beau-Janette Fleming and Mrs. Claire Cosgrove, along with my wife, Susan, and especially the Random House advisor in sociology, Charles Page, worked hard in helping me improve the book—for which they have my sincere gratitude. Ted Caris, Carol Green, and Claire Adams, and others of the Random House staff gave editorial assistance and personal assistance for which I am most grateful. My typists, Mrs. Betty Gallant, Mr. Arthur Harris, Mrs. Therese Johnson, Miss Wilma Liebman, Miss Lucretia Martinet, Miss Sandy Palmer, Miss Jean Robertas, Mrs. Suzanne Silverman, Miss Joanne Sweeny, and Miss Margaret Tunnell, contributed much beyond what their job title would suggest. Summer session financial support from Drexel Institute of Technology in 1967 and 1968 made possible the completion of necessary revisions, even as a Ford Foundation Faculty Research Fellowship for the summer and fall of 1965 made possible my release from teaching and consultant commitments, an invaluable aid in the four-year-long process of completing this book.

Contents

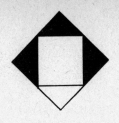

Part I

1

BLUE·COLLAR
PROFILE

*Rich man down and poor man up—they
are still not even.* —YIDDISH PROVERB

Typical of the kind of man this volume is concerned with
is a New Jerseyite, forty-one-year-old Leonard P. Scheno, a
maintenance machinist. Mr. Scheno was chosen by the federal
government in February 1967 to symbolize the twenty-five-
millionth voter to have participated since 1935 in a National
Labor Relations Board election. He serves equally well to
symbolize this volume's leading character, the contemporary
male Caucasian blue-collarite.

Leonard P. Scheno was born in 1928 in Nyack, New York, a
semirural upstate setting. The press report of his selection in
the *AFL-CIO News* notes that he met his wife Grace in Nyack

at a reunion for immigrant families whose forebears had come from the town of Cisternino, Italy. A Navy flight engineer in World War II, Mr. Scheno logged 2,000 flying hours, and was honorably discharged in 1948 at twenty years of age. He worked for two years thereafter under the GI Bill as an apprentice stereotyper on a local newspaper. In 1950 Mr. Scheno was recalled for Korean War service. After a stateside tour at a Naval Air Station, he married in 1952 (at twenty-four years of age) and began a family that now includes three youngsters (Geraldine, 15, and twins Nicolas and Grace, 14). In that year he also began a brief career as a manager of service stations on the New Jersey Turnpike and on the Garden State Parkway. He later operated a Cities Service retail dealership in Avenel, New Jersey, and at present works as a maintenance machinist at a new Reynolds Metals Co. aluminum can plant at Woodbridge, New Jersey, where he joined his first labor union, and was soon elected union treasurer.[1] Mr. Scheno now resides with his family in a comfortable blue-collar suburb in Carteret, New Jersey.

Note that Leonard Scheno's personal history contains the following sociological elements: semirural origins, ethnic and "foreign stock" ties, endogamous mate selection, and considerable job-switching, with more lateral than vertical occupational mobility. Correspondence with the gentleman has further established his Catholic religious preference, his upbringing in the home of a blue-collarite, and his moderate educational attainment (high school plus one year of technical school), all items likely of occurrence on the basis of what is known of male Caucasian blue-collarites as a whole.

More specifically, five demographic characteristics exemplified in Mr. Scheno's case especially set off the blue-collar sample of concern in this book. These five characteristics—"foreign stock" origins, rural origins, Catholic origins, blue-collar origins, and moderate educational attainment—are by no means exclusive to or even concentrated in blue-collar ranks. Proportionately more of the white poor than of white blue-collarites may have rural origins or low educational attainment, and proportionately more of the lower-echelon white-collarites

than of all blue-collarites profess a Catholic religious preference. Nevertheless, as far as this study's sample is concerned,
the extraordinary frequency with which these five particular
demographic characteristics occur, both separately and in
combination, compels further attention and analysis.

DEMOGRAPHIC CHARACTERISTICS

Foreign Stock Origin. Americans of foreign white stock (foreign-born or native-born of foreign or mixed parentage) are
greatly overrepresented in blue-collar occupations. These 33
million new Americans (61 percent are first generation) are
drawn especially from Italy, Germany, Canada, Poland, Russia,
and England. In the classic "Ellis Island" pattern, many of
these newcomers entered the American labor force at the
lower levels of the occupational ladder, and large numbers of
their first-generation progeny have not yet advanced significantly beyond their blue-collar origins. Indeed, so strong is the
ethnic influence in blue-collar affairs that sociologist Bennett
Berger concludes that we have no clear image of an "American
working-class style" precisely because our images here are
dominated by ethnic motifs, by bits and pieces of an "old
country" working-class style.[2]

Ethnicity retains much of its hold across generations, and
the persistence of a foreign and traditional ethos, or "flavor,"
in the life style of many blue-collarites becomes more understandable for this fact. Journalist Nicholas Pileggi, for example,
writes with affection of New York's many "Saturday Italians,"
or those prospering overweight sons of leaner immigrant
fathers who drive in now from suburbia to New York City's
Little Italy on weekends to replenish their ever-diminishing
ethnic supplies:

> They return, after all, not only for the bread, tiny bitter onions,
> bushels of snails, live eels and dried cod, but also to enjoy a
> weekend heritage that their education, blonde wives, and the
> English language have begun to deny them . . . it is only with

a trunk filled with Italian market produce that a Saturday Italian can face six days in the suburbs.[3]

Many other Americans seem to have a similar deep-rooted need to maintain some parochial marks—and to have them acknowledged as such by outsiders.

Support for religion, along with immersion in European traditions, support of in-group conviviality, and rejection of certain self-denigrating standards set by "Yankees" are related to the ethnicity of many blue-collarites. Also important is the practice whereby different ethnic groups exclude outsiders from blue-collar posts they monopolize, and pass the positions from father to sons through their control of the apprentice or hiring system (certain longshore locals, for example, are reputed to "belong" to a particular Italian or Polish neighborhood). Contrariwise, and equally significant, other ethnic groups bent on assimilation and upward class mobility diligently direct their offspring away from the once-honored lives of blue-collar toil. Writer Jimmy Breslin caustically observes that "the Irish in New York represent a way of life that never was Irish. The Irish always were poor and they measured value by other than material things. They sang and told stories and used words for entertainment. Their descendants in New York can't wait to get into the banking business." [4]

Ethnic affairs at present are in considerable flux. In July 1968 a new Immigration Act took effect, and immigration has begun to change as increasing numbers of Italians, Greeks, Chinese, Portuguese, and Filipinos replace declining numbers of English, Irish, Dutch, and Germans. (During 1968 approximately 444,000 immigrants were admitted, the highest number since 1924.) [5] The long-range effect of the new ethnic shift and build-up on the contemporary blue-collar style cannot be known. Altered patterns of immigration, however, and the steady pressure for assimilation on those foreign white stock Americans long here may combine to weaken the influence of ethnicity on blue-collar culture. Nevertheless, there remains at present a strong association between the style of life and the ethnic attachments of many blue-collarites. The striking persistence in the blue-collar mass of culturally differentiated ethnic blocs explains much of the record of the worker—and his future prospects.

Rural Origin. The rural origin of many foreign-born and of many native-born blue-collarites, while commonly overlooked, warrants serious attention. These blue-collarites have spent their childhood and adolescence on the farm or in rural communities, some on the Midwest prairies, some in the Northwest wheat belt, some on the Mississippi Delta, and others in the Appalachian thirteen-state area. The only national data available, gathered in 1958 and published as "still reliable" in 1964 by the U.S. Department of Agriculture, suggest that over 5.75 million of the nation's nearly 30 million blue-collarites (1958), or 18 percent, were born and raised on the nation's farms. Overrepresentation of ex-farm dwellers in urban blue-collar occupations is clear in the fact that in 1958, 60 percent of the nation's farm-born men had found their way into blue-collar jobs.[6] This, of course, is consistent with the farm-bred competence many have in mechanical and construction matters, their limited educational attainment, and their habituation to manual work.

The fact that blue-collarites were often raised in abject poverty on farms helps account for the present-day sense of achievement of many ex-rural city workers. (Whereas one person in eight is poor in the city, and one in fifteen in the suburbs, one of every four is poor in rural areas.)[7] In the countryside it is likely that a distinct set of values and attitudes earned reinforcement:

. . . [the farmers] are more traditional in religious beliefs, ascetic, work-oriented, puritanical, ethnocentric, isolationist, uninformed, unlikely to read books or newspapers, distrustful of people, intolerant of deviance, opposed to civil liberties, opposed to birth control, and favorable to early marriage and high fertility than all or most classes of urban workers. However, the evidence on political attitudes and interest is ambiguous, and farmers rank between urban manual and nonmanual workers in authoritarianism.[8]

Apropos the drift of the younger men away from farming, it is especially revealing that a smaller percentage of farmers than of any broad urban occupational category consider themselves "very happy." [9]

A number of contemporary blue-collar attributes are remarkably like those of rural dwellers and are regularly reinforced by the steady influx into manual work of people who have left the land. Relevant here are such items as parochialism in religion and politics, the presence of self-sufficient females in quasi-patriarchal homes, the development of large families, and the choice of outdoor recreational pursuits with a violence/ruggedness component. Opposition to trade unionism is also significant. Ingrained individualism, ignorance, isolation, mobility, apathy, poverty, and suspicions of outsiders impede the rural worker's capacity to act collectively—whether he lives on the land or in the city.

The ongoing exodus of 17 million farmers from the land in the last twenty-five years and the current influx of hill folk from the Southern Appalachian region into Northern industrial cities and Northern factories have bolstered the general blue-collar style of life in such important components as individualism, Puritanism, and stoicism. For example, many of the new blue-collarites shy away from dependency on public welfare; most endorse the Puritan ideal of industry and uprightness; and large numbers refrain from the personal expression of any sad, lonely, or anxious feeling (outside of their country "blues" music). These former ruralites figuratively link forces with the second-generation "foreign stock" sons of European immigrants to impress on the nation's blue-collar style of life the peasant ways and preference of (former) earth tillers everywhere.[10]

While nearly 11 million Americans remain in the farm population, the figure is down considerably from the 1950 total of 23 million, and the annual decline regularly approximates a 6 percent loss.[11] In time the Appalachian and Delta stream of "refugees" may reduce drastically, and the peasant legacy of the sons of foreign immigrants may fade with each intervening generation. Until then, however, the impact of the rural or hill culture on blue-collar ways remains a most significant one.

Catholic Origin.   Roman Catholics, much like individuals of white foreign stock and of farm origins, are greatly overrepresented today in blue-collar occupations. Although 47 million Roman Catholics make up only 4 percent of the nation's population, most reside in urban areas (80 percent of all Catholics, as compared with 60 percent of all Protestants) where they are usually employed in manufacturing and mining industries.[12] Sociologist Gerhard Lenski in 1958 compared white Protestants in Detroit with white Catholics in the city who began life at the *same* point in the class system; Catholics wound up in the lower half of the working class more often than did Protestants three times out of four.[13] Similarly, a 1960 national sample of 2,390 Catholics, when divided into three social classes, located 66 percent of the Catholics in the lower, 25 percent in the middle, and 9 percent in the upper class.[14] In an exceedingly controversial generalization Lenski suggests that "Protestantism is conducive to more positive attitudes toward those positions in society which are more demanding (and also more rewarding), while Catholicism is conducive to more positive attitudes toward the less demanding (and less rewarding) positions." [15]

Religious group membership is now recognized as a variable comparable to social class membership both with respect to its potency where style of life is concerned and with respect to the range and extent of its general influence. For example, although sociological data here are thin, a revealing picture of Catholic–non-Catholic differences can be constructed:

> In general, the American Catholic is less likely than his non-Catholic neighbor to become a social activist, more likely to vote Democratic (until he moves to suburbia), less likely to excel in the academic world (particularly the sciences), more likely to have a large family, less likely to make "Who's Who."
>
> If he reaches the top in American society, he is more likely to have made it through politics, the professions or show business. He is likely to stress order more than freedom, and more likely to favor strict laws enforcing sexual mores—though the pattern here seems to be breaking down.[16]

Accordingly, the significance of a "Catholic influence" on the life style of many blue-collarites becomes more understandable.

Strong ethnic ties, along with strong religious concern, traditional family patterns, a preference for large families, and endogamous mate selection take on new meaning when their association with the Catholic background of many blue-collarites is recognized. Although there is cause to recognize diversity in people's relationship to their religious experience and in the character of local urban parishes, there remains a solid core of Catholic "culture" that influences the life style of a sizable bloc of blue-collarites.

Blue-Collar Origins. Americans of blue-collar origins are greatly overrepresented in blue-collar occupations. Despite a popular mythology of considerable social mobility for Horatio Alger types from humble origins, the record of the past century suggests that blue-collar work has been a common legacy among the generations of a working-class family. Historian Stephan Thernstrom's exacting analysis of occupational mobility between 1850 and 1880 suggests that the climb upward from the bottom rungs of the social ladder was seldom rapid or easy. As a matter of fact, most of the upward occupational shifts made by workingmen one hundred years ago left them manual workers still. Few of these men and few of their children rose very far on the social scale.[17]

Current data indicate that "occupational inheritance" among the generations remains considerable, albeit the measuring and analysis of data pose very difficult problems. Studies by sociologists Natalie Rogoff, Seymour Martin Lipset, and Reinhard Bendix, among others, suggest that sons of every social class in America can generally be found in occupational levels that are the same as or are similar to those of their fathers.[18] In particular, men who start their working lives in manual jobs experience relatively little net intergenerational mobility, clearly less than those who begin careers in farm or white-collar jobs. Their erratic job changes serve only to take these men back to the occupations of their origins.[19]

In short, while enough variation occurs so that our social

mobility system cannot be considered rigid and unyielding, mobility nevertheless remains confined largely *within* the manual occupational strata (sons may hold skilled blue-collar jobs where their fathers held only unskilled jobs). This fact is thought to account for "perhaps the most fundamental cleavage in American society." [20]

Given the well-documented significance of the family as a prime agent for personality maintenance, status conferral, and socialization, the reinforcement of blue-collar ways across blue-collar generations becomes understandable. Sociologist Mirra Komarovsky notes of the fifty-four blue-collar families she studied in 1959 that the "impressive fact about them was their narrow generational cleavage":

> The parental family . . . remains their major reference group after marriage. The mother, for example, may be considered old-fashioned about sex and religion but in most respects the married woman's guide is still her mother and certainly not Dr. Spock nor even her own peer groups. . . . [The parents and relatives in general] may not have the motivation or the resources to regulate the lives of the young couples, but they do influence them. Their continuing impact stems from the lack of competing pressures. It is power by default because the relative insulation of the young couples from other social influences heightens the importance of relatives and, in turn, strengthens continuity of traditional patterns. [21]

Komarovsky adds later that her interviewers "felt transported, as if by a Wellsian Time Machine, into an older era . . ." [22]

Such attributes as dependency on one's immediate family and early marriage as an escape from one's parents, along with a materialistic evaluation of education's rewards and a tendency to take labor's side in labor-management conflicts, take on new meaning when their roots in a cross-generational blue-collar culture are recognized. Although individual family styles may vary within and across generations, much contemporary blue-collar behavior reflects the impact of a childhood spent immersed in a common blue-collar culture.

Moderate Educational Achievement. Finally, and in full recognition of the considerable overlap among the preceding categories (foreign white, rural-born, Catholic, and blue-collar origins), it is not surprising that Americans of moderate educational attainment are greatly overrepresented in blue-collar occupations. Whereas the median years of schooling completed by all white males in all occupation groups in 1968 was 12.4, the figure was only 12.0 for Caucasian male craftsmen, 11.3 for operatives, 10.1 for laborers (except farm and mine), and 11.9 for service workers, excluding private household.[23] Blue-collarites have a disproportionately large share of the 8 million members of the 74-million-member labor force without an eighth-grade education and of the 30 million other labor force members without a high school diploma. Some 67 percent of all Caucasian male blue-collarites in 1960 were high school dropouts, as compared to 35 percent for white-collarites and 9 percent for professionals.[24]

The picture does not change appreciably after formal schooling is completed or rejected. For example, little job-related education was uncovered in a rare nationwide survey conducted by the Department of Labor in 1963 to find out how adult workers (ages 22–64) had been trained for their occupational roles. Nearly 60 percent of blue-collar craftsmen in construction reported that they had not learned their specialties through much-touted apprenticeships, and nearly 90 percent of all semiskilled workers in factories had not received any formal job training.[25] Poorly schooled before beginning work, most blue-collarites receive little more schooling after starting work: The undereducated remain just that.

Given the importance of education and training in conditioning mental abilities, in shaping personality, and in helping to determine one's life chances, much of the blue-collar style not otherwise comprehensible becomes so.[26] An uncertain quality of mental reasoning, a depressed level of self-esteem, and a bleak record of vocational aspirations and career achievement take on new meaning when the poor educational history and meager training record of many workers is brought to mind. While campaigns to keep students at school, to upgrade schooling, and to advance men through on-the-job schooling may change the blue-collar educational record, the impact of the educational underachievement that characterizes millions of blue-collarites is presently considerable.

SUMMARY

Convinced that certain demographic features help shape much of the blue-collar workers' style of life, the chapter has focused on five such features: ethnicity, agrarianism, religiosity, occupational inheritance, and educational attainment. These demographic features complement and reinforce one another in various ways, their resonance going far to explain the hardiness and persistence of the blue-collar style of life in general and of its "old-fashioned" bias in particular. Later chapters will explore the many consequences of this built-in bias for the worker's struggle to maintain his bearings in our troubled times.

Notes to Chapter One

1. Eugene A. Kelley, "25-Millionth Vote Cast in Labor Board Ballot," *AFL-CIO News,* February 27, 1967, pp. 1, 5. See also Frank T. Paine, *et al.,* "Relationship Between Family Backgrounds and Work Values," *Journal of Applied Psychology* (August 1967), pp. 320–323.

2. Bennett M. Berger, *Working-Class Suburb* (Berkeley: University of California Press, 1960), p. 95. Berger adds: "But the end of mass immigration from Europe may promote the development of an indigenous white working-class culture in the United States in the near future" (p. 95). Cf. Joshua A. Fishman, *et al., Language Loyalty in the United States: The Maintenance and Perpetuation of Non-English Mother Tongues by American Ethnic and Religious Groups* (The Hague: Mouton and Co., 1966).

3. Nicholas Pileggi, "Saturday Italians," *New York World Journal Tribune,* January 15, 1967, pp. 12, 14. See also Leonard Co-

vello, *The Social Background of the Italo-American School Child* (Leiden, Netherlands: E. J. Brill, 1967); Nathan Glazer and Daniel A. Moynihan, *Beyond the Melting Pot* (Boston: Harvard University Press, 1963); John Greenway, *The Inevitable Americans* (New York: Knopf, 1963).

4. Jimmy Breslin, "The True Irish Export," *New York World Journal Tribune*, March 12, 1967, pp. 6–7. See also Mario Puzo, "The Italians, American Style," *The New York Times Magazine*, August 6, 1967; Norbert Wiley, "The Ethnic Mobility Trap and Stratification Theory," *Social Problems* (Fall 1967), pp. 147–159.

5. Press Associates, Inc., "Washington Window," *AFL-CIO News*, March 29, 1969, p. 5. See also John Corry, "Immigration Shows an Ethnic Change," *The New York Times*, March 18, 1968, pp. 1, 16; Norman Sklarewitz, "New U.S. Immigration Law Draws a Flood of Applicants and a Different Ethnic Mix," *The Wall Street Journal*, April 16, 1968, p. 34.

6. Calvin L. Beale, *et al.*, *Characteristics of the U. S. Population by Farm and Nonfarm Origin*, Agricultural Economic Report No. 66 (Washington, D.C.: U.S. Department of Agriculture, 1964), p. 13. Note that "blue-collar" here includes service workers.

7. President's National Advisory Commission on Rural Poverty, *The People Left Behind* (Washington, D.C.: Government Printing Office, 1967), p. 3.

8. Norval D. Glenn and Jon P. Alston, "Rural-Urban Differences in Reported Attitudes and Behavior," *The Southwestern Social Science Quarterly* (March 1967), pp. 381–400. See also Leo F. Schnore, "The Rural-Urban Variable: An Urbanite's Perspective," *Rural Sociology* (Fall 1966), pp. 138–139; Iowa State University Center for Agricultural and Economic Development, *Family Mobility in Our Dynamic Society* (Ames: Iowa State University Press, 1965).

9. Norman M. Bradburn and David Caplovitz, *Reports on Happiness: A Pilot Study of Behavior Related to Mental Health* (Chicago: Aldine, 1965); Stuart Chase, *American Credos* (New York: Harper & Brothers, 1962), p. 98, *passim*.

10. William E. Powels, "The Southern Appalachian Migrant: Country Boy Turned Blue-Collarite," in A. Shostak and W. Gomberg (eds.), *Blue Collar World: Studies of the American Worker* (Englewood Cliffs, N.J.: Prentice-Hall, 1964), pp. 270–281. Bernice Goldstein and Robert L. Eichhorn, "The Changing Protestant Ethic: Rural Patterns in Health, Work, and Leisure," *American*

Sociological Review (August 1961), pp. 557–565; S. M. Lipset, "Social Mobility and Urbanization," *Rural Sociology* (September–December 1955), pp. 220–228.

11. Douglas E. Kneeland, "The Growing Farm Exodus: Land Loses Its Hold," *The New York Times,* November 27, 1967, pp. 1, 72.

12. Ben J. Wattenberg and Richard M. Scammon, *This U.S.A.: An Unexpected Family Portrait of 194,067,296 Americans Drawn from the Census* (Garden City, N.Y.: Doubleday, 1965), p. 46.

13. Gerhard Lenski, *The Religious Factor* (New York: Anchor Books, 1961), p. 84.

. . . the differences may not stem *merely* from lingering cultural traditions of the past, but conditions of life in the modern metropolis may actually generate, or magnify, differences between socio-religious groups. This is a rather startling finding, quite contrary to the predictions of most students of the urban community, who constantly stress the homogenizing tendencies of the metropolis and metropolitan institutions [p. 114] [author's italics].

14. Herbert Schneider, *Religion in 20th Century America* (Cambridge, Mass.: Harvard University Press, 1962), Appendix, p. 228; see also N. J. Demerath, III, *Social Class in American Protestantism* (Chicago: Rand McNally, 1965).

15. Lenski, *op. cit.*, p. 114, *passim.*

16. John Leo, "The American Catholic Is Changing," *The New York Times Magazine,* November 14, 1965, p. 45.

17. Stephan Thernstrom, *Poverty and Progress: Social Mobility in a Nineteenth Century City* (Cambridge, Mass.: Harvard University Press, 1964).

18. For a thoroughgoing review of the relevant literature, see Chapter 10, "Occupational Mobility," in Walter L. Slocum, *Occupational Careers* (Chicago: Aldine, 1966), pp. 159–185. See also Seymour M. Lipset and Reinhard Bendix, *Social Mobility in Industrial Society* (Berkeley: University of California Press, 1959), pp. 197–198.

19. Peter M. Blau and Otis Dudley Duncan, *The American Occupational Structure* (New York: Wiley, 1967), pp. 55–56, *passim.* "The occupational world of these blue-collar starters seems to be epitomized by the remark the Queen made to Alice: 'Now, *here,* you see, it takes all the running *you* can do, to keep in the same

place. If you want to get somewhere else, you must run at least twice as fast as that!' " (p. 56).

20. S. M. Lipset and R. Bendix, "Social Mobility and Occupational Career Patterns," *American Journal of Sociology* (January–March 1952), p. 371. See also James L. Stern and David B. Johnson, *Blue- to White-Collar Job Mobility* (Madison: University of Wisconsin, Industrial Relations Research Institute, 1968).

21. Mirra Komarovsky, *Blue-Collar Marriage* (New York: Random House, 1964), pp. 34, 37.

22. *Ibid.*, p. 78. See also S. M. Miller and Frank Riessman, "The Working-Class Subculture: A New View," in A. Shostak and W. Gomberg (eds.), *op. cit.*, pp. 24–35.

23. *Statistics on Manpower: A Supplement to the Manpower Report of the President, March 1969*, U.S. Department of Labor, Table B–12, p. 41.

24. "Dropouts Found Capable in Jobs," *The New York Times*, February 24, 1965, p. 56.

25. *Manpower Report of the President, 1964*, U.S. Department of Labor, pp. 66–72.

26. For an overview of relevant literature see John Evanson, *et al.*, "Literature on the American Working Class," *Radical America* (March–April 1969), pp. 32–55.

2

BLUE-COLLAR
ODYSSEY

*Could we know what men are most apt to remember,
we might know what they are apt to do.*—HALIFAX

Much of what the median-age worker is today reflects his adaptations to the forty-three years of history his life has spanned. Born in the late 1920s, the median-age blue-collarite has intimately known the economic challenge and opportunity of the Depression, World War II, the postwar recessions, and the postwar economic boom. Each of the critical time periods involved is discussed below, attention being paid the legacy blue-collar workers may take with them from the experiences that are peculiarly their own.

THE UNEVEN TWENTIES

American mythologies about the "golden past" revolve about "the Roaring Twenties," when the country's peacetime economy was strong, prices stable, and employment and production levels rising. A million stock market speculators expected to get rich quite soon. Many who had never owned stock before—chauffeurs, taxicab drivers, housewives, speakeasy bartenders, elevator operators, waiters, college students, and barbers—were confident that luck, good times, and, in some cases, tips from wealthy customers would make them rich. Overlooked then, as even now in the mythology, was the plight of the blue-collar man. "Although on the surface American workers appeared to share in the material advantages of the time, the serious maladjustments within the economic system fell upon them with disproportionate weight. This interplay between illusion and reality is a key to the period." [1] America contained an exceedingly uneven society, and its workers enjoyed few of its benefits.

Trouble built up steadily, though few seemed to notice. A building boom was overextended and it provided more empty office space than was needed for the next generation (it was 1942 before building construction again reached the level achieved in 1928). Automobile manufacturers were slow to realize that they had saturated the market and secondhand dealers could not clear their lots (it was 1949 before car manufacturing again reached the level achieved in 1927). A factory expansion effort was overextended, investment bankers in 1928 and 1929 literally forcing money on manufacturers to expand capacity.[2] Astute observers believed that everyone who could afford a house, a car, or a radio had one already, and they feared industry was dangerously overproducing.

Trouble was also building up around the great labor issues that were to absorb the nation in the 1930s. Behind the false glitter there was regional poverty, hard-core unemployment, and inadequate relief. Unanswered were critical questions of labor standards—of low wages, long hours, night work for women and children, factory sanitation, company housing, and workmen's compensation. Unanswered also were open issues in labor relations, including the fundamental right to organize. Related was the problem of the rigidity of the American employer who opposed labor unions with force or resorted to the use of company union paternalism. "And here, finally, was a central issue of a democratic society—whether the majority or merely a few of its members were to make its basic economic decisions."[3]

In 1929 the fantastic spiral of false prosperity and unreal wealth ended in the crash of the stock market. Huge blocks of stock went unsold at any price. Construction stopped, car manufacturing halted, plants closed, and debtors defaulted. Between 1929 and 1932, consumers' goods fell off 23 percent, capital goods 50 percent, and house construction 80 percent.[4] Other disasters accompanied the financial collapse: In 1930 giant dust storms devastated the land in many agricultural states, and the related closing of country banks spread financial hardship far beyond the direct sphere of Wall Street influence. The labor issues, long unfaced, erupted into full view, with industrial espionage, strike-breaking, and labor violence exacting high tolls everywhere. By New Year's Day, 1931, *The New York Times* reasoned that things had become so bad they simply had to become better.[5]

THE DEPRESSION THIRTIES

Writer David Cort maintains that "probably nobody can understand America, or hence himself, if he does not understand the Great Depression."[6] Another close student of the subject, writer Caroline Bird, suggests that the Depression "packed a bigger wallop than anything else that happened to America between the Civil War and the atomic bomb."

It had more far-reaching consequences . . . than either of the World Wars. Nobody escaped . . . The twelve years in between [1929 and 1941] were filled with lower-case tragedies: mean stratagems, unspeakably petty economies, lost time, lost hope, lost opportunities, monotony, envy, and bitterness . . .[7]

Summing it up, Mrs. Bird suggests that while the total human bill for the Depression has never been added, a tally would show it contained thousands of sizable items.

Focusing on the blue-collar scene at the height of the Depression, we find that some 34 million Americans lived in families whose head was without steady work and often without hope.[8] One in five workers was unemployed or underemployed and lived with a "dull misery in the bones." Careful studies at the time showed that such men were ill more often than the employed, were less self-confident, were more unhappy, were more distrustful, and were more suicidal.[9] When work became available, many men took anything they could get. Skilled blue-collarites laid off by factories turned to wrapping packages, swept out beauty parlors, and washed dishes, their skills rusting with disuse. Others found that employers had shifted operations to piecework, burdening the worker with any time lost due to machine breakdown or lack of planning. (Between 1930 and 1934, workers suffered an income loss of 43 percent.) Millions of ex-blue-collarites were pathetically enterprising. They borrowed on life insurance or used their last few hundred dollars to go into small businesses of their own—where almost all failed. (Between 1930 and 1934, small businessmen who stayed "alive" suffered an income loss of 41 percent.)[10]

In the latter half of the grim 1930s, the "New Deal" administration of President Franklin Delano Roosevelt moved to offset the persistently high unemployment level with an unprecedented series of legal and social reforms. Backed by solid blue-collar support, the FDR administration earned Supreme Court approval (previously denied) for laws that promised work for all seeking it, financial aid for those between jobs, and the maintenance of an "income floor" under the standard of living.

For example, the Works Progress Administration (WPA), the largest and most heavily underwritten corporation established up to that time, combined with the Tennessee Valley

Authority (TVA) to put millions back to work. The Social Security Act of 1935 led the state governments to establish a system of unemployment insurance while the federal government moved to provide "income floor" pensions for the aged. In addition the Civilian Conservation Corps (CCC) (the original model for today's Job Corps), the National Labor Relations Board (NLRB), the U.S. Employment Service, and other such newborn agencies contributed to a slow but steady restoration of confidence.

The nation's manual workers entered the 1930s as laissez-faire individualists comfortable with the values of "Main Street" merchants. Unemployment, to be sure, had been high for seamen, textile workers, coal miners, and other blue-collarites even during the prosperous 1920s. At that time, however, the superfluous people thought themselves to be largely victims of bad luck. Most were confident their luck would change and the social order would soon provide jobs for them.

The nation's manual workers left the gross catastrophe of the 1930s considerably changed by the experience. With dreams shattered, skills gone rusty, and children undereducated and therefore unlikely to achieve much more than their fathers, blue-collarites had suffered much. Many left the decade of the Great Depression impressed as never before with society's built-in, structural deficiencies, with the enormous interrelationships that explain how a collapse in speculation on paper margin could close real factories and sponsor human starvation. Many left the decade impressed with the philosophic and political differences that set them off from merchants and employers where human and property rights seemed to conflict. Class consciousness reached new heights, and class hostilities were keenly felt. Journalist Murray Kempton suggests in reminiscence that "there were no neutrals . . . [it was] a landscape blighted more than anything else by the absence of pity and mercy." [11]

It was also a landscape marked by a new sense of urgency, at least on the part of many blue-collarites. It had become increasingly necessary to surrender a characteristic faith in the natural order and in the Horatio Alger myth of individual success. It was increasingly apparent that things did not always turn out right. No longer reliant on the automatic workings of the economy, blue-collarites sought a new kind of control over their destinies. Many workers, impressed with the post-1935 gains of the FDR administration, tested and came enthusiastically to endorse welfare economics and New Deal social planning.

Blue-collarites also moved with evangelical enthusiasm to join the new industrial unions led by John L. Lewis, Philip Murray, Walter Reuther, and others. For the first time, large-scale labor organizations were established in the nation's mass-production industries. From insignificance and near-extinction in the 1920s and early 1930s, the industrial unions soared to prominence, their success with new tactics like that of the Sit-In and the NLRB Representation Election helping the unions to double their membership by 1940. Historian Sidney Fine observes that "what had been a dispirited and demoralized labor movement became a vital and powerful force on the American scene . . . The decade of the 1930's was the most significant decade in the history of the American labor movement." [12]

THE WARTIME FORTIES

Those economic hardships not reached by New Deal welfare economics or by blue-collar union control efforts were reached with unexpected suddenness in the winter of 1941. On December 8, the day after the Japanese attack on Pearl Harbor, this nation declared a war that put almost every employable man and woman to work. What came as a shock developed quickly into an economic bonanza.

Blue-collarites went back to work and by 1944 everyone who could hold and wished to have a job had one. With the government seeking ever more workers, skilled labor was in special demand. Women, the aged, the handicapped, and others were drawn into gainful employ in an unprecedented fashion, and an enormously productive confusion abounded everywhere. Playwright Arthur Miller recalls:

It was like a baseball game with five hundred men playing the outfield at the same time, sweeping in a mob toward the high arching ball, which was caught somewhere in the middle of the crowd, by whom no one knew, except that the game was slowly and quite inconceivably being won.[13]

Economic prosperity spread, and by the war's end in 1945, the tightly rationed civilian population was nevertheless consuming considerably more than it had been able to get during the Depression.

Governmental controls were the key to prosperity, and the point was probably not lost on the blue-collarite. As the Office of Price Administration rationed essentials and set price ceilings, blue-collarites were able to compete with the wealthy for consumer goods. As the War Manpower Commission trained and deployed skilled labor, blue-collarites were able to take advantage of distant job opportunities. As the administration required it, war plants were located in pockets of poverty and welfare provisions were routinely written into war contracts. And, as the War Labor Relations Board helped settle labor disputes, unions and employers were able to avoid bitter and crippling strikes.

Blue-collarites made their own distinct contribution. In reaction to the patriotic demands of the war effort, many workers relaxed work rules and production-regulating norms: Men worked in hazardous but productive ways—a swashbuckling tone came to characterize their efforts. Absenteeism fell, large numbers worked enormous amounts of overtime, and no personal sacrifice was denied if it might serve "our boys over there." The forty-eight-hour workweek was not unknown, and blue-collarites drew together in a way that many can even now recall with warmth and nostalgia.

Overall, it appears that the nation's blue-collarites entered the decade of the 1940s unexpectedly excited by the prospects of economic prosperity and the related recovery of self-esteem and pride—pride fed both by patriotic sacrifice and by gainful employment. Much of the sting was temporarily taken out of Depression-bred class consciousness, and new confidence was secured from the continued success of the worker-endorsed Roosevelt administration and the labor movement led by Philip Murray—the new CIO. Men advanced in their jobs, gained seniority, and most significantly of all, experienced unprecedented job satisfaction from the patriotic "give-your-all" character of war work.[14]

With the death of FDR in 1944 and with the end of the war in 1945, many Americans feared the arrival of a new depression. Certain experts predicted that returning servicemen would swell unemployment to all-time highs and that social chaos would result. Instead, however, the general consumer moved to cash in his war savings bonds and began an enormous buying spree, one strong enough to bolster the entire economy. Women workers ("Rosie the Riveter" and "Winnie the Welder") left the factory for home, and this opened up many new posts for male job-seekers. Employers clamored all the time for new workers to help meet the consumer demand pent up during the war. The Gross National Product dropped very little in 1946, a critical year, and unemployment did not rise above a tolerable 3 percent.

Earnings fell, however, and the spirit of patriotic trust and cooperation among labor, management, and government quickly faded from the scene. With the termination of lucrative "cost-plus" war contracts, business rushed in to reduce the amount of overtime worked, and the average workweek was cut down from forty-five to forty-one hours. Men continued to work, but they earned much less than they had between 1942 and 1945. The federal government compounded developing problems by lifting price and rent controls and, in 1948, by actually withdrawing a significant amount of its support from the nation's economy. Without this prop, the economy faltered and production and employment declined. By 1949 the satiation level of consumption was reached, and consumer demand sagged. Weaknesses showed up in the market, and production contracted. Unemployment rose to a postwar high of nearly 6 percent of the labor force.

Blue-collar response to the period's various disappointments was both heated and sharp. In 1948 over a million manual workers "hit the bricks," or walked out on strike. Labor strife peaked in the 1948–1950 period, and industrial strikes set records for average duration and bitterness. Workers also split among themselves as the CIO in 1949 and 1950 expelled eleven labor unions on grounds of Communist party domination; fathers and sons were set against one another, and much violence accompanied the new internecine "dual union" struggles.

The federal government added fuel to the flames of discontent by responding with an exceedingly weak legislative program. While a Full Employment Act was forced through a reluctant Congress in 1946, its content was diluted, its implementation was partial, and its impact was slight. Similarly, an enormous blue-collar demand for new housing resulted in path-setting housing legislation, but once again the rhetoric produced little of real consequence. In 1947 blue-collar disillusionment reached a new height with federal passage of the bill labeled a "slave labor act" by the unions, the Taft-Hartley Act. President Harry S Truman vetoed the bill and, in a sharp lesson to organized labor, a conservative coalition in Congress overrode the veto and Taft-Hartley became the law of the land.

A Presidential election in 1948 heightened feelings of class rivalry that had been relatively dormant since 1941, feelings stirred considerably by the lingering impact of the Great Depression of the 1930s. Reduced hours, reduced earnings, reduced union solidarity, and reduced blue-collar confidence in the federal government combined throughout the post-1945 period to sober and alarm a blue-collar bloc lulled by the security and gains of the 1940–1945 war period. The future in the late 1940s seemed cloudy to most and hazardous to many.

THE TURBULENT YEARS

Economic reversals were unexpectedly set right in 1951, as they had been in 1941, by the start of a war. The new production demands of the Korean conflict initiated an economic boom that has continued with little interruption through to the Vietnam production demands of the late 1960s.

In the early years of the boom, however, its benefits were very unevenly distributed, many blue-collarites suffering a frequency and duration of unemployment that recalled memories of the Depression. Automation began to take hold in American industry, and the absolute number of blue-collar production workers fell by a half-million between 1948 and 1960. As the years went by, the pace and impact of automation intensified: Between 1953 and 1960, some 80 percent of the decline in factory job openings was attributed to the technological displacement of automation. Between 1951 and 1963, steel employment fell 28 percent, but the industry's labor force—minus 80,000 blue-collarites—produced as much steel at the end of the period as at the start. Between 1953 and 1963, auto employment fell 20 percent, but a million more trucks and cars were produced in 1963 than a larger work force had turned out in 1953. What little new growth in job availabilities occurred took place in the public sector of the labor force and involved increases in the number of government employees, schoolteachers, policemen, and others. Between 1957 and 1963, only 5 percent of the 4 million new jobs created were full-time jobs generated by private industry, the kind of job blue-collarites generally fill.[15]

In the years since the Korean War, the nation's labor force intensified its long-term shift from employment in goods-producing and associated industries to employment in the service-producing industries (finance, education, public administration, and professional and personal services). From 1957 to 1967, the number of white-collar jobs increased 30 percent, while the blue-collar figure stayed at 8 percent.[16] Indeed, 1956 marked the first time in American history, if not in the history of industrial civilization, that the number of white-collar workers in a nation outnumbered the blue-collarites.

The shift away from blue-collar employ was accompanied by severe dislocation for many, and Depression-like unemployment rates throughout the 1950s and early 1960s rarely dipped below 5 percent and reached as high as 6.8 percent.[17] Experience from 1950 to 1965 showed that every five years the percentage of jobless increased by about one-half a percentage point, the proportion of the unemployed growing slowly but perceptibly.[18] Unemployment also changed in character: Between 1957 and 1962 the number of unemployed increased 36 percent, but the number of long-term unemployed (twenty-seven weeks or more) increased 145 percent.[19] Furthermore, recovery from both of the recessions in 1958 and 1960–1961 left the country with a higher rate of unemployment than had each preceding recovery.

Only in recent years has the picture improved. Relevant here have been the impact of the tax cut of 1964 and the additional impact in mid-1965 of rising military orders and the placement of Vietnam defense contracts. In 1966 the nation experienced its first significant improvement in blue-collar job totals since 1953; the number, which had dropped 1.5 million between 1953 and 1963, rose by about 1.5 million between 1963 and 1967.[20] (Provocative, however, was the fact that in 1967 the major employment gains were made only by skilled craftsmen: The Department of Labor reports that "there were virtually no additional opportunities for unskilled and semi-skilled workers.")[21]

Unemployment levels, while remaining at the 1966 level, oscillated sharply in 1967, and the growth in blue-collar jobs was halved by the nation's "mini-recession." [22] Recovery came swiftly, however, and by January 1969 unemployment reached a fifteen-year low.[23] Unemployment levels throughout 1968 averaged a low 3.6 percent, but the total labor force increased by only 750,000, the smallest increase since 1961.[24] Unclear also was the possible impact here of a cessation of the Vietnam War, with the loss of perhaps a million domestic jobs directly linked to that international conflict.[25]

As part of one of the most dramatic redistributions of income that any nation has gone through in so short a time, the average weekly gross wage for production workers went to $123 in 1968—a figure more than quadrupling the 1939 gross wage. Earnings of factory workers, which had passed the $2-an-hour level in 1956, finished a twelve-year climb to finally achieve the $3-an-hour pinnacle.[26] Alterations in the economy's price structure also made it possible for a worker to labor only 4,000 hours to purchase a home that would have required 10,000 hours in 1900; the average worker also earned in 3 hours enough to pay for a market basket of food that required 11 hours in 1909.[27] This kind of thing encouraged writers like John Brooks to advance an ever-more common notion: The comfortably off, including blue-collarites, have become our great central mass.[28] (That consumer installment-buying debts are growing astronomically, and beginning to look like the giddy margin buying of stocks in the pre-crash 1920s, bothers all too few.)

Overlooked in Brooks' rosy version of blue-collar economics is the critical fact that blue-collarites have actually lost the economic momentum they had in the early 1940s. Continued price increases have reduced the worker's wage increase over the past twenty-five years to only a doubling in terms of buying power.[29] And the picture is not improving: The cost of living in 1966 took its greatest rise in a decade and cut down real spendable earnings of factory workers for the first time since 1960.[30] In 1968 the Consumer Price Index recorded an ever greater climb than in 1966, and spendable earnings of workers reached their lowest level since 1964. In terms of constant 1957–1959 dollars, the typical nonsupervisory worker with three dependents in 1968 averaged $77.62 in take-home pay, 32 cents less than in 1967, and 40 cents less than in 1966.[31] Reduced "real spending power" has also had to contend with particular price boosts in critical purchases: While the overall increase in prices between 1958 and 1968 amounted to approximately 20 percent, the *Wall Street Journal* (October 22, 1968) recorded these constituent increases: Daily hospital service, 101 percent; movie admissions, 70 percent; auto insurance rates, 44 percent; postal charges, 42 percent; physicians' fees, 38 percent; men's haircuts, 37 percent; property insurance rates, 36 percent.

It is true that in 1968 labor unions secured their largest negotiated wage increases in several years (increases, by the way, that the *Journal* article mentioned above evaluates as far less significant a contributory element in inflation than is commonly believed). An impressive 12-cent rise in 1967 hourly earnings, however, was completely wiped out by inflation; the worker's purchasing power actually fell by 27 cents a week.[32] Blue-collarites could only buy less with the same dollars than in 1965, paycheck purchasing power having shrunk regularly over the ensuing three years.[33] Experts at the year's start (and in June 1969, at the time of this writing) were predicting the largest increases since 1951 in price rises, in inflation, and in the erosion of purchasing power.[34]

One terse comparison may sum up the entire situation: Between 1960 and 1967, the weekly after-tax take-home pay of an average factory worker with three dependents increased by 11 percent.[35] In the same time period, however, the amount of money such a family needed to "live moderately" rose by 24 percent: The Bureau of Labor Statistics City Worker Budget actually rose from $6,100 in 1960 to $9,439 in 1967. The budget itself was held to *very* moderate standards ($1.50 a day for food, $6 a month for recreation, $15 a month for clothing; no allowance for college expenses, savings, or installment buying). Nevertheless, the budget in 1967 required a net income of $3,400 more than the 1967 earnings of the average blue-collarite.[36]

Budget inflation, inadequacy, and disparity demonstrate the serious erosion that has occurred in the worker's economic position. For all the talk of joining the "great central mass," most workers have actually failed to share in the semiaffluence of the postwar years; many in 1967 could not even manage a stringent "moderate" living budget.

SUMMARY

Historical events of consequence have occurred since the late 1920s that have had a direct and important influence upon blue-collar workers. As later chapters will emphasize, in light of the past forty years' history, it is not surprising that the style of life of the blue-collarites reflects much uneasiness where current events are concerned. (Workers were disproportionately overrepresented among the 47 percent of Americans who in 1967 told Gallup pollsters that another depression was either "possible" or even "likely.")[37]

Today's event-shakened blue-collarite maintains his distance from many contemporary modes of thought, preferring instead the time-honored maxims and myths that helped see him through the grim 1930s, the bitter late 1940s, and the half-dozen different recessions America has known since 1945. Above all, many such men remain anxious about the developments unfolding around them, especially developments that challenge the status quo and compel them to reexamine how far they have come, where they are heading, and how satisfying they are finding the lives they have thus far made for themselves. The immediate past gives these men little confidence in the immediate future—or in their own role as shapers of that future. Their forty-year history helps explain much of their anxiety and insecurity—even as it underlies their sober and solid preference for "haste made slowly" and caution-in-all-things.

Notes to Chapter Two

---

1. Irving Bernstein, *The Lean Years: A History of the American Worker, 1920–1933* (Boston: Houghton Mifflin, 1960), p. 47. See also George Rawick, "Working Class Self-Activity," *Radical America* (March–April 1969) pp. 23–31.

2. The data are drawn from Caroline Bird, *The Invisible Scar* (New York: McKay, 1966), pp. 1–21. I owe Mrs. Bird much as I have drawn extensively from her insights. See also Louise Tanner, *All the Things We Were* (New York: Doubleday, 1967).

3. Bernstein, *op. cit.*, pp. 42–43. See also David Alexander, *Panic!* (Evanston, Ill.: Regency, 1960); James O. Morris, "The AFL in the 1920's: A Strategy of Defense," *ILR Review* (July 1958), pp. 572–590.

4. Stuart Chase, *Idle Money Idle Men* (New York: Harcourt, Brace and Co.), 1938, p. 86.

5. Bird, *op. cit.*, p. 17. See also David A. Shannon (ed.), *The Great Depression* (Englewood Cliffs, N.J.: Spectrum Books, 1960); Malcolm Cowley, *Think Back on Us* (Carbondale: Southern Illinois University Press, 1967).

6. David Cort, "The Money That Money Can't Buy," *The New York Times Book Review*, March 24, 1968, p. 38. See also Milton Derber and Edwin Young (eds.), *Labor and the New Deal* (Madison: University of Wisconsin Press, 1967).

7. Bird, *op. cit.*, pp. xii, xiv, xvii. On p. xvii, Bird adds:

It changed the balance of power in family life in favor of women while discouraging marriage and motherhood. It held back and isolated Negroes, Jews, and women by making it easy to discriminate against them in employment, and it converted the public school from stepping-stone to refuge for the unemployed. It turned intellectuals to the left, slowed the application of technology, kept most of the nation ill-housed, and prevented the natural spread of population to suburbs . . .

8. Chase, *op. cit.*, p. 87. See also John Kenneth Galbraith, *The Great Crash: 1929* (Boston: Houghton Mifflin, 1954).

9. See Clinch Calkins, *Some Folks Won't Work* (New York: Harcourt, Brace and Co., 1930); Grace Adams, *Workers on Relief* (New Haven: Yale University Press, 1939); Nels Anderson, *Men on the Move* (Chicago: University of Chicago Press, 1940); E. Wright Bakke, *The Unemployed Worker: A Study of the Task of Making a Living without a Job* (New Haven: Yale University Press: 1940); Mirra Komarovsky, *The Unemployed Man and His Family: The Effect of Unemployment upon the Status of the Man in 59 Families* (New York: Dryden Press, 1940).

10. Chase, *op. cit.*, p. 87.

11. Murray Kempton, *Part of Our Time: Some Monuments and Ruins of the Thirties* (New York: Delta Books, 1967), pp. 1, 11. See also Geoffrey Gorer, "What's the Matter with Britain?: One Trouble Is That the British Working Class Can't Forget the Depression," *The New York Times Magazine*, December 31, 1967.

12. Sidney Fine, "The History of the American Labor Movement with Special Reference to Developments in the 1930's," in William Haber (ed.), *Labor in a Changing America* (New York: Basic Books, 1966), p. 105. See also Irving Bernstein, *The Turbulent Years* (Boston: Houghton Mifflin, 1969); Frances Perkins, *The Roosevelt I Knew* (New York: Viking, 1946).

13. Arthur Miller, *I Don't Need You Any More* (New York: Viking, 1967), p. 177.

14. On the entire War period, see A. A. Hoehling, *Home Front, U.S.A.: The Story of World War II Over Here* (New York: Crowell, 1966). Note especially the author's impatience with labor's record during the war years, an impatience this writer does not share. See also Milton Derber, "Labor-Management in World War II," *Current History* (June 1965), pp. 340–345; "Fitter's Night," in Miller, *op. cit.*, pp. 175–223.

15. The data in this section are drawn from Ben B. Seligman, *Most Notorious Victory: Man in an Age of Automation* (New York: Free Press, 1967).

16. Paul M. Ryscavage, "Changes in Occupational Employment Over the Past Decade," *Monthly Labor Review* (August 1967), p. 27.

17. Albert Rees, "Discussion," in Arthur M. Ross (ed.), *Unemployment and the American Economy* (New York: Wiley, 1964), p. 136.

18. Guy Tyler, *The Labor Revolution* (New York: Viking, 1967), p. 75.

19. John Brooks, *The Great Leap: The Past Twenty-five Years in America* (New York: Harper & Row, 1966), p. 44.

20. Nathaniel Goldfinger, *Labor's View of Manpower Policy*, Department of Labor (Washington, D.C.: Government Printing Office, 1967), p. 8.

21. *Manpower Report of the President, 1968*, Department of Labor (Washington, D.C.: Government Printing Office, 1968), p. 184.

22. Anon., "Labor Letter," *Wall Street Journal*, June 4, 1968, p. 1.

23. Eileen Shanahan, "Jobless Rate Down to 3.5% in January, Lowest in 14 Years," *The New York Times*, February 8, 1968, pp. 1, 26.

24. Anon., "Washington Dateline: Jobless Rate Stays at 3.6 Pct.," *Philadelphia Inquirer*, November 7, 1968, p. 2.

25. Anon., "Million Jobs Created by Intensification of War," *The New York Times*, September 14, 1967, p. 18.

26. Department of Labor Press Release, July, 1968; *Manpower Report of the President, 1967*, Department of Labor (Washington, D.C.: Government Printing Office), p. 13. See also Brooks, *op. cit.*, p. 31; H. M. Douty, *Labor Issues in Perspective: Trends in Labor*

Compensation in the United States, 1946–1966 (Washington, D.C.: Government Printing Office, 1968); *Bureau of Labor Statistics, Employment and Earning Statistics for the United States, 1909–1968* (Washington, D.C.: Government Printing Office, 1969).

27. Bernard C. Meltzer, "Wrong, Old-Thoughts," *Philadelphia Evening Bulletin,* October 1, 1967, p. 32; Anon., " '66 Workers' Pay Buys More Food," *The New York Times,* July 30, 1967, p. 43.

28. Brooks, *op. cit.,* p. 132. See also Joseph Bensman and Arthur Vidich, "Business Cycles, Class, and Personality" in P. Olson (ed.), *America as a Mass Society* (New York: Free Press, 1963), pp. 441–454.

29. Brooks, *op. cit.,* p. 132. See also "Living Costs Get Critical Again," *Business Week,* February 11, 1967, pp. 62–64.

30. "Biggest Jump in Decade: '66 Living Cost Rise Outstrips Wage Gains," *AFL-CIO News,* January 18, 1967, p. 12.

31. Jerry M. Flint, "Car Workers Find Prices Too High," *The New York Times,* June 1, 1969, p. 29. See also Anon., "Boom Keeps Building for Business, but Worker Keeps Dropping Behind," *AFL-CIO News,* March 23, 1968, p. 5. See also Anon., "Wallace Cashes In on the Dollar Issue," *Business Week* (October 26, 1968), pp. 122–124.

32. David R. Jones, "Consumer Prices Rise 3.1% in Year; Slowup Doubted," *The New York Times,* January 26, 1968, pp. 1, 16.

33. Alfred L. Malabre, Jr., "Boom for Whom?," *Wall Street Journal,* February 28, 1968, pp. 1, 14.

34. Morton Paulson, "A Year of Uneasy Prosperity?" *National Observer,* January 8, 1968, p. 10. See also Anon., "Cost of Living Increase Sets 17-Year Record," *New York Post,* October 29, 1968, p. 3; Edwin L. Dale, Jr., "Prices Rise 0.6%; October Increase Highest Since '62," *The New York Times,* November 28, 1968, p. 1.

35. Anon., "Boost in Worker Buying Power Called Vital to Balanced Economy," *AFL-CIO News,* December 9, 1967, p. 3. See also Walter P. Reuther, *The Economy in 1967* (Detroit, Mich.: United Auto Workers Union, 1968); Council of Economic Advisers, *Economic Report of the President, 1968* (Washington, D.C.: Government Printing Office, 1968).

36. David R. Jones, "A Family's Needs Found 50% Higher," *The New York Times,* October 26, 1967, pp. 1, 47. The 1968 budget figure was set at $9,570. Anon., "Costs Average $9570 for City Family of 4," *Philadelphia Inquirer,* March 17, 1969, p. 1.

37. Max Gunther, "How We Feel About Our Money," *Saturday*

Evening Post, December 16, 1967, p. 72. See also Leonard D. Cain, Jr., "Age Status and Generational Phenomena: The New Old People in Contemporary America," *The Gerontologist* (June 1967), pp. 83–92.

Part II

3

BLUE-COLLAR
WORKERS

*A man at work at his trade is the equal of the most
learned doctor.*—HEBREW PROVERB

Perhaps nothing is as determinative and revealing of a
blue-collarite's style and quality of life as the answer to the
question, What is his general skill rating? Manual workers are
differentiated by the Census, the public, and the working class
itself into three broad skill blocs: unskilled laborers, semiskilled operators, and skilled craftsmen. To better understand
why and how the American Caucasian manual worker lives as
he does, it is important to consider these skill bloc issues: How
do the skill blocs differ? How do they rank over time and at
present? Why is a man found in one or the other? What challenges and strains preoccupy each bloc? And how is automation

changing the picture? Each is briefly considered below, the entire chapter seeking to shed new light on the worker's very stringent state of affairs.

SKILL BLOCS

In 1968 blue-collar men were distributed among the relevant census categories as indicated in Table 1.

TABLE 1   **Employed Men by Occupational Category, 1968**

Craftsmen, foremen, and kindred	9,696,000
Operators and kindred	9,687,000
Laborers (except farm and mine)	3,429,000
Service workers (except private household)	3,273,000

SOURCE: *Statistics on Manpower: A Supplement to the Manpower Report of the President, March 1969*, U.S. Department of Labor, Table A–9, p. 11.

Examples of the kind of jobs that men in each category pursued included the following:

Craftsmen	*Operators*	*Laborers*	*Service Workers*
Bakers	Assemblers	Car Washers	Barbers
Bookbinders	Attendants	Fishermen	Cooks
Bricklayers	Auto Service	Garage Laborers	Counter Men
Cabinetmakers	Blasters	Gardeners	Elevator Men
Carpenters	Boatmen	Groundskeepers	Guards
Cement Masons	Brakemen	Longshoremen	Janitors
Decorators	Bus Drivers	Warehousemen	Waiters
Electricians	Checkers; Inspectors	Utility Workers	Watchmen
Painters	Deliverymen		
Plumbers	Machine Operators		

Each of these census categories approximates a skill bloc that is something of a world unto itself ("service workers" divide among the other three).

Unskilled laborers, for example, characteristically work on auto-assembly lines. There they spend the day clambering up on the auto bodies that glide by every few minutes to clamp twenty-pound hooks and chains onto them, so that when the car bodies reach the end of the line they can be swung into the air and hoisted into the bonderizing booth. Other laborers on highway construction work may spend their work lives pushing long-handled wooden floats to level imperfections, or dragging stiff-bristled brooms to give the concrete a skid-resistant surface, or spraying on a surface membrane to protect the road as it cures. Laborers in a sugar refinery may spend their time waiting at the bottom of a four-story tube to catch the funneled sugar in twenty-five- or one hundred-pound bags, swing them onto scales and adjust the weight of the bags, and then lift the bags onto conveyor belts for later sewing by a semiskilled worker.

In short, low-skill or unskilled work has as its chief characteristics its heavy reliance on brawn and its insignificant training requirement. Men can spend their lives at a task taught to them their first day in less than thirty minutes. The routine is generally fixed and unchangeable: Manual dexterity, manipulative ability, physical strength, and physical stamina exhaust the human potentialities most often called upon. From predominance in the early industrial years, this type of labor has now shrunk in significance to a point where perhaps only one in twenty jobs requires more than average physical prowess.

The chief characteristics of medium or semiskilled work are reliance on rudimentary mental skills and minimal training requirements: While several months of practice may be required for real proficiency, no formal apprenticeship is generally involved. Some of the work is highly repetitious, as in operating a semiautomatic stamping and fashioning machine in a metal-fabricating shop or in making the same cut all day long in the carcasses of pigs that are conveyed along in a meat-finishing plant. Other kinds of semiskilled work are less routine; two examples include that of the assembly-line utility man—an all-around worker who is slipped into spots made vacant by absenteeism or emergencies—and that of the "clean-hands" chemical operator—a blue-collarite who makes regular tours of panels and valves; takes readings of temperatures, pressures, and rates of flow; records these data in log data sheets; and occasionally turns a valve. Whether as machine tender, bench assembler, taxi driver, or restaurant cook, the semiskilled blue-collarite generally experiences considerable physical *and* mental involvement.

The major features of skilled work are the considerable reliance placed on brainpower and on extensive training requirements (long and arduous apprenticeships are allegedly commonplace in the craft occupations). Very little of the work is repetitious; most of it demands initiative and requires responsibility. Plumbers may spend the day high up on a skyscraper still in the girder stage, moving carefully around the beams, taking sights, dropping plumb lines, making sure the bay is going up vertically, wrapping the whole bay around with guy wires, and tightening turnbuckles on the guy wires to line the bay up with the one beneath. Hand compositors may spend much of their work lives reading from manuscript copy and setting type by hand, preparing metal trays of "galley" type, arranging the type "pages," breaking down the type forms after use, and storing the foundry type for reuse. The skilled blue-collarite, in short, experiences considerable personal, satisfying, and privileged involvement.[1]

DISTRIBUTION OF BLOCS

Across time the distribution of the skilled craftsmen in the blue-collar sector has remained remarkably stable. Contrawise, the proportion of semiskilled blue-collarites in the labor force has doubled, even as the proportion of unskilled blue-collarites has been more than halved over the past fifty-five years. (See Table 2.) Given the fact that assembly-line modes of production and continuous-process modes of production have been vastly expanded over the fifty-five-year period, the redistribution of blue-collarites away from brawn employment of laborers in favor of machine-integrated employment of more skilled men becomes understandable.

Looking now at the proportion of blue-collarites inside the blue-collar sector, and excluding for the moment white male service workers, the distribution of 21 million white males in

TABLE 2   Employed Male Blue-Collarites by Skill Type, Both Races, 1910–1966 (Percent of Labor Force)

	1910	1920	1930	1940	1950*	1960*	1965*	1966†
Skilled	15%	17%	16%	15%	18%	19%	19%	20%
Semiskilled	11	13	14	18	21	19	21	20
Unskilled	18	18	16	11	8	8	8	6

* U.S. Department of Labor, *Manpower Report of the President, 1966*, p. 165.
† Bureau of Employment Security, Department of Labor, *Employment and Earnings*, January 1967, p. 102.
SOURCE: U.S. Department of Labor, *The Skilled Labor Force*, Technical Bulletin T-140, April 1954, p. 18.

1965 (the last year for data) found 44 percent in the skilled bloc, 41 percent in the semiskilled bloc, and only 15 percent in the unskilled category.[2] This distribution sharply challenges the image of the burly, dim-witted, muscle-bound "horny-handed son of toil" that misleads in newly made folk songs or in occasional Sunday supplement articles on America's "men of steel." Insofar as the vast majority of blue-collarites (white males) are concerned, it is first and foremost a skilled assembly, to a lesser degree a semiskilled one, and least of all a brawny laborer's work force.

Finally, there is the matter of concentration among specific occupational types. Among white men employed as blue-collarites in 1960, the following occupations predominated (in order of decreasing size):[3]

Skilled	Semiskilled	Unskilled
Mechanics, repairmen	Truck drivers, deliverymen	Unspecified
Carpenters	Assemblers	Lumbermen, raftsmen, woodchoppers
Machinists, jobsetters	Attendants, auto, service and parking	Longshoremen, stevedores
Painters	Welders, flame cutters	Fishermen, oystermen

Note how revealing are the absolute majority types: The skilled bloc is led by an occupational type that requires vocational aptitude and training, an apprenticeship of sorts, and crisp tests of personal performance. The semiskilled bloc is led by an occupational type with a commonplace salable claim (driving, navigating, and delivery skills), the appearance of easy interchangeability of personnel, and the fact of routine, repetitive tasks. The unskilled go "unspecified" by the Department of Labor, a most striking commentary on the low social status and seemingly low social valuation of this bloc of 3½ million Americans.

SKILL BLOC PLACEMENT

Two factors in particular help explain why a man is found in one or another of the three skill blocs—and why he generally remains there over his work life.

Education, the country's major status-allocation mechanism, initially determines the ability range of most manual workers. Generally ill-prepared by their families, schools, and communities for the realities of the labor market, young workers take whatever is available—and find almost immediately that their "last year of education completed" largely determines their chance of ever moving up the job ladder and getting anything better. For example, three-to-six-year apprentice programs confront the would-be skilled craftsman, programs complete with classroom instruction in fairly complex vocational matters (instrument repair apprentices now study mathematics, physics, electronics, chemistry, blueprint reading, and instrumentation theory; hammersmith apprentices are required to learn about the properties of metals, the operation of power hammers and furnaces, and the reading of blueprints). This is no small point, for the earnings of a worker correlate strongly with his educational background inside each skill-level category (that is, a laborer with a high school diploma is likely to earn more than a semiskilled worker who dropped out of primary school). Advanced education does not always assure maximum earnings. However, there is a close connection among educational level, skill level, and earnings.

More surprising than the correlation between education and earnings is the fact that men do not achieve more over their work lives, that more do not surmount their handicaps (educational and otherwise) and move upward to higher ability levels —although many try. Work force mobility is considerable, and job turnover is very high. For example, an analysis of 1962 data for male workers has established that 60 percent of the men then employed as skilled blue-collarites had not started out in that skill type, but only later secured entrance into skilled employ. Similarly, 72 percent of all semiskilled workers began elsewhere in the labor force, as did 85 percent of all laborers.[4] The Department of Labor now expects the average worker to change jobs six or seven times during his work life and spend only about five and a half years on each job. But few blue-collarites have well-ordered work lives. Rather, after considerable moving about, they generally wind up not very far from where they started. Many are "going nowhere in an unordered way. [They] can expect a work life of nearly unpredictable ups and downs." [5]

SPECIAL SKILL BLOC CONCERNS

Consistent with differences in their work are differences among blue-collarites in their experience of three major pressures, namely, worries about adequacy of pay, worries about job security, and worries about job satisfaction. Unskilled workers appear the most concerned about their earnings. Semiskilled blue-collarites seem more concerned with remaining employed. Skilled workers appear preoccupied with protecting and even increasing the control and status-linked satisfaction they enjoy in and from their work.

Unskilled male workers earn considerably less than do other blue-collarites. As year-round, full-time employees, they had a median income in 1965 of $4,651. Service workers, excluding private household help, topped this by $233; semiskilled workers, by $1,131; while craftsmen earned $2,100 more.[6] Even these figures understate the full disparity, however, for only 53 percent of the unskilled worked the year-round at full-time jobs, as compared with 65 percent for men in the "service" bracket, and 71 and 79 percent for semiskilled operatives and skilled craftsmen. The 47 percent of all male laborers without steady employ help bring the median income figure in 1965 for all male laborers down to a poverty-level Depression-like low of $2,410. Important also is the considerable range of income among the unskilled themselves: In 1959, the last year for which data are available, the lowest-paid laborer (wholesale and retail trade) earned only an average median income of $1,318, or some $3,392 less than the best-paid laborer, the longshoreman who earned $4,710.[7]

It is hardly surprising therefore to learn that 21 percent of laborers employed year-round full time in 1966 earned under $3,000 and struggled to support families on an income below the federal poverty line (the figure was only 9 percent for semiskilled, and 4 percent for craftsmen).[8] Significant here is the additional fact that, of the three blue-collar types, laborers have the largest families to support.[9] That the families of the unskilled must suffer considerable financial strain is underlined by a comparison of their 1965 median income of $2,410 with the $6,418 the Labor Department's 1964 City Worker's Family Budget required for a "modest but adequate" standard of living.[10]

Unskilled workers made the greatest relative wage gains of all three blue-collar skill blocs in the years between 1939 and 1950, but in more recent years, or since 1950, the unskilled bloc has made the smallest gain (the greatest gains are now being made by the highest-paid workers). What is even more, the narrowing of wage differentials inside the bracket of the un-skilled (and of the other two skill blocs, for that matter) has slowed to a standstill since the late 1940s.[11] Unskilled workers, in short, earn little, often so little as to leave many poverty-stricken. As a whole, they have made no progress in their efforts to catch up or to draw the lesser-paid among them toward the middle of the wage spread of their skill bloc. Little wonder many seem preoccupied with their level of earnings and with related dollar matters.

In contrast, semiskilled workers seem preoccupied by job security matters. Proportionately more of the semiskilled have spent more time on the street seeking work in recent years than has been true of any other blue-collar skill bloc type. While the unskilled have a higher rate of unemployment, much of this is seasonal and traditional. More disturbing is the irregular situation of semiskilled operatives, who, as recently as 1963 needed seventeen years' seniority to be reasonably sure of their jobs at the Ford Motor Company plants in Detroit. While unemployment rates swing wildly (1969 marking fourteen-year lows for many blue-collar occupations), semiskilled workers have reason to be concerned over the fact that proportions of unemployment among the three blue-collar ability types and between industries have not varied greatly over the past ten years. Irregular unemployment is an integral part of the recent history of the semiskilled worker.

Ironically, the blue-collarites with the greatest job satisfaction are also those who appear to worry most about job satisfaction. Clearly, unskilled and semiskilled blue-collarites experience the most restrictive work conditions: Many are unable to control their immediate work processes (as do skilled building craftsmen), develop a sense of purpose and function (as do skilled engravers), find support in industrial communities (as do skilled printers—who socialize together after work), and experience work as a mode of personal expression. Nevertheless, while large numbers of skilled craftsmen enjoy these advantages over other blue-collarites, they apparently experience much more conflict and psychological stress than do the unskilled and the semiskilled. The expectations from work of skilled blue-collarites appear higher than those of other manual workers, and their anxiety concerning real and imagined challenges to their job satisfaction is often considerable. Alert and concerned, the craftsmen guard their work prerogatives with all the zeal commonly associated only with tradition-bound management groups.

Unique in their interest in passing along their own occupations (or even their particular jobs) to their sons as a filial legacy, skilled craftsmen remain apprehensive that fate will somehow trick them into defaulting on an intergenerational pledge that has helped rationalize an entire lifetime of manual labor. It is not enough that cybernation spare the craftsman's post: It is most important that none of "the enemy" (such as the noncraftsmen who enviously seek craftlike wages, or the industrial engineers who seek to build craft skills into machines that noncraftsmen can operate) transform the job so as to make it unworthy of occupational inheritance—and thereby shame the father in the eyes of his sons.

SKILL BLOC DEVELOPMENTS

Leaving to Chapter 6, "Blue-Collar Unionists," the account of skill bloc reactions to adversity, certain major technological changes that impinge at present on the skill bloc types will be examined here.

The major technological changes in 1969 are basically related to the intensification of the drive to automate industry.[12] Discrete production processes in the product lines of the twenty-one-industry aggregate are being converted into a flow; feedbacks and servomechanisms are being added, a computer is attached, and the job is done. In the 1930s, for example, an automobile engine block came from the foundry to an assembly line where 300 blue-collarites performed discrete operations that transformed the block into an engine in three and a half weeks. Nowadays the block is carried on a conveyor belt from the foundry to a series of computer tape-guided mechanical units, and in fifteen minutes an engine block is machined, untouched by human hands. Auto workers in this instance only monitor lights and dials to help adjust the line. Everyone involved is affected by change of this sort, the skill-level blocs in particular coming to look more and more like one another.

Typical of the upgrading in unskilled work going on at present is the job situation of a blue-collarite, Elmer McNeal, whose job-finding experience was recently reported by journalist Ben Bagdikian. In 1965 the twenty-nine-year-old McNeal left the ranks of the temporarily unemployed for the lowest-paid, lowest-status blue-collar job available in a nearby chemical plant. To land the job, McNeal first turned up among 500 others who had passed the company's screening interview and test battery (4,500 test takers were not hired, their scores being too low on the arithmetic test, aptitude test, personal vocational-interest test, IQ test, and the Minnesota Multiple Personality Inventory). As an unskilled packer working alone in a section of the shipping department, McNeal is sent a steady stream of Teletype messages in complex company jargon that has him select the proper size and type of drum, look up coded specifications, and mix the desired formula in triplicate combinations. While not especially difficult, the job remains quite nerve-racking, and as Bagdikian points out, "it is unlikely that 30 years ago this would have been required of the bottom-grade worker in any large industrial plant." [13]

The change involved in the ethos of unskilled work is also interesting. Where it once claimed the distinction of testing certain masculine attributes such as endurance, strength, hardiness, and vigor, it is becoming increasingly more mechanized, protected, and even commonplace. Typical is the change on the waterfront docks that eliminated manhandling of the cargo in favor of the highly mechanized loading and unloading of prepackaged metal containers of cargo. Writer Harvey Swados expects the containerization on the waterfront to alter the unskilled laborer's job there in several ways: "He will become more like other American workers, whether manual or white-collar: he will go to work more regularly, more steadily, more habitually, he will do what he is told—and in consequence I suspect he will come to like it less." [14]

Unlike unskilled work, semiskilled work is being neither upgraded nor downgraded, but is instead being altered in a rather skill-neutral way. For example, no significant change in necessary prejob schooling, on-the-job schooling, or physical exertion is involved in the replacement of twenty-five semiskilled riveters with one semiskilled tender of a giant automated riveting operation. A vital clue to the skill requirements of automated functions is clearly the training time they require, and where semiskilled workers are concerned, in-plant training programs of a rather brief duration seem to meet the need. An ordinary mechanic is readily trained to operate a numerically controlled machine tool, and the Department of Labor does not hesitate to recruit people with average educational records to train for computer-related or console-monitoring tasks. In short, while job content may change somewhat in form, it remains little altered in substance (that is, in the little discretion left to, and the considerable pressure for production placed on, the worker).

On the other hand, job settings are changing, and the semi-skilled automation console operator in the textile dye works, for example, now sits at ease in officelike surroundings where a short time ago he sweated among the steaming vats.[15] Nevertheless, color-matched officelike furniture and piped-in music notwithstanding, the console operator is paid semiskilled hourly or weekly wages, has probably reached the peak of his possible advancement, and may, with laborer Elmer McNeal, think with nostalgia on occasion of a romanticized past when a man strained only his muscles and could effectively reserve his mind at work for private reveries—rather than possibly experience his muscles grown soft and his mind grown weary from the strain of "babysitting" for a console dial board.

Skilled workers are presently in high demand, as many new maintenance and technical jobs are created during the introductory phase of the automation cycle. As the installation is debugged, however, many of these jobs prove transitory. Further advances lead machines into control positions over other machines, measurement is done electronically, and computers take over more and more of the data-logging and even data-analysis functions. For example, the production of various metal billets, electronic circuits, and machine subassemblies has already been taken entirely out of the hands of skilled workers and put under the guidance of computers.

Like the semiskilled worker the skilled blue-collarite enjoys an improvement in his work environment. The master roller in the steel industry, for example, rides in an air-conditioned cab where his predecessors sweltered. Unlike the semiskilled worker, however, the skilled blue-collarite may be losing important and arcane elements of his craft to still craftier machines. The master roller no longer uses controls in his cab to delicately manipulate massive levers below, but now appraises orders, surveys conditions, and (delicately?) feeds punched cards into a computer. The "new craftsman" may not see the product or work on it directly with his hands. Instead, he may only monitor the automatic control dials, inspect machinery, adjust valves, and record the data that describe the operations of a continuous-process operation. In place of the skilled craftsman one finds an alert and "skilled" attendant or watchman, a man capable of accepting machine-determined discretion, initiative, and responsibility.[16] While sharing some things with his immediate and direct predecessor, the "new worker" is much more his own man.

In short, as economist James Bright points out, high skill requirements tend to rise during the early installation and trial stages of automation, but may decrease thereafter.[17] Cost-reduction pressures motivate management to build skill into machines, and this ancient incentive is as operative in a Buck Rogers-like factory today as it was in the first large American factories of a mere 150 years ago.

SUMMARY

Few distinctions in the world of work are as significant today as is the distinction among the three skill-level blocs of blue-collarites, a distinction among a declining number of upward-bound unskilled workers, a growing number of stable semi-skilled workers, and an uncertain number of craft-fading skilled workers. Laborers find today that old-fashioned unskilled jobs are disappearing and that the remaining posts are being upgraded so that "unskilled" seems increasingly inappropriate as a designation. Semiskilled jobs are holding constant as a proportion of the labor force, and, aside from the substitution of some mental for much physical strain, remain as before. Skilled jobs are growing in number and in proportion. Additional evidence, however, raises the possibility that post-

automation development may include a far-reaching diminu-
tion in the special skills possessed—and perhaps even in the
numbers involved.

Notes to Chapter Three

1. For profiles of the three skill types, see Ira Wolfert, *An Epidemic of Genius* (New York: Simon and Schuster, 1960); W. F.
Whyte, *Men at Work* (Homewood, Ill.: Dorsey Press, 1961); Sig-
mund Nosow and William H. Form, *Man, Work, and Society: A
Reader in the Sociology of Occupations* (New York: Basic Books,
1962).

2. *The Negroes in the United States, Bulletin No. 1511, 1966,*
Bureau of Labor Statistics, p. 107.

3. *Statistical Abstract of the United States, 1965*, Department of
Commerce, Table 316, pp. 230–232. Most perplexing is the as-
sumption the data compel that all craftsmen are skilled, all operatives are semiskilled and all nonfarm laborers are unskilled. While
probably true in the largest number of cases, the amount of possible discrepancy remains unknown and vexsome. The Department
of Labor has recently abandoned the classification scheme employed in this chapter for this reason, and now uses six new and
five old occupational categories: The only old categories retained
are those of professional, clerical, sales, and service workers. See
the 1965 edition of the *Dictionary of Occupational Titles.*

4. In comparison only some 35 percent of the men employed in
1962 as professionals and some 50 percent of the managers had
not started out as such. Contrariwise, some 84 percent of all sales
workers and 81 percent of all clerical workers began in other
employ, an unknown number presumably starting out as blue-
collarites. Walter L. Slocum, *Occupational Careers, A Sociological
Perspective* (Chicago, Ill.: Aldine, 1966), pp. 174–175.

5. Harold L. Wilensky, "Orderly Careers and Social Participation," *American Sociological Review* (August 1961), pp. 525–526.
For a discussion of related studies, see Slocum, *op. cit.*, pp. 159–
185.

6. Department of Commerce, *Current Population Reports, Series
P-60, No. 51,* January 12, 1967, p. 40.

7. *Statistical Abstract* . . . , *op. cit.*, Table 316, pp. 230–233. See also C. C. Hodge and J. R. Wetzel, "Short Workweeks and Underemployment," *Monthly Labor Review* (September 1967), pp. 30–35.

8. *Manpower Report of the President, 1968,* Department of Labor (Washington, D.C.: Government Printing Office, 1968), p. 30. See also Mollie Orshansky, "More About the Poor in 1964," *Social Security Bulletin* (May 1966), Table 2, p. 6; Mollie Orshansky, "Counting the Poor: Another Look at the Poverty Profile," *Social Security Bulletin* (January 1965), Table 9, p. 10.

9. *U. S. Census 1960: PC (2)–3A,* Department of Commerce (Washington, D.C.: Government Printing Office, 1964). See "Women by Number of Children Ever Born."

10. Labor Research Association, *Labor Factbook No. 17* (New York: Labor Research Association, 1966), p. 31.

11. *Income Distribution in the United States,* by Herman P. Miller, U.S. Bureau of the Census (A 1960 Census Monograph) (Washington, D.C.: Government Printing Office, 1966), pp. 78, 80, 87, 91.

12. Unless otherwise noted, the data and illustrations that follow are drawn from Ben B. Seligman, *Most Notorious Victory: Man in an Age of Automation* (New York: Free Press, 1967). See also Bureau of Labor Statistics, *Tomorrow's Manpower Needs* (Washington, D.C.: Department of Labor, 1969).

13. Ben Bagdikian, "I'm Out of a Job, I'm All Through," *Saturday Evening Post,* December 18, 1965, p. 40.

14. Harvey Swados, "West-Coast Waterfront—The End of an Era," *Dissent* (Autumn 1961), p. 453.

15. For the case that environmental and other changes are "bleaching the blue-collar," see Thomas R. Brooks, *Toil and Trouble: A History of American Labor* (New York: Dial Press, 1965), p. 277. See also Mark Lefton, "The Blue Collar Worker and the Middle Class Ethic," *Sociology and Social Research* (January 1967), pp. 158–169. Cf. Richard F. Hamilton, "The Behavior and Values of Skilled Workers," in A. Shostak and W. Gomberg (eds.), *Blue Collar World* (Englewood Cliffs, N.J.: Prentice-Hall, 1964), pp. 42–58. On the British scene see W. G. Runciman, *Relative Deprivation and Social Justice: A Study of Attitudes to Social Inequality in 20th Century England* (Berkeley: University of California Press, 1966).

16. For an evaluation of the situation of the "new craftsmen" in

the continuous-process industries, see Robert Blauner, *Alienation and Freedom: The Factory Worker and His Industry* (Chicago: The University of Chicago Press, 1964).

17. James R. Bright, "The Relationship of Increasing Automation and Skill Requirements," in *The Employment Impact of Technological Change, Appendix, Volume II,* National Commission on Technology, Automation, and Economic Progress (Washington, D.C.: Government Printing Office, 1966), pp. 207–221. See also Paul Sultan and Paul Prasow, "Technology and Talent," *The Western Economic Journal* (Summer 1965), pp. 247–273.

4

BLUE-COLLAR WORK:
SUBJECTIVE FACTORS

Not failure, but low aim is crime.—J. R. LOWELL

While the preceding chapter has considered divisions among blue-collarites, there are certain commonalities that warrant attention as well. This is particularly true of four subjective features of blue-collar work—work status, work meaning, work satisfaction, and worker relationships—that clearly contrast with commonalities of white-collar work. Each of these blue-collar distinctions is discussed below, attention being paid throughout to the consequences entailed both for the blue-collar group and for society as a whole.

WORK STATUS

Blue-collarites begin and end the workday with the knowledge that their employ could hardly have less status. Manual workers occupy the bottommost rungs on the occupational status ladder. What is worse, their status may have even declined further with time. With regard to the five components of occupational status level (money, power, prestige, nature of the work, and amount of prerequisites, like education), blue-collar work clearly earns a low ranking in the judgment of the general public.[1]

Blue-collarites are sensitive to their low status. They are especially resentful of the debasing stereotypes that frequently accompany it: Longshoremen, for example, are commonly thought "craggy, tough, suspicious, close-mouthed, uncompromising, often one step ahead of the law, ready to strike at the drop of a baling hook." A New York longshoreman challenged this image of his occupation in a recent discussion with a newspaper journalist:

> The longshoreman always gets the blame whenever anything happens on the waterfront. We built up this industry with our backs and brawn, but we never get the credit, only the blame. I don't know what kind of people they think work down here . . . Everybody is right some of the time, but we're never right.[2]

Other reactions of workers toward the public include accenting selected aspects of the job, as with janitors who seek status in their boast that the safety of the building's inhabitants depends on them, or accenting the upgrading of job titles (waitresses become "food service specialists"; garbagemen become "sanitation aides").

Business often supports the process of enhancing blue-collar status: Typical is the copy of a new series of ads sponsored in 1967 on behalf of the American trucking industry. The ads praised the safety-conscious heroism of the blue-collar teamsters, men who have "earned their title, 'knights of the road,'" and concluded: "The American Trucking Industry is proud of its drivers." Similarly, a number of vocational schools seek to raise the image of the trades they prepare men for. A prominent school for truck drivers recently took nationwide ads urging readers to "put yourself in the 'Commander's Cockpit' ":

> Earn as much as $10,000 yearly and *more!* Enjoy the excitement, adventure, and prestige that can be yours as a pilot of giant over-the-highway transport rigs! Join the exclusive corps of keen-eyed, quick-thinking, professional men who help maintain America's life-line.[3]

The imagery speaks to issues of manliness, responsibility, elitism, professionalism, and patriotic contribution—a handsome list of alleged occupational attributes, all of a marked status-enhancing character.

Within the work group itself, blue-collarites seek status increments from variations in seniority, work skills, "pull" with management or with the local union, knowledge of baseball statistics, and the like. Many gain respect for an ability to mediate between the rigid specifications insisted upon by customers or supervisors and their own knowledge that much looser specifications will do. The informal association of workers enters in here, assigning in-plant status to "wise old gray-hairs" and others valued in the work group. The informal association also operates to assign low status to whole categories of coworkers, such as Negro or women workers, who thereafter constitute a negative reference group. Blue-collarites spared membership in the disparaged reference group gain much in-plant status from this fact alone, and the gradations here, however "invisible" to casual visitors to the workplace, can be very significant to the status-hungry men involved.

With all of this, the discomforts of low status remain serious. The situation is further compounded by the rising level of educational attainment of many younger workers, the rising standard of living of all workers, and the rising level of material expectations of many workers. As a significant increase in job status can lag far behind these other developments, blue-collarites may suffer the additional discomfort of status inconsistency: They may earn enough to "command respect," but the low blue-collar origins of their high earnings may undermine both their self-esteem and the respect they command from others.[4] (See Table 3.)

TABLE 3   Status Consistency of White Family Heads, 35 to 54 Years of Age, Living in Central Cities, by Socioeconomic Status: 1960

	All Statuses Consistent	One Status Inconsistent	All Statuses Inconsistent
Upper Class	64%	36%	—%
Middle Class	19	68	13
Working Class	12	72	16
Lower Class	61	39	—
All Classes	28	62	11

Source: Charles B. Nam and Mary G. Powers, "Variations in Socioeconomic Structure by Race, Residence, and the Life Cycle," *American Sociological Review* (February 1965), p. 100. Reprinted. I have added the class labels to their SES Score division of 0–19, 20–49, 50–79, and 80–99.

Intriguing is the finding above that blue-collarites, more so than any other occupational type, currently experience a great deal of status inconsistency. Irregularities of personal and social behavior are traced by researchers to such inconsistency, and these irregularities further set many blue-collarites off from persons with more consistent statuses. As sociologist Everett C. Hughes points out, the "dilemmas and contradictions" so posed nourish the roots of much discontent.[5]

Finally, in a relentlessly acquisitive society like our own, blue-collarites are always challenged by the example of similar but "better-off" men. Tony Calabrese, Shipfitter First Class, a fictional character in a new short story by Arthur Miller, has many such encounters:

> There was no mystery what the good life was, and he never lived a day without thinking about it, and more and more hopelessly now that he was past forty; it was being like Sinatra or Luciano, or even one of the neighborhood politicians who wore good suits all day and never bent over, kept two apartments, one for the

family, the other for the [woman] of the moment. He had put his youth into trying for that kind of life and had failed . . . He knew he was simply not smart enough. If he were, he wouldn't be working in the Brooklyn Navy Yard.[6]

Workers cannot avoid making dissonant comparisons, and often conclude they enjoy less status than they legitimately should. Envy edges along here very close to shame and anger, all three commingling on dramatic occasion.

Little wonder, then, that in the longshore interview situation referred to earlier, no dock worker listening dissented when the spokesman revealed much of his own situation in speaking of his dream for his son. In response to the suggestion that his son might some day come to the pier and be a longshoreman, the dock worker quietly informed the reporter: "I'll break his legs if he ever comes down here to work." [7]

WORK MEANING

To further compound the situation of the worker, his blue-collar work may also be in the process of losing its once-distinct and always precious ability to affirm manhood. Men especially rely on their work to confirm their sex role identity: Both in their own minds and in the judgment of others this constitutes an increasingly troublesome issue for blue-collarites.[8]

Work can affirm manhood, sociologist Robert Blauner explains, when it entails responsibility, control over tools and machinery, certified skill, initiative and self-assertion, the use of some intelligence, and the securement of the relatively high wages that symbolize masculine adequacy within the family and the larger society.[9] Craft jobs in particular encompass these characteristics. Moreover, they generally take place in an all-male setting and rely on a long apprenticeship that "separates the men from the boys." Little wonder then that being on a craft job in the first place more or less affirms masculine identity.

The situation is very different for the vast majority of blue-collarites who are semiskilled men working at machine-tending tasks (as in textile mills) or on assembly lines (as in auto, meat-packing, or rubber plants). Here the subdivision of labor has often permitted women to enter the labor force, and their presence as peers can threaten the firm sense of maleness of certain blue-collar men. The simplification of job tasks also means that not only women but "mere boys" are now capable of doing the work. Close supervision further implies the worker himself is still a child and is not yet mature enough to responsibly use freedom and autonomy. Finally, mechanization threatens the distinction men desire to preserve between themselves and their own machines (à la Chaplin in *Modern Times*). To the extent to which mechanization lessens the worker's control over technology and cuts down on the responsibility and mind-reliance of the job, the blue-collarite may find new meaning on the job hard to confront.

As if in desperation, workers earnestly play out the drama of manliness in work settings. Blue-collarites infuse their language with obscene oaths of Anglo-Saxon origin, stockpile impressive collections of off-color jokes, and traffic in pornography—all in an attempt to make the workplace "feel" more like a gathering place of men.[10] Others react to the encroachments of technology by inventing unofficial means of reasserting some degree of personal control (such as working out of sequence). The defense pattern here consists of rationalizations (work has no meaning for anyone), denial (reluctance to identify with the job), projection (the work force includes others still worse off), aggression (verbal and mitigated hostility toward the work process, the work, and the supervisors), withdrawal (horseplay, daydreams, fantasies of leaving to set up a small business), and compensation (emphasis on discussions of off-work sources of meaning, including sex relations, family life, and leisure activities). Most of the blue-collarites involved eventually adjust their identity to the erosion of work meaning (acquire an "occupational personality") or shift out of work roles that excessively punish them.

Blue-collarites, in short, may find the meaning of work as

often as not a negation rather than an affirmation of a basic sense of worthiness. Certain blue-collar work may and often does reduce manhood potentials, the vast majority of workers adopting a stance of indifference as a form of self-protection. If blue-collarites appear preoccupied with "playing it cool" at work, they may be so animated by the paucity of meaning of other possible responses. The typical worker appears lightly committed to his work, and his work appears to grow ever lighter in meaning for him.

WORK SATISFACTION

Research data, especially that collected and interpreted by psychologist Frederick Herzberg and his associates, suggest the novel conclusion that blue-collarites may know little of either dissatisfaction or satisfaction from their work.[11]

There are apparently three states of being where job-related sentiments are involved: Workers can be dissatisfied, or they can be satisfied, or they can be neither. Satisfaction is viewed as resulting primarily from the challenge of the job itself, through such factors as achievement, responsibility, growth, advancement, and earned recognition. Dissatisfaction more often springs from workplace factors peripheral to the task, such as conditions of work, character of supervision, level of pay, and others.

All of these workplace items conjoin with important external variables, including the worker's frame of reference (a steadily employed worker thinks himself well off in a depressed area), to form a complicated calculus of job sentiment. This calculus is further conditioned by the worker's history (for example, former rural dwellers find change in blue-collar work more unsettling than do comparatively inured urbanites), the comparative performance of "significant others" (usually the worker's male relatives of the same age cohort), and the worker's estimation of available or future realistic alternatives to his present job.[12]

Taking all this into account, the research of Herzberg and

associates suggests blue-collarites by and large are neither dis-satisfied or satisfied, but are instead uneasily in-between. They "make do." Such men often tell researchers work is not a "central life interest" for them; they are working only to insure an after-work pursuit of happiness.[13] Many such men remain vaguely aware and uneasy about the possibilities for job satis-faction that they never totally experience. In their situation satisfaction at the job has apparently become less significant (for being less attainable) than satisfaction from consumption, and success at one's job has become less important than success in one's after-work style of life.

WORKER RELATIONSHIPS

So significant is the need for positive association with fellow workers, for communication with others who can be counted upon to understand, that men regularly rank this need very near the top of their list of significant situational items at work. This is not to suggest that things are always rewarding when blue-collarites are in continuous contact with one an-other. On the contrary, a number of tradition-bound animosities divide blue-collarites in many work situations, animosities by no means as characteristic of white-collarites.

Typical here is the strain that sets men and women against one another in the workplace. Constant wrangling character-izes situations where women give orders to status-anxious blue-collar men. Male kitchen help, for example, resent taking orders from female waitresses. The men demand social insula-tion and insist that orders be written down rather than shouted loudly about the place.[14] More generally, blue-collar men resent the possibility that working women might be displacing other men from gainful employ. A woman's place, they believe, is in the home with her kids, away from the competitive labor market. Her presence as a workplace peer is thought to jeop-ardize the physical and emotional health of her children, undermine the self-esteem of her husband, and provide indus-try with a competitive menace it will use to depress wages, dilute skills, and remove men from their "natural" work roles. Women who want to remain in the plant are condemned for "trying to get ahead of the Joneses." Married women are thought to stay in the shop because they "spend indiscriminately, consume conspicuously, and overextend household income in their nervous desire for social status." [15] Working women, of course, deny and resent these allegations, the battle of the sexes raging both on and below the surface in many a blue-collar setting.

Race differences also set blue-collarites against one another and, as with sex antagonisms, appear more characteristic of blue- than of white-collar relationships. This is probably related less to relative degrees of sex or race prejudice than it is to the fact that there are more women either originating orders for men or working as peers in blue-collar settings than in white-collar workplaces; similarly, there are far more Negro manual than Negro white-collar workers.

Sociologist Sidney M. Peck's 1959 study of the attitudes of union shop stewards sheds light on the anti-Negro sentiment that moves as an undercurrent throughout the ranks of Caucasian blue-collarites.[16] Some workers are resentful of an over-reaction of Negro workers to the race issue in work matters (if Negroes would not "cry" or "holler" so quickly, there would be "no trouble at all"). Some criticize an alleged lack of incentive for educational self-improvement and emphasize the poor work habits of certain Negroes. Many of the shop unionists Peck interviewed considered Negro workers immature, childish, impetuous, and generally irresponsible. Above all, white blue-collarites fear that as Negroes gain education and training they may be willing to work for half the going wage rate. This could lower wage standards and might mean that Negroes would replace white workers.

Equally significant, though not affecting union or blue-collar cohesiveness, is the general relationship and mutual antagonism of contingent blue- and white-collarites. Clerks, typists, technicians, office workers, and low-echelon supervisors engage in daily face-to-face relationship with blue-collarites, relationships rich in clues to the culture of the workplace.

Many blue-collarites are critical and disdainful of the white-collar men they refer to as "desk jockeys" and "pencil pushers." (Sociologist Robert Blauner suggests that the traditional distrust and mutual feeling of distance here is probably as old as the division between the literate and nonliterate strata that emerged with the invention of writing.)[17] Blue-collarites frequently "write off" office workers as men who have sold out their masculine heritage for the dubious merits of a white shirt and higher social status. At the same time, however, blue-collar derision of white-collarites does not preclude many from selecting the white-collar post as an appropriate occupational target for their sons. Indeed, blue-collarites seriously differ among themselves in the character of their jealousy of white-collarites. In the last analysis, many would rather have their sons follow the white-collarite into a technical, professional, administrative, or even clerical post than follow the "old man" into the plant. (One wonders at what price to family solidarity and father-son relations comes the presence of the father as a negative reference model, a man who insists his career is not to be emulated, but is to be avoided?)

Sex, race, and class tensions only begin to suggest the kind and quality of divisions where blue-collarites are concerned. Other divisive items include age, educational attainment, religion, region of origin, marital status, political opinions, leisure preferences, and occupational aspirations.[18] Informal relationships, of course, cut across these demarcations, linking younger, better-educated men regardless of race, or older deep-sea fishing enthusiasts regardless of religion, marital status, or political opinion. The divisive items are ever-present, however, and remain both a challenge to local union solidarity and a drain on affable relationships among shoulder-rubbing manual workers.

SUMMARY

Every line of work has its particular subjective factors. Large numbers of blue-collarites know the corrosive humiliation of low status and unmanly work. They share fully in the many animosities that cross-cut the workforce. Many know an absence of either work dissatisfaction or work satisfaction. And they may lose ground in the struggle to keep the idea of themselves as human beings from getting itself stamped, ground, hammered, buffed, or chiseled entirely away.

A number of blue-collarites, in sum, are challenged to grow beyond the subjective limitations of their present work. In the fact that many are unequal to this challenge can be found the origins of much of their discontent and much of their anxious behavior and attitudes off the job. Many of these men spend their lives at jobs beneath their dignity, jobs barely redeemed by any genuine social purpose or relation to real human need. They do not simply adjust or fail to adjust to work, but are deeply and continually changed by their work.

Notes to Chapter Four

---

1. National Opinion Research Center, "Jobs and Occupations: A Popular Evaluation," reprinted in Reinhard Bendix and Seymour M. Lipset (eds.), *Class, Status and Power* (Glencoe, Ill.: Free Press, 1963). See also Albert J. Reiss, Jr., *et al.*, *Occupations and Social Status* (Glencoe, Ill.: Free Press, 1961); Robert W. Hodge, *et al.*, "Occupational Prestige in the United States, 1925–1963," *American Journal of Sociology* (November 1964), pp. 286–302; A. P. Garbin and F. L. Bates, "Occupational Prestige and Its Correlates: A Re-Examination," *Social Forces* (March 1966), pp. 296–302. A useful beginning for a new perspective is available in Richard T. Morris and Raymond J. Murphy, "The Situs Dimension in Occupational Structure," *American Sociological Review* (April 1959), pp. 231–239.

2. All quotations in the paragraph are from Frank Sugrue, "Longshoremen's Beef: Image Muddied Up," *World Journal Tribune*, March 26, 1967, pp. 1, 24.

3. See, for example, the Bostrom Corporation ad, in *Business Week*, March 25, 1967, p. 26. See also the March 1967 ads of the National Professional Truck Driver Training School, Philadelphia, Pa., and the July 1967 *Saturday Evening Post* ads of the Whirlpool Corporation on their factory-trained repairmen.

4. For discussion, see Charles B. Nam and Mary G. Powers, "Variations in Socioeconomic Structure by Race, Residence, and the Life Cycle," *American Sociological Review* (February 1965), pp. 97–103. See also Elton F. Jackson, "Status Consistency and Symptoms of Stress," *American Sociological Review* (August 1962), pp. 469–480.

5. Everett C. Hughes, "Dilemmas and Contradictions of Status," *American Journal of Sociology* (March 1945), pp. 353–359: Lee Braude, "Work: A Theoretical Clarification," *Sociological Quarterly* (Fall 1963), pp. 343–348.

6. Arthur Miller, "Fitter's Night," in *I Don't Need You Any More* (New York: Viking, 1967), pp. 177–178.

7. Sugrue, *op. cit.* Note also that a 1957 Roper Poll found that 72 percent of the professional people polled, 50-odd percent of the white-collarites, but only 37 percent of the blue-collarites not in factories and 30 percent of those in factories would choose their present occupation again. As reported by Stuart Chase, in *American Credos* (New York: Harper & Brothers, 1962), p. 98.

8. See in this connection, Ely Chinoy, "Manning the Machines—The Assembly-Line Worker" in Peter L. Berger (ed.), *The Human Shape of Work* (New York: Macmillan, 1964), pp. 75–80. See also David L. Miller, "The Individual as a 'Cog' in a Machine or in a System," *The Southwestern Social Science Quarterly* (Fall 1966), pp. 297–308: Lewis Mumford, *Technics and Civilization* (New York: Harcourt, Brace & World, 1934).

9. Robert Blauner, "Work, Self, and Manhood: Some Reflections on Technology and Identity," a paper presented to the 1964 Meeting of the American Sociological Association, Montreal, Canada. See also "The Themes of Work and Play in the Structure of Freud's Thought" in David Riesman, *Individualism Reconsidered and Other Essays* (Glencoe, Ill.: Free Press, 1954), pp. 301–333; "The Role of Work" in Sol W. Ginsburg, *A Psychiatrist's Views on Social Issues* (New York: Columbia University Press, 1963), pp. 162–177; Braude, *op. cit.*; Arthur B. Shostak, "The Impact of Business on the Meaning of Work," in Ivar Berg (ed.), *The Impact of Business on American Life* (New York: Harcourt, Brace & World, 1968), pp. 338–360.

10. Lalia Phipps Boone, "Patterns of Innovation in the Language of the Oil Fields," *American Speech* (February 1949), pp. 26–35. "Amongst workers such words have . . . everyday use which almost empties them of derogatory significance" (p. 31).

11. Frederick Herzberg, *Work and the Nature of Man* (Cleve-

land: World, 1966). See also Alex Carey, "The Hawthorne Studies: A Radical Criticism," *American Sociological Review* (June 1967), pp. 403–416; F. Herzberg, *et al., The Motivation to Work* (New York: Wiley, 1959). Cf. "Work and Its Satisfactions" in Ginsburg, *op. cit.*: G. P. Fournet, *et al.*, "Job Satisfaction: Issues and Problems," *Personnel Psychology* (Summer 1966), pp. 165–183; Frank Friedlander, "Motivations to Work and Organizational Performance," *Journal of Applied Psychology* (Spring 1966), pp. 143–152.

12. Charles L. Hulin, "Effects of Community Characteristics on Measures of Job Satisfaction," *Journal of Applied Psychology* (1966), pp. 185–192; William A. Faunce, "Social Stratification and Attitude Toward Change in Job Content," *Social Forces* (December 1960), pp. 140–148.

13. Robert Dubin, "Industrial Workers' Worlds: A Study of the Central Life Interests of Industrial Workers," *Social Problems* (1956), pp. 131–142; Robert Dubin, *The World of Work* (Englewood Cliffs, N.J.: Prentice-Hall, 1958).

14. See in this connection, "From Kitchen to Customer," in W. F. Whyte, *Men at Work* (Homewood, Ill.: Dorsey Press, 1961), pp. 125–135.

15. See in this connection, "A Woman's Place Is with Her Kids" in Sidney M. Peck, *The Rank-and-File Leader* (New Haven: College and University Press, 1965), pp. 180–208. "Practically every suggested remedy [made by the white male union stewards] resolves to eliminate women from industry" (p. 205).

16. "Some of the Best Guys I Know Are . . . ," *ibid.*, pp. 152–172. See also "The Chance to Get Ahead" in T. V. Purcell, *Blue Collar Man* (Cambridge, Mass.: Harvard University Press, 1960), pp. 119–136. On the factual basis of the fears of white workers, see Alma F. Taeuber, *et al.*, "Occupational Assimilation and the Competitive Process: A Re-analysis," *American Journal of Sociology* (November 1966), pp. 273–285. Cf. Robert W. Hodge and Patricia Hodge, "Comment," *ibid.*, pp. 286, 289. See also Charles S. Johnson, "The Conflict of Caste and Class in an American Industry" in S. Nosow and W. H. Form (eds.), *Man, Work, and Society* (New York: Basic Books, 1962), pp. 142–149; Robert W. Hodge and Patricia Hodge, "Occupational Assimilation as a Competitive Process," *The American Journal of Sociology* (November 1965), p. 264; Herbert Harris, "The Riddle of the Labor Vote," *Harper's Magazine* (October 1964), p. 45.

17. Robert Blauner, *Alienation and Freedom: The Factory*

Worker and His Industry (Chicago: University of Chicago Press, 1964), p. 179. See also E. P. Thompson, *The Making of the English Working Class* (New York: Random House, 1963).

18. For rare comment on the division engendered by fears of homosexuality among anxious, overcompensating blue-collarites, see Gerald W. Haslam, "The Language of the Oil Fields," *Etc.* (June 1967), p. 197, *passim*.

5

BLUE-COLLAR WORK: OBJECTIVE FACTORS

To the worker who cannot receive technical gratifications fron his work, its market value is all there is to it.
—C. WRIGHT MILLS, *White Collar*

Blue-collarites are not only set off from the rest of the workforce by the subjective matters reviewed in the preceding chapter but also by four objective matters that confer a very dubious distinctiveness on them. Each is discussed below, with the question of cost and consequence being raised in turn about wage levels, shift hours, work safety conditions, and work security. Together their significance helps explain what George Bernard Shaw may have had in mind when he wrote: "The very last thing the ordinary industrial worker wants is to have to think about his work."[1]

WORK COMPENSATION

Blue-collarites share disproportionately in the lower levels of the fringe benefit division and in the comparative ranking of occupations by compensation.

Fringe benefits have grown considerably. They now average about 82.2 cents per hour, or 26.6 percent of average hourly pay, up from 50 cents an hour or 17 percent twenty years ago. The National Industrial Conference Board now counts more than fifty kinds of fringes, including such well-known items as vacations; medical, life, and accident insurance; pensions, Christmas bonuses, production savings payments, and education allowances. Rockwell Standard Corporation, for example, points out to its employees that their fringe benefits, if individually acquired, could absorb up to half of their wages.[2]

It is also true, however, that 48 percent of the blue-collarites in the latest (1966) national survey of the Department of Labor have to work more than ten years to gain an annual vacation of three weeks; 22 percent have to work over fifteen years to qualify for this benefit. Some 70 percent have only seven or fewer paid holidays; 12 percent have six or less. Some 25 percent have no medical insurance, 60 percent have no catastrophe insurance, and 20 percent have no sick leave. As for retirement pensions, 27 percent of the blue-collarites can work their entire 45-year work lives without any pension waiting for them at the end.[3] To put this in sharper perspective, note that the comparable percentages for white-collarites are as follows: 34, 13, 78, 5, 18, 27, 21, and 18 percent; in other words, a clear-cut advantage for white-collarites.

The unevenness of the fringe benefit situation only begins to tell one side of the work compensation story. Blue-collarites occupy the bottommost rungs in the compensation ladder, as documented in Table 4. Note also that during the year referred to in Table 4 the average city family of four people required well over $8,000 to secure a "modest but adequate level of living."

TABLE 4   Median Earnings, Males, Both Races, Year-Round Full-Time Workers, 1965

Professionals	$8,459
Managers	7,895
Clerical	6,280
Sales Workers	7,226
Craftsmen (excluding foremen)	6,583
Semiskilled Operatives	5,782
Service Workers (excluding private household)	4,874
Unskilled Laborers (excluding farm and mine)	4,651

Source: Department of Commerce, *Statistical Abstract of the United States, 1967* (Washington, D.C.: Government Printing Office, 1968), Table 338, p. 240.

The degree to which an adequate income standard eludes many blue-collarites is made clear in Table 5.

TABLE 5   Income of Families by Occupation of Head, Both Races, 1960

	Under $3,000	$3,000– $4,999	$5,000– $9,999	$10,000 and Over
Professional and Managerial	14.7%	17.4%	26.5%	57.0%
Clerical and Sales	7.3	13.5	16.0	12.7
Craftsmen	9.0	16.9	24.7	15.5
Operatives	14.3	24.2	20.5	8.4
Laborers	16.5	10.0	4.3	1.5
Service Workers (including private household)	14.1	10.1	5.6	3.0
Farmers and Farm Managers	24.1	8.0	2.4	1.9

Source: U.S. Bureau of the Census, *Income Distribution in the United States*, by Herman Miller (A 1960 Census Monograph), (Washington, D.C.: Government Printing Office, 1966), Table II–1, p. 34. No control for race.

Not surprisingly, then, blue-collarites do not have the kinds of possessions and living circumstances they desperately want for themselves, as suggested by Table 6. Many blue-collarites are anxious to replace items they do have; a national survey finds the peak of economic discontent is reached by those in the in-

TABLE 6   Households Reporting Specified Items, by Occupation of Employed Male Head, and Dominant Income Bracket, Both Races, 1959

	Auto Available	Telephone Available	Hot Piped Water	House in Sound Condition	All Four Items
Professionals and Managers	98%	98%	100%	99%	94%
Clerical and Sales	92	92	99	93	80
Craftsmen and Operatives	82	62	80	72	40
Service Workers and Laborers	70	57	75	65	37

SOURCE: James D. Cowhig, *Urban and Rural Levels of Living: 1960* (Washington, D.C.: Department of Agriculture, Agricultural Economic Report No. 79, 1965), Table 5, p. 17. Data are for Dominant Income Bracket, as established in Table 1 of this chapter. No control for race.

come range of $5,000 to $7,499, where two-thirds wish to buy or replace items.[4]

In the marketplace blue-collarites know a host of constraints on "the good life." Price rises continuously erode real income gains and few blue-collarites attempt in any systematic way to stay abreast of quality variations. Mass media pressures to acquire material goods by time-and-credit buying are especially compelling, as work provides few rewards beyond wage compensation itself.

Typical is the record of Frank H., a Seattle blue-collar warehouseman earning $7,000 a year, who was "profiled" in 1966 as part of a *Wall Street Journal* series on how Americans are contending with inflation.[5] To help reduce $800 in outstanding debts and to cover the expenses of his wife and five children, Frank tries to save money by having his hair cut at a barber school, shopping only at discount stores, stretching milk by blending it half and half with powdered milk and water, taking a boarder into his home, hauling home his own fuel oil, and doing all his own household repairs in return for a rent deduction. His wife contributes by preserving fruits and jam, sewing most of her clothes and those of the children, and preparing especially economical dishes.

Their marketplace problems are several. For one, the family must make do with second-grade items ("The meat is utility-grade beef. You have to beat hell out of it, tenderize it, hang it out for a couple of days, and hope. It's cheap."). Many popular items are by-passed entirely ("Seattle is supposed to be the salmon capital, and it's 99 cents for one little, tiny can of salmon. I've quit buying it, it makes me so mad."). Secondhand buying frequently betrays them, and has left them owing $400 on a 1954 car they purchased in 1961. Frank agreed to pay about 25 percent interest on his auto loan, and the car gave out after four months of use. Subsequently they have gone through three other used cars, and presently own a 1954 truck and a rundown 1957 Plymouth. The $9,500 home they purchased in 1957 they lost soon after to a mortgage company. During a then-current recession Frank had taken a demotion to remain employed, but the babies and bills kept coming:

> I tried some moonlighting. I went on the graveyard shift at Boeing, then worked for two weeks as a Fuller Brush man in the daytime. I drove a truck for a month. I couldn't hack it; that's no way to beat inflation or bills, to have two paychecks.

While the family had $3,500 equity in the house, they only received $900 out of it, and all of that went for unpaid bills.

Frank now has no savings, but hopes to soon join a new company savings plan. His special worry involves how he will eventually finance the college education of his youngsters. Overall, however, his payday-to-payday existence apparently causes no bitterness: "I make a good living; nobody asked me to have five kids. If I could afford it, I'd fill this house with kids." Here is where Frank's typicality may fade, both in his easy accommodation and in his desire for still more children. The question of family size is the subject of a later chapter; here it may be noted that many other blue-collarites, living much as Frank does, are more bitter.

WORK HOURS: SHIFT WORK

Blue-collarites share disproportionately in the growing ranks of men required or induced to work after-5-P.M. shifts. While various benefits of late afternoon and night work are well known (10 to 15 percent pay differentials, looser supervision, easier commuting and parking, and so on), other drawbacks are less obvious.

An extensive folklore exists among blue-collarites to the effect that shift work depresses the worker's life, that night workers have more illnesses, and that men age more rapidly doing shift work. Also associated with night work are absenteeism, lateness, and more accidents. Survey results bear out various drawbacks of shift work. A 1962 national survey found afternoon-shift workers complaining of going days without seeing their school-age children, while night workers reported difficulty in such role performances as sexual relations and protection of the wife from harm. Shift workers reported few memberships in voluntary associations and little participation in those joined. Shift workers also complained that they were fatigued much of the time, that their appetites were dulled, that they were frequently constipated, and that they had trouble sleeping. Significantly, age and length of service on a shift were not related to complaint level: One does not necessarily "get used to it." [6]

To be sure, some workers volunteer for shift work to escape from family responsibilities, or a henpecking wife, or "unappreciative" children, or the din and roar of small living quarters overrun by children. Some prefer shift work for its easygoing air and the thin number of men in the workplace and plant cafeteria. But others—a large, if precisely unknown number— never get used to the shift work they did not volunteer for but share in as a condition of employment.

Shift differentials, or extra pay for working late hours, are commonly offered as the major solution for shift-related problems. Although the extra money is always welcomed, it does not resolve the physical, psychological, or social problems that shift work creates. A palliative, the financial differential lulls workers for a short time, and when they stir restlessly again, they discover they can transfer to a day job only at a marked financial loss. A new dilemma is added to the blue-collarites' problems. Increased income means a greater ability to pay bills and possibly buy necessities or even luxuries. Continued shift work, however, means a lack of time in which to enjoy such advantages, a lack of family life, and a lack of community involvement. Many men remain on night work for economic reasons long after they might prefer to transfer to more normal work hours for physical, mental, or social reasons.[7]

WORK HAZARDS

Blue-collarites share disproportionately in the so-called hazardous occupations. These include the cleaning of machinery in motion, the operation of cranes or freight elevators, the manufacture or use of explosives, the operation of certain types of power-driven machines, repair of electrical wires, work in mines or quarries, work on scaffolding, and work with poisonous dyes or gases. Nearly 100,000 Appalachian coal miners suffer from "black lung," a preventable disabling chest disease caused by their work. More than 7 million blue-collarites work in noisy jobs that seriously endanger their hearing. Another 4 million blue-collarites in manufacturing, construction, and automotive repair labor under conditions either immediately dangerous to their health or hazardous enough to require continual inspection. Yet it is estimated that 80 percent of the nation's workers are employed in places where no type of employee health service is now provided.[8]

Work injuries this year will involve 7 million employees, another 2 million being disabled by occupational accidents, while still 500,000 more are disabled by occupational diseases. Annually, some 85,000 are permanently maimed, and more than 14,500 are killed on the job.[9] In other words, every working day finds 55 men killed, 8,500 disabled, and over 27,200 injured on the job. Every minute of the working day 18 to 20 people are hurt severely enough to have to leave their jobs, some of them never to work again. Overall, accidents at work cost blue-collarites far more lost time than the better-publicized and guarded-against work stoppages. In 1966 the ratio was ten to one in favor of work accidents.[10]

What is even more alarming, additional risks are also created every year by thousands of new gases, acids, ores, chemical compounds, and radioactive substances. (In the state of Pennsylvania, for example, state health officials are trying to keep tabs on 8,000 industrial sources of ionizing radiation alone.) New uses of cadmium mean new hazards for storage battery makers, ceramic makers, dental amalgam makers, engravers, lithographers, and solderers. Benzene, an increasingly popular solvent, threatens to afflict the central nervous system, and will include among its victims this year a growing number of dry cleaners, furniture finishers, oil processors, painters, welders, printers, photographic chemical makers, bronzers, cobblers, and degreasing workers. Even with advance warning, the situation nevertheless allows for much improvement. All the more dire, then, is the fact that voluntary exposure limits exist for only 400 of the 6,000 industrial chemicals in substantial use, and, the total of federal and state safety inspectors averages out to about 17 inspectors for each state in the union.[11]

Safety programs in industry are estimated to have resulted in a 67 percent decrease in accidental deaths on the job between 1912 and 1965.[12] Unfortunately, many small plants of 500 or fewer employees, a type equal to 98 percent of all working establishments and to the employ of 67 percent of all workers, contain little in the way of modern safety programs. (Even more alarming is the fact that one-third of the labor force is not covered by any workmen's compensation.) Safety efforts, in any case, vary widely in character and quality. As Congress continues to refuse to set national standards in an Occupational Health and Safety Bill, the joint labor-management committees in some plants have secured reforms of consequence, while in other plants a superficial committee is little more than a sinecure for certain "politicians" among the workers who value time away from their own routine jobs.

In many plants considerable strain has come to characterize employee-employer relations in this area. This is especially true where workers have explained to a supervisor that a particular repair was called for before production should proceed, only to be ordered to make the (safety-related) repair at some future "slack" time and to keep production rolling. Supervisors concerned with safety often find it difficult to withstand constant pressures for production and to weigh objectively the hazards of a given situation. Furthermore, company emphasis on good safety records has been known to lead to an open conspiracy on the part of management personnel to conceal the actual extent of accidents and to pressure workers not to report accidents.

WORK SECURITY

More so than white-collar, managerial, or professional types, blue-collarites are threatened with short- and long-term layoffs. Workers have no property right to their jobs, either by law or, as in industrial Japan, by social convention. Certain employers adjust to economic pressures by reducing the variable cost of labor, and, as Table 7 makes plain, blue-collarites live with uncertainty where job security is involved.

As journalist Paul Jacobs puts it, "to people for whom the only really important inquiry is not 'What is your field?' but 'Where do you work?' the threat of unemployment is a spectre that haunts them." [13] Some workers may refuse to accept the prospect of future unemployment, as if accepting such a possibility somehow destroyed their belief in their own value as individuals with a work function that they perform uniquely. Still others turn to the union, but their solidarity often weakens when internal disputes break out in the local over seniority and layoffs. Above all, employed blue-collarites watch warily for clues to their dispensability. Every management move is ap-

TABLE 7 Distribution of the Unemployed, Percent and Rate, by Occupation, Both Races, 1950–1968

	1950	1955	1960	1965	Unemployment Rate: 1965, 1968*	
Professionals	3.1%	2.2%	3.4%	3.8%	1.5	1.2
Managers	3.2	2.2	2.5	2.4	1.1	1.0
Clerical	8.2	8.0	9.8	10.8	3.3	3.0
Sales	4.9	3.6	4.2	4.7	3.4	2.8
Craftsmen	13.8	12.8	12.1	9.9	3.6	2.4
Operatives	26.9	28.2	26.5	22.4	5.5	4.5
Laborers	14.2	15.3	13.3	10.2	8.6	7.2
Service	10.3	11.7	9.9	11.9	5.5	4.6
Others (Farm; Private Household; No previous work experience)	15.4	16.0	18.3	23.9	2.6 (Farm only)	2.1

* Data from *Statistics on Manpower: A Supplement to the Manpower Report of the President, March 1969,* U.S. Department of Labor, Table A–14, p. 16. No control for race.
SOURCE: Department of Labor, *Manpower Report of the President, 1966,* Table A-16, p. 170.

praised for its significance to the prime desire of all: remaining gainfully employed. Many a blue-collarite fears he will discover in his middle age that his skills are no longer needed, that he is suddenly and emphatically a surplus commodity, a "discontinued model."

These reactions—protective disbelief, anxious self-seeking through union seniority protection, and wariness—have two major consequences. First, the blue-collar workforce is seriously divided by the issue. Older workers rely on accrued seniority for protection and middle-aged workers rely on accrued skills to insure speedy reemployment. Younger workers are left especially vulnerable, and this difference makes itself felt in patterns of friendship among workers and in patterns of local union politics. Second, the fundamental philosophic skepticism of the blue-collarite is fed by job insecurity. The worker never quite trusts the security of his livelihood.

SUMMARY

Every line of work has its own particular objective factors. Large numbers of blue-collarites, for example, know daily exposure to hazardous conditions. Their work hours are inadequate to their income needs and are often irregular in character. Their compensation runs behind both their bills and their consumption goals, even while their hold on the work itself seems tenuous to many of them. These blue-collarites, quite possibly a representative type, are clearly not honored by their work: The talmudic adage, "Great Is Work, for It Honors the Workman," is apparently known to few and experienced by even fewer.[14]

Notes to Chapter Five

---

1. Quoted by Edward F. Murphy, in "Quotes: Labor," *The New York Times Magazine,* September 6, 1964, p. 54.

2. "Employers Toot on the Horn of Plenty," *Business Week* (January 28, 1967), pp. 94, 99; "Should Wages Embrace Fringes?," *Business Week* (February 15, 1969), p. 53.

3. Bureau of Labor Statistics, *Handbook of Labor Statistics* (Washington, D.C.: Government Printing Office, 1967), Tables 96, 98, 99, pp. 193, 195. See also W. Kolodrubetz, "Employee-Benefit Plans in 1966," *Social Security Bulletin* (April 1968), pp. 23–40.

4. James N. Morgan, *et al., Productive Americans* (Ann Arbor: Survey Research Center Monograph 43, 1966), p. 278. "There is presumably some basic stock and some potential saturation at the highest income levels."

5. Harold H. Brayman, "Inflation and a Working Man's Life," *Wall Street Journal,* August 8, 1966, pp. 1, 9.

6. Paul E Mott, *et al., Shift Work: The Social, Psychological, and Physical Consequences* (Ann Arbor: University of Michigan, Institute for Social Research, Survey Research Center, 1963).

7. Floyd C. Mann and L. Richard Hoffman, *Automation and the Worker* (New York: Holt, 1960). See especially Chapter 5,

"Continuous Operation: Patterns and Effects," pp. 105–140. See also "The Night People," *Wall Street Journal*, January 4, 1967, pp. 1, 10.

8. Neil W. Chamberlain, *The Labor Sector: An Introduction to Labor in the American Economy* (New York: McGraw-Hill, 1965), p. 537. See also "New Dangers: Job Health Risks Tied to Technology," *AFL-CIO News*, June 4, 1966, p. 2.

9. "For Dual Approach: LBJ Asks Increase in Job Health Funds," *AFL-CIO News*, March 11, 1967, p. 8.

10. Benjamin Aaron, "The Strike: A Current Assessment" (Los Angeles: Institute of Industrial Relations, University of California at Los Angeles, April 1967, unpublished mimeographed paper), p. 2. See also Anon., "Higgins Hits C of C on Job Safety Lies," *AFL-CIO News*, May 11, 1968, p. 5.

11. Ralph Nader and Jerome Gordon, "Safety on the Job," *New Republic* (June 15, 1968), p. 23. See also Murray C. Brown, "Health Hazards in the Workplace," *AFL-CIO Federationist* (May 1966), pp. 16–19. The inspector estimate is from the *AFL-CIO News*, June 7, 1969, p. 8.

12. "Industry Doctors Try New Approach," *Business Week* (May 13, 1967), pp. 81–82. On the union tie-up, see Joseph Ershun, "Death of a Steelworker," *The Nation* (January 16, 1960), pp. 50–52. On problems in accident rehabilitation, see A. J. Jaffee, *et al.*, *Disabled Workers in the Labor Market* (Totowa, N.J.: Bedminster Press), 1964.

13. Paul Jacobs, "A View from the Other Side: Unemployment as Part of Identity" in W. G. Bowen and F. H. Harbison (eds.), *Unemployment in a Prosperous Economy* (Princeton: Industrial Relations Section, 1965), p. 59. See also Don Marsh, "Chaos in the Coal Fields," *The Nation* (January 26, 1963), pp. 69, 72.

14. Daniel Bell, *Work and Its Discontents: The Cult of Efficiency in America* (Boston: Beacon Press, 1956). See also A. Shostak, "The Impact of Business on Meaning of Work," in Ivar Berg (ed.), *The Impact of Business on American Life* (New York: Harcourt, Brace & World, 1968), pp. 338–360.

6

BLUE-COLLAR UNIONISTS

The American Labor Movement, one has been repeatedly told in recent years, is either dead or dying. In fact, it may well be stirring to new life.
—Michael Harrington, *Toward a Democratic Left*

Beneficiaries of bloody struggles in the 1930s that secured the right to form labor unions, some 60 percent of the nation's blue-collarites are presently trade unionists.[1] Members of the largest joint voluntary association in the nation, the blue-collar unionists leave their clear stamp on 150,000 labor-management contracts, 60,000 local unions, 190-odd international unions, and the 14-million-member AFL-CIO itself.[2] This chapter, focusing especially on the grass-roots level of the local unions, discusses significant types of blue-collar unionists and considers related contemporary issues in union democracy, militancy, and political affairs. A closing section looks at the plight of the blue-collar shop steward, a man who more than any other symbolizes Labor to the worker—and whose plight reveals much about the strengths and weaknesses of grass-roots unionism in our country.

UNION MEMBERS

To help make sense of the otherwise dizzying array of 16 million rank-and-file trade unionists, students of the subject have devoted considerable effort and ingenuity to the construction of membership typologies. Especially useful in underlining the important diversity that marks the rank and file is a classification that distinguishes among loyal Patriots, critical Gripers, uncommonly fearful Fence-Sitters, and independent-minded Pickers and Choosers.[3] Of these, the largest number of blue-collarites are thought to be of the Pickers and Choosers variety, and it is this bloc of manual workers that probably holds the balance of power in local union decision-making. Members of this bloc characteristically reserve the right to ponder and evaluate every union option available to them.

Blue-collar Accommodators—or, as discussed elsewhere in the volume, those who acquiesce early in their own blue-collar destinies and take the path of least resistance in all things—probably provide the largest number of Pickers and Choosers. Many are too urbane or wary to join the Patriots in an immediate commitment to labor. However, having generally come from blue-collar families themselves, the Pickers and Choosers are sufficiently immersed in blue-collar culture to avoid the uncomfortable indecision of the rootless Fence-Sitters. Rather, they have their own modern version of trade union loyalty: Their loyalty is at once informed on issues of personal concern; it is independent of a priori judgments and the ideological urgings of others; and it is demanding in its high expectation of regular material gains. This particular mix helps to preserve and promote whatever rank-and-file vitality there is to contemporary local union affairs.

At the same time, Pickers and Choosers bring to local union affairs an ambivalence about unionism that especially draws on elements of the general blue-collar style. First, they are inclined to search for the middle ground in conflict situations —such as labor-management disputes—and often think compromise is indicated by an impasse in negotiations. Hence, many blue-collar unionists decline to take seriously the "hard" bargaining talk of Big Labor and Big Management, and the class-based "fighting" rhetoric of vote-seeking politicians. Second, Pickers and Choosers have mixed feelings concerning the relative merits of collective advancement versus individual ascent. Some fear that too great an identification on their part with the union may lead to, or signify, an abandonment of their own dream of individual social class mobility. Third, some are concerned that labor's demands and strikes put it too often in conflict with society, and particularly with government. As a good number patriotically believe the national government is operated in their interest and distributes rewards relatively fairly, these blue-collar unionists are wary of positions that appear antigovernment in any important way. Such challenges of the blue-collar style to union power are deeply significant, and serve to check the growth of union power even in an industrial, urban, working-class community.[4]

Not surprisingly, then, the relation of Pickers and Choosers to their union locals is very much like that of the average citizen to government. "Bigness" is feared, complexity is disliked, and involvement is casually dismissed ("We pay others to run the show."). Meetings are rarely attended. Taxes (or dues) are grudgingly paid. New taxes are resisted. And the election polls are visited only if the issues on the ballot are dramatized enough and if there is little personal inconvenience. In short, Pickers and Choosers, like most adult Americans, normally act only when their own particular interests are threatened. Should a crisis develop, however, and the union's survival be threatened, the Pickers and Choosers—and even some Fence-Sitters and a converted ex-Griper or two—will generally rush to demonstrate their loyalty and sense of fraternal unity with their union "brothers."

UNION DEMOCRACY

One of the rare experiences a blue-collarite can have with "maximum feasible participation" is through active involvement in his local union. Especially at the level of the local the worker can generally find officers who are responsive to his pressure, an opportunity to express himself on issues of consequence, and a chance to influence the secret-ballot vote of others on basic issues. That more blue-collarites do not take advantage of the opportunity is sometimes erroneously thought a warning that corruption or antidemocratic pressures are distorting an otherwise natural rank-and-file interest in participation.

For the large majority of blue-collar rank-and-filers, neither corruption nor antidemocratic oligarchic pressures are necessarily vital concerns. Instead, as Pickers and Choosers these blue-collarites distinguish carefully between the intimate and immediate character of their own affairs and of those of their local and of their international union. It is vital that a man get the effective support of his shop steward for his own grievances, whether in fact or in a highly stylized sociodrama. It is also vital that a man feel he can safely go above the heads of his immediate union representatives to effectively appeal a local decision. If these two items are secure, the general union situation is likely to be judged as acceptable.

This is not to say that the blue-collarite involved is ignorant of antidemocratic features of his local and of his international union.[5] Rather, the blue-collarite downgrades the absence of a legitimate opposition party, the conversion of elective posts into sinecures, or even occasional intimidation in comparison with the more personal matters of perceived opportunity to compel two results, that is, union protection against the local employer and personal justice for himself from the local and from the international itself. (Economist Neil Chamberlain notes in this connection: "Despite the cogency of the [results, rather than democracy] argument, it is difficult to avoid an uneasiness that a membership which is concerned only with ends and not means carries dangers to the broader society of which it is a part.")[6]

The blue-collarite's highly personalized approach to evaluating local union affairs partially explains why the racketeers and union autocrats are of less concern to many local unionists than is still a third source of jeopardy to union democracy. This third source of jeopardy, complacency and excessive reliance on benevolent union "managers," is much more difficult to correct. Journalist Michael Harrington, for example, wonders if one of the nation's fastest growing unions, the Retail Clerks International Association, does not pay a special price for the lack of dissent within its rank-and-file membership:

> The union's situation has provided the basis for a kind of benevolent union paternalism, for an administration which unquestionably enjoys the support of the bulk of the rank-and-file, but which employs IBM cards for policy decisions . . . the RCIA is a disturbing symptom of the development of efficient welfarism within our society without the participation of the people who belong to the institution.[7]

Ironically, much of the paternalism that labor fought to replace with industrial democracy in the 1930s now threatens labor's own internal situation. It is far from clear that thirty years later a cadre of activists can again be found to take to the field to fight the "good fight."

What is clear is that the least-often discussed danger is clearly the most insidious ("Who can argue with success?"), even as it is also the one that especially tests the mettle and values of the rank and file. If labor has gone from brickbats to briefcases, many rank-and-filers have gone from involvement to indolence. Whether or not the potential activists among them can soon be involved again—or, as Walter Reuther puts it, whether or not the unions can unionize their unionists—remains to be seen. The prospects for labor success in vitalizing strategic numbers, in transforming Gripers into Fence-Sitters, and in moving many of the latter into the ranks both of Pickers and Choosers and of Patriots remain uncertain, at best.

UNION MILITANCY

Linked to the decline in rank-and-file spirits and to the attractiveness of benevolent union paternalism is the current transformation of labor union militancy. Blue-collar unions seldom strike any longer over such dramatic and class-linked items as union recognition or the interpretation and application of existing agreements. Instead, labor increasingly relies on the NLRB or its own union-management grievance machinery to resolve such matters. Indeed, blue-collar unions seldom "hit the bricks" for any of the causes that animated labor in the 1930s. Economist John Kenneth Galbraith notes in this connection that "since World War II, the acceptance of the union by the industrial firm and the emergence thereafter of an era of comparatively peaceful industrial relations have been hailed as the final triumph of trade unionism. On closer examination it is seen to reveal many of the features of Jonah's triumph over the whale." [8]

Historically, from the first labor strike in Philadelphia in 1799 to the present-day unofficial (and often popular) "wildcat strikes" led by local union insurgents, the character of labor militancy has been intimately linked to the state of the unions. Labor-management negotiations have steadily become more complex and more centrally handled by top-level union specialists. Contracts—complete with "no-strike" pledges—are written for longer periods (three or more years), are reopened for negotiations long before termination, and are sometimes negotiated in privacy without the benefit of meaningful consultation with rank-and-filers.

Accordingly, union militancy today takes two major forms: Rank-and-filers are setting new records in their initial rejection of contracts offered for ratification (see Chapter 2, "Blue-Collar Odyssey"). They are also setting new records in their willingness to "hit the bricks" in defiance of both union and company leaders thought to be indifferent to an intensified interest in deep-reaching workplace reforms. (In 1966 there were 4,200 strikes involving 1.8 million workers, as compared with 3,963 strikes involving 1.5 million workers in 1965.[9] In 1967 the working time lost due to strikes was 50 percent above the three previous years and the highest since 1959.)[10]

Official strikes, or those called by the international union as part of a scenario for a labor-management engagement, are lightly regarded by the rank and file, except for inconvenienced and bitter Gripers. Most blue-collarites are content to do their turn on the picket line, reassured by the knowledge that union strike benefits will help until rarely needed unemployment checks can be had (The Steelworkers Union spent over $6 million in strike benefits during the 8½-month copper strike of 1967–1968; the Auto Union spent $54 million in the last 6 months of 1967).[11] Cynics among the rank and file assure coworkers that many official strikes work out to everyone's advantage, the wage increase "reluctantly" agreed to being used as an excuse to raise prices and help lower corporate break-even points (the lowest percentage of operating capacity needed to make a profit). Indeed, some local unionists consider their rare strikes a "service" to business, even as some businessmen welcome an occasional "official" strike as an opportunity to dispose of inventories.

Similarly, rank-and-filers have grown increasingly skeptical about the time-honored union tradition of honoring a picket line and refusing to cooperate with a strikebound employer. The tactic has historically reinforced class identification and solidarity. At present, however, unions agree to honor the picket lines of allied unions only and do not hesitate to order members to ignore the pickets of unfriendly labor organizations or of wildcat strikers. Here, as elsewhere in labor affairs, selectivity comes increasingly at the price of sentiment and mutual strength.

Much more seriously regarded are the bitter, terse, and emotionally charged unofficial strikes that dominate the contemporary labor-management scene. Top-level negotiations can cope fairly adequately with disputes concerning the benefits that surround a job—higher wages, vacations, and so on—but it is at the level of the local union that plant management and blue-collarites must work out management's new interest in reasserting control over the work done. Encouraged by automation and its own rich backup resources, many plant managers are now busy challenging long-established work practices. As the largest number of such practices reflect local union victories in countless subterranean battles fought out daily in the workshop, the bitterness and intransigence on both sides run very deep.

Indeed, no other single work-related matter stirs class consciousness and promotes an otherwise latent interclass hostility as much as does an unofficial strike. Few involve wages, hours, or working conditions. Instead, wildcat strikes (and the illicit extension of official strikes) frequently develop over emotionally laden "little issues"—such as the sudden designation of a certain work area as off limits to cigarette smoking or the unexpected firing of a controversial or "handicapped" worker (such as one who persists in lateness or drinking, but is known to be having "wife problems"). A Steel Union official explains: "Today's steelworker has cultural concepts influenced by his TV-type, middle-class kind of living. He has real sensitivities, and he wants to be treated well in the plant." [12]

Better-known dispute issues here include overtime penalties; lines of demarcation between incentive and nonincentive and between skilled workers; requests for extra release and wash-up time; job bidding and promotion procedures; and requests for extra union committeemen to handle backed-up grievances. Even more volatile, if much more rarely known matters include a demand for air-conditioning coverage or the provision of occasional benches for a man to take a brief rest on. (Little-known issues of this sort lead a writer to suggest that "the 'true sociology' of the American worker is to be discovered in the fact no one sees fit to clean the filth off a factory floor rather than in terms like 'other-directed consumer' or 'upward social mobility.'")[13]

The emotional and ideological intensity of the "last-straw" walkouts or of the "rebel-local holdouts" cannot be exaggerated. Somewhat like the delinquent acts that lure the youthful blue-collar rebels (see Chapters 9 and 10), the contract-violating wildcat strikes offer routine-weary blue-collarites a rare chance to affirm that they can make things happen. Enthusiasts practice the art of social protest and learn how to suppress dissensions inside the work group in pursuit of common goals. These men lose some of their sense of isolation and powerlessness and gain new respect for themselves.

In an ironic way, and in some respects not unlike certain property riots and ghetto insurrections of the summers of 1966, 1967, and 1968, wildcat strikes invoke among participants a "humanistic" mood and thereby help to reform the moral order. For a small number of volatile rank-and-file leaders, the wildcat strike appears to affirm their masculine prowess, serving as a symbol of restored potency and virility: No one dares call a wildcatter "boy." Although parentlike officials of both labor and management punish the "immature" offenders, the psychological gains of the participants, which are normally unavailable, lead at least some individuals to believe that the militant effort is well worth its price.

Labor's officialdom is embarrassed and exasperated by the unruly, undisciplined conduct of rank-and-file "hotheads." Particularly angered are the front-line union professionals, or business agents and international representatives, who are charged by the higher echelons of the union bureaucracy with "keeping the men in line." Little appreciated is this insight from labor journalist Thomas R. Brooks:

> . . . there is a thin, uncertain line that runs from the early journeymen cordwainers, who struck to save their craft, to Goldfield, Arizona, where the Wobblies defiantly posted the terms of work on the union hall bulletin board for employers to come, read, and observe, down to the New York City schoolteachers, who recently threatened to strike to win a reduction in class size. Each of these events had to do with a worker's dignity, his pride in the quality of his work. On this slender threat rests whatever there is of lasting value in the struggles of American Labor.[14]

Should the rank-and-file insurgents finally be contained, should union militancy be thoroughly converted into mere stagecraft, the victory will finally be to the indifferent, who have never really expected otherwise. At present many Patriots and certain Pickers and Choosers are seeking to prevent such a development. But here, as elsewhere in the struggle against rank-and-file complacency and drift, the prospects for keeping alive rank-and-file involvement and autonomy are uncertain.

UNION POLITICAL AFFAIRS

Given the gradual increase in the ratio of Pickers and Choosers to Patriots, the decrease in the significance of many local union stewards, the enthronement of benevolent union paternalism as a primary governing mode in many local union situations, and the dominance of officially harmonious union-management relations, it is little wonder that rank-and-filers increasingly take labor and their own local union for granted. In many ways labor's coming of age has helped to dampen enthusiasm among those who, in the 1930s, might have been Patriots rather than Pickers and Choosers or Fence-Sitters. In many ways labor's new acceptability and accommodation have encouraged blue-collarites to feel quite casual about a limited-purpose organization they regard less and less as a significant part of their lives.

Rank-and-file leaders see only one possibility of change in an otherwise bleak political picture. A rare study of the political attitudes of 553 unpaid rank-and-file leaders completed in 1960 by Alton C. Bartlett, a professor of labor relations, found the leaders agreeing that the labor movement had a legitimate, but a meticulously defined and limited, political role: Only where collective bargaining could not advance an appropriate goal of the union, and only where the goal was capable of being specifically stated, would the rank and file approve of the union taking political action to secure the goal. That is, only where the goal was linked to "wages, hours, and working conditions," and only where the goal was a concrete one, rather than espousal of "clean government" or "votes for Friends of Labor," would the grass-roots leaders expect a positive rank-and-file response.[15]

Accordingly, when labor attempts in familiar, and even

shopworn, ways to extend its mission beyond ordinarily accepted work-related limits, when labor seeks to play a more significant part in the lives of its rank and file, it is as often as not ignored or even rebuked. For example, unionists are regularly approached by organized labor and asked to register and to vote in this way or that. In 1966, for example, the AFL-CIO's Committee on Political Education concentrated on sixty-seven House seats that candidates had won by narrow margins in 1964; the candidates backed by COPE lost in thirty-two of these contests. Overall, the AFL-CIO score was only 54 percent in House races, 57 percent in the Senate, and 31 percent in governorships. The average score of 52 percent was down sharply from the 65 percent figure achieved in the off-year 1962. The 1968 figures tell a similar tale: The average score rose only to 57 percent. The AFL-CIO scored 57 percent in House races, 56 percent in the Senate, and 35 percent in governorships.[16]

Equally significant was the extent in 1966 of explicit rank-and-file disregard of labor's political preference. In California, for example, state-level union leaders endorsed Edmund Brown for governor, but city-level shop stewards worked hard for eventual winner Ronald Reagan. In Michigan, Walter Reuther's politically astute United Auto Workers Union campaigned for Senatorial candidate G. Mennen Williams; in Illinois the UAW worked hard for the reelection of Senator Paul H. Douglas. Their successful opponents, Republican Robert P. Griffin (coauthor of the labor-opposed Landrum-Griffin Act) and Republican Charles Percy (industrialist) ran extremely well in UAW and labor-oriented areas.[17] (It should be understood that rank-and-filers generally support Democratic party nominees, 72 percent of polled unionists having voted Democratic in the 1958 Congressional election, 70 percent in 1960, and 65 percent in 1966.[18] Similarly, a 1967 poll of 1,700 representative unionists found 58 percent identifying themselves as Democrats, 16 percent as Republicans, 17 percent as Independents, and 9 percent as "not sure.")[19]

The single major exception to the constrictions on labor's political maneuvering involves the generally overlooked char-

TABLE 8   Presidential Vote of Union Member Families, 1936–1968

	Democratic	Republican	Independent
1968	56%	29%	15*
1964	73	27	
1960	65	35	
1956	57	43	
1952	61	39	
1948	74	26	
1944	72	28	
1940	72	28	
1936	80	20	

* 15 percent of union families voted for George Wallace. George Gallup, "Campaign Shift by Labor Found," *The New York Times*, December 1, 1968, p. 48.
SOURCE: "The Gallup Poll," *Philadelphia Evening Bulletin*, September 11, 1968. Used with permission and by special arrangement with the American Institute of Public Opinion, November, 1968.

acter of city and state politics. Blue-collarites, while liberal in their position-taking on national domestic issues, are often more conservative on certain local issues. This permits local unions to back Republican or even third-party candidates on occasion and to threaten to "sit on their hands" and depress the Democratic vote if candidates of that party do not respect their conservative interests.

Many unionists fail to vote at all, however, and local unions regularly run "register-and-vote" campaigns with impressive effort and expense. Where successful, the local union manages to draw to the polls extra-large numbers of pro-Democratic Pickers and Choosers, the Patriots, of course, voting the union line in solid ranks. This can be significant in especially close elections. For example, labor's efforts in 1960 in New Jersey allegedly increased registration by 227,000, primarily in industrial cities and among manual workers and their relatives. Labor-backed John F. Kennedy carried the state by only 22,000 votes.[20]

In a smaller number of cases the unions may have succeeded in concentrating rank-and-file attention on the positions candidates have taken on labor and on shop issues. Such cases are fewer than those involving an effort to get indifferent men to vote their own (union-endorsed) preference because many rank-and-filers are exceedingly bored by thirty or more years of a steady diet of union political advice. Not simply Gripers and Fence-Sitters, but many Pickers and Choosers as well, "turn a deaf ear" to incessant labor appeals for rank-and-file support of this or that candidate or ballot issue. Boredom mixes here with skepticism, many grass-roots unionists skeptical that their individual vote really makes a difference.

At the level of state- and city-wide politics many union officials are known to be loosely aligned with the more conservative elements among people influential in political and industrial circles. This is especially true of the largest single type of local union, the AFL craft union locals. These skilled-worker groups are dependent upon local markets for their welfare and are very responsive, for example, to shifts in the construction of area housing or in the success of civic efforts to win the holding of conventions in the city's hotels. The state and city political positions of AFL locals, according to sociologist James R. Hudson, are "in a sense conservative." The craft union lobbyists "seek to maintain the status quo by job protection for AFL members in the same way that the State Retail Merchant Associations seek to protect themselves from unfair competition." [21]

It is not surprising, then, that certain AFL local union leaders have come to be known for their opposition to, or hampering of, city antipoverty efforts. They believe certain programs of this type menace the economic interests of their membership (the ambitious ex-poor, once equipped with new job skills, are feared likely to undercut wage levels, displace unionists, or effectively compete with the job-seeking sons of local members). [22] Contributing to bitterness here is the failure of certain city-wide antipoverty programs to insist that employers using program-referred workers be paid the union scale, and the stridency of charges of race prejudice aimed at the unions. Local union officials also withhold support from the militant programs designed to enhance the "maximum feasible participation" of the poor. In such situations union disinterest or even veiled opposition is linked both to labor's empathy with the City Hall interests attacked by elements among the poor and to the identification by the Caucasian rank and file of an unknown quality (Poor Power) with an allegedly known and very much disliked quality (Black Power).

Even on the national level the political conservatism of the rank and file makes itself apparent. The intense and extreme anticommunist policies of George Meany, AFL-CIO president, which sometimes puts him to the right of the Pentagon, are consistent with much shop floor patriotism. This is particularly true where the conspiratorial politics of ethnic blocs among the rank and file (as with second-generation East Europeans) urges militant support of clandestine anti-regime elements behind the Iron Curtain.[23] Encouraged by Catholic and other religious urgings, rank-and-filers identify communism with evil. Most oppose it unrelentingly, and do so without patience for subtle distinctions among various types of communists or brands of communism. President Lyndon B. Johnson's use of the "domino theory" in his support of intensified military operations in Vietnam, Thailand, and elsewhere falls on receptive ears. With many a man's son or sons fighting in Vietnam, sentiment runs strongly in favor of an all-out hawk-like policy of "win now," conservatism here taking the form of aggressive militancy. A variation on the theme urges the immediate withdrawal of American troops and the creation at home of a Fortress America, indifferent to, and invincible against, developments anywhere else.[24]

On the domestic scene the record is similarly revealing, even as it also draws deeply on elements of the general blue-collar style. A 1967 poll of 1,700 representative local unionists found only 76 percent in agreement with the AFL-CIO contention that workmen's compensation laws should be improved, only 71 percent supporting higher minimum wage laws, and only 54 percent approving the Labor Federation's effort to win repeal of the anti-Closed Shop clause of the Taft-Hartley Act, which prohibits making union membership a condition of employment. In the first and second cases the low level of rank-and-file support may draw on the infrequency with which a well-off unionist expects to profit from higher accident benefits or from a rise in the floor under wages. Striking here are the self-centeredness of poll respondents and their disinclination to endorse traditional labor policies likely today to primarily benefit the less fortunate. The low vote on the Taft-Hartley reform may reflect boredom with labor's twenty-year-old struggle in the matter or confusion in the face of the whole complex issue of conditional or compulsory union membership.

On the nonlabor domestic scene the same 1967 poll underlines considerable political conservatism. Reflecting especially deep-seated anxiety over the possibility of having to raise one's children alongside of the children of new neighbors from the Negro lower class, the rank-and-file respondents gave only 43 percent support to the AFL-CIO's bold espousal of Open Housing legislation. Reflecting especially a disinterest in further tax rises and a belief that men should individually sacrifice for the education of their own children, the rank-and-file respondents gave only 67 percent support to the AFL-CIO's endorsement of expanded Federal Aid to Education. Contrariwise, on relatively noncontroversial national issues the rank and file provide much stronger poll support for the Labor Federation's public positions: Some 94 percent agreed that water pollution control should be sought, 91 percent approved of seeking truth-in-lending legislation, 91 percent supported truth-in-packaging legislation, and 91 percent approved of air pollution control.[25] These last few "safe" issues to the contrary and notwithstanding, it becomes easier to understand the judgment here of labor journalist A. H. Raskin: "The typical worker —from construction craftsman to shoe clerk—has become probably the most reactionary political force in the country." [26]

The AFL-CIO in short appears today to speak politically— and with some accuracy—for a rank and file that is progressive on impersonal public issues, conservative on personal and quasi-private issues, and fainthearted and self-centered on issues of once-removed, if class-linked, mutual-aid items. In this context former AFL-CIO Vice-President and UAW head Walter Reuther rails against "complacency, indifference, ad-

herence to status quo, lack of social vision, . . ." [27] But Msgr.
George C. Higgins explains that organized labor may actually
lead rather than lag:

> I have great admiration for many rank-and-file union members,
> but I have yet to come across any reliable evidence that union
> rank-and-filers, on the average, are more progressive than the
> allegedly sclerotic officials who preside over the House of Labor.
> On the contrary, every available scientific study of rank-and-file
> attitudes on current social issues—and notably in the field of race
> relations—clearly indicates that this is definitely not the case.
> . . . Surely the labor movement is too conservative in many re-
> spects, but if the rank-and-file are, on the average, more con-
> servative than their elected officers (in the UAW incidentally, as
> well as in some of the old line crafts), where do we go from
> here? [28]

Answers are far from clear. This is especially so in light of
George Meany's representative scorn for those "loud-mouth
critics who say we are not doing too well; that the AFL-CIO
. . . has failed to display an adequate sense of social consciousness—whatever the hell that means." [29]

UNION STEWARDS

Coming to the shop level of trade unionism, it is now possible to trace the interconnectedness of union types and issues
in democracy, militancy, and politics as they affect the man
who, more than any other, means labor to the average blue-
collarite.

Rank-and-filers may see the international union president
only as infrequently as he is interviewed on a television news
show or as regularly as his picture and prose are featured in
the adulatory union press. International union representatives,
sometimes ironically known as business agents, visit the locals
on schedule, but spend the bulk of their time with local union
officers and company representatives. Only members of the
first-line echelon of nonprofessional shop stewards are com-

monly available for rank-and-file contact; their superiors in the local union's leadership are generally pleased to leave to the stewards the daily routine and "grind" of rank-and-file blue-collar affairs.

At first glance the post of shop steward would seem to have much to recommend it to an ambitious blue-collarite. Annually some 100,000 workers assume elected terms with high personal expectations and considerable pride in placement on a new status rung in the factory hierarchy. The worker-turned-steward can now break the monotony of his work routine by tending daily to vaguely defined "union business," and he can also expect to spend some subsidized time off or evenings at special union training courses for shop stewards. Should he be interested, it is even possible for him to use his steward's post as a launching pad for a new career inside labor's professional ranks. Contrariwise, he may win a career with a management team impressed with his peer-endorsed leadership promise. Above all, and in the immediate present, the post of shop steward carries with it the prestige of a new standing in the society of the workplace: To be able to summon the foreman or to have the division superintendent paged, to prevent an "illegal" supervisory action or to give the boss a "talking to"— all of this makes the steward a man among men, or so it would seem. Reality, however, departs considerably from the textbook job description outlined thus far.

Shop stewards, according to sociologist Sidney W. Peck, generally seek or accept their posts so as to aid and defend their coworkers.[30] Linked originally to fellow blue-collarites through a sense of ideological identity and mission, many stewards nevertheless come to identify with the upper union leadership or with the employer rather than with the local shop's union membership. Their gradual alienation from fellow workers can be traced in large part to the centralization of power at the level of the international union. This development has left the blue-collar steward with a bare shadow of the significance he enjoyed in the raw organizing years of the 1930s. In response, many stewards defensively withdraw from the fellowship of coworkers and instead seek the backup support of the international membership. Contemptuous attitudes toward the rank and file become common, as do also condescending and paternalistic attitudes.

Many stewards have the related problem of providing and protecting the considerable support that marginal companies receive from the local and international union. Certain labor unions go out of their way to shore up businesses verging on collapse. Anxious to protect the jobs of members, these unions make concessions in the writing and policing of contracts to help hard-pressed firms reduce labor costs, increase labor productivity, and fight to stay competitive. Although "dual loyalties" to both union and employer are commonplace among workers, rank-and-filers do not always appreciate every particular instance of union statesmanship. Apathy, cynicism, and job dissatisfaction can be traced to covert and lingering strain between local union members and leaders over this little-publicized matter.

It is at the level of the stewards' dealing with antagonistic local management that the limits of local union power are clearest—and are most painful for the rank and file. Stewards are generally powerless to compel accommodation of production demands to safety demands or to secure a new agreement that local work will not be subcontracted out of the plant, both of which are extremely sensitive matters. Furthermore, short of the extreme sanction of calling a strike, the alternatives available to the steward in dealing with foremen almost always necessitate the dutiful performance of disputed work pending the filing of a formal grievance. This in turn means involvement of successively higher levels of labor and management and the eventual resolution some months or even years later of the long-since altered matter. Hard-pressed intermediaries, stewards appear in some respects classic "men in between."

To be sure, stewards have evolved various defensive techniques of enhancing their status and expanding their power. For example, many capitalize on their ability to move freely about the workplace to carry gossip and manipulate rumors, both important components of the informal communications

network of the workshop. Many stewards also seek advantage
from the prestigious fact of their attendance at university extension courses in labor subjects. The "book-learning" involved
comes in handy in "putting down" opponents in sensitive and
public disputes on the shop floor. Finally, union shop stewards
trade on their first-name familiarity with high-level union professionals. Such "contacts" are used to impress workplace col-
leagues and company men. They are also helpful in securing
unofficial "favors" outside conventional union affairs (including
political backing in campaigns to secure reelection or selection
as shop steward).

In all, however, a good many problems of blue-collar trade
unionism have their roots in a serious rift that frequently
divides men on the shop floor from the part-time labor spokesman and full-time co-worker on whom the union relies. Shop
stewards, with their tutored knowledge of the union contract,
labor affairs, and labor's past, constitute a change-making,
character-shaping bloc of critical significance to the present
state and future prospects of blue-collar unionism. Most provocative, therefore, is the finding that built-in sources of role
strain regularly alienate many such men from the rank and
file. Accordingly, if blue-collarites manifest a distrust of leadership both in *and* outside of work, if they greet the promises of
political candidates with skepticism, the experience that certain local unionists have with "once-promising" local shop
stewards may not be far from the minds of many.

SUMMARY

No other private association includes as many blue-collarites and as directly and indirectly reflects and shapes the
worker's style of life as does organized labor. Notwithstanding
its unusual shop-level focus and its supportive legalistic and
social framework, however, local unionism leaves much to be
desired—to judge from the complacency of some and from
the discontent of other blue-collarites. Many local union

members fear events are passing them by and that decisions are steadily being made for them. Moreover, occasional grass-roots revolts against "puppetry" may do little more than stimulate the demand for ever-greater insurgency—to no special or rewarding end.

The fortunes of the labor movement may well be decided at the local union level. Much money and effort is put into union-izing the 45 percent of blue-collar labor and 90 percent of "gray-collar" service workers who remain outside labor's ranks, but it is the informally communicated satisfaction of local union neighbors with labor that often spells the difference in union organizing campaigns. While much bargaining is cen-tralized, day-to-day contract administration nevertheless re-mains a local union matter. However large the union treasury grows, the enhancement of group cohesion remains a local union matter. And no matter how well staffed the union head-quarters may become, only the local union can develop rank-and-file concern, participation, and support. In short, whether influential local unionists soon choose to help labor expand its vistas or decide instead to settle for more of the same—includ-ing the steady decline in significance of the local union—is a critical matter. The life issues contained in the rank-and-file pressure to rehabilitate work may yet turn the drift of local union affairs in a new and positive direction. Contrariwise, continued emphasis on escapism from work, accommodation in union-management relations, conservatism in local politics, and erosion of the steward's autonomy may mean the further decline of the local union—and the national loss of an inval-uable opportunity to help blue-collarites help themselves to a new manhood.

Blue-collar unionists are torn at present between the option of more or less "welfare paternalism" and "auto club" trade unionism on the one hand and involvement in, contribution to, and sacrifice for a bold and imaginative new labor movement on the other. Their plight in trying to decide whether to "sit back" or "stand up" is a major dilemma of contemporary American society. The decision they reach will help to shape the society we all share.

Notes to Chapter Six

1. Anon., "Labor Notes," *Wall Street Journal*, August 15, 1967, p. 1.

2. For supportive data see the *AFL-CIO American Federationalist* (July 1967). See also *Handbook of Labor Statistics, 1967*, Department of Labor (Washington, D.C.: Government Printing Office, 1967); Ruth Kornhauser, "Some Social Determinants and Consequences of Union Membership," *Labor History* (Winter 1961), pp. 30–61.

3. Hjalmar Rosen and R. A. Hudson Rosen, *The Union Member Speaks* (New York: Prentice-Hall, 1955). On the Griper, see Paul Sultan, *The Disenchanted Unionist* (New York: Harper & Row, 1963). See also Daisy L. Tagliacozzo and Joel Seidman, "A Typology of Rank and File Union Members," *American Journal of Sociology* (May 1956), pp. 546–553; Jack Barbash, *Labor's Grass Roots* (New York: Harper & Bros., 1961); Scott Greer, *Last Man In: Racial Access to Union Power* (Glencoe, Ill.: Free Press, 1959); Fred Blum, *Toward a Democratic Work Process* (New York: Harper & Bros., 1953), pp. 123–157.

4. Robert E. Lane, *Political Ideology: Why the American Common Man Believes What He Does* (New York: Free Press, 1962), p. 135, *passim*.

5. See, for example, M. A. Verick, "Rebel Voices in the NMU," *New Politics* (Summer 1966); John Cole, "SIU: The Shortchange Artists," *New Politics* (Summer 1966); Murray Kempton, "Hoffa the Pure: 'Everything Can Be Bought and Fixed!'," *New Republic* (January 18, 1964). See also Charles Gregory, "Government Regulation or Control of Union Activities," in W. Haber (ed.), *Labor in a Changing America* (New York: Basic Books, 1966), pp. 224–237; "Crooks, Communists, and Legislative Reforms," in Thomas R. Brooks, *Toil and Trouble: A History of American Labor* (New York: Dial Press, 1964), pp. 223–230; "Politics in Labor" in Gus Tyler, *The Labor Revolution: Trade Unions in a New America* (New York: Viking, 1967), pp. 229–256; Ralph and Estelle Dinnerstern James, *Hoffa and the Teamsters* (Princeton: Van Nostrand, 1965).

6. Neil W. Chamberlain, *The Labor Sector: An Introduction to Labor in the American Economy* (New York: McGraw-Hill, 1967), p. 207.

7. Michael Harrington, *The Retail Clerks* (New York: Wiley, 1962).

8. John Kenneth Galbraith, *The New Industrial State* (Boston: Houghton Mifflin, 1967), p. 281.

9. Robert W. Fisher, "Labor in the Economy of 1967," *Monthly Labor Review* (December 1967), p. 7.

10. David R. Jones, "Union Aim: Ballot Box, Lunch Box," *The New York Times*, January 8, 1968, p. 19.

11. Anon., "Labor Letter," *Wall Street Journal*, April 2, 1968, p. 1.

12. Anon., "Steel Bargaining Gets Local Spin," *Business Week* (March 23, 1968), p. 94.

13. Midge Decter, "A Good Man Is Hard to Find," *New York Review of Books* (October 31, 1963), p. 5. See also Michael K. Drapkin, "Hot 'Local Issue,'" *Wall Street Journal*, June 12, 1968, pp. 1, 14; Anon., "In Steel, a Conflict of Priorities," *Business Week* (January 27, 1968), pp. 63–64, 68; Peter Millones, "Labor Tactics," *The New York Times*, February 7, 1968, p. 35.

14. Thomas R. Brooks, *op. cit.*, p. xx.

15. Alton C. Bartlett, "How Rank and File Leaders View Union Political Action," *Labor Law Journal* (August 1966), p. 494. See also Deutsch, *op. cit.* For a contrary position see Sidney M. Peck, "The Friendly Enemies," *The Rank-and-File Leader* (New Haven: College and University Press, 1965), pp. 277–318; "The Political Consciousness of Rank-and-File Labor Leaders," *Studies on the Left*, Vol. 4, No. 4 (1961), pp. 43–51.

16. Anon., "Unions Fail to Deliver the Goods," *Business Week* (November 19, 1966), pp. 103, 106–107. The 1968 data are from *AFL-CIO News* (November 1968), p. 12. See also Chapter 10, "Labor in Politics," in Gus Tyler, *op. cit.*, pp. 198–228. Note that COPE reported spending over $1 million in 1968. Anon., "Labor Letter," *Wall Street Journal*, November 5, 1968, p. 1.

17. Anon., "Unions Fail to Deliver the Goods," *op. cit.*

18. Gallup Poll, "Republicans Doing Better with Labor," *New York Herald Tribune*, October 16, 1966, p. 17.

19. David R. Jones, "Poll Finds Most Members Support Labor Policies," *The New York Times*, July 16, 1967, p. 27.

20. Charles M. Rehmus, "Labor in American Politics," in Haber (ed.), *op. cit.*, p. 264.

21. James R. Hudson, "The Political Perspectives of Local Union Officials" (State University of New York, Stony Brook, Long Island, unpublished, undated paper). See also Paul R. Eberts,

"Political Cleavages on Local Political Issues," unpublished paper read at the 1966 Miami Meeting of the American Sociological Association (Cornell University); Edward C. Banfield and James Q. Wilson, *City Politics* (Boston: Harvard University Press, 1963), p. 285.

22. See, for example, Herbert Hill, "Sewing Machines and Union Machines," *The Nation* (July 3, 1967); Charles J. Levy, "Scripto on Strike: The Race-Wage Picket Line," *The Nation* (January 11, 1965). See also Steven E. Deutsch, "Perception of and Attitudes Toward Automation: A Study of Local Union Leaders," *Labor Law Journal* (July 1967), pp. 396–405; Anon., "Union Investors Stick to Blue Chips," *Business Week* (January 13, 1968). Cf. David Sullivan, *Labor's Role in the War on Poverty* (Washington, D.C.: Department of Labor, 1967); Michael Harrington, "The Labor Movement and Social Change" (Iowa City: Center for Labor and Management, University of Iowa, 1967).

23. On the AFL-CIO entanglement with the CIA, see Paul Jacobs, "How the CIA Makes Liars out of Union Leaders," *Ramparts* (April 1967); David Langley/A.G., "Labor Officialdom and the CIA," *New Politics* (Spring 1966).

24. In January 1968, Gallup pollsters found that 47 percent of union families, and only 39 percent of all families approved of the way President Johnson was handling the situation in Vietnam. Gallup, "Poll Finds Labor Split on Vietnam," *The New York Times,* January 3, 1968, p. 3. On the opposition of a bloc of 500 union staffers from 60 unions to labor's pro-Vietnam position, see Anne P. Draper, "Unions and the War in Vietnam," *New Politics* (Summer 1966).

25. Anon., "Members Back Union Policies, LBJ," *AFL-CIO News,* July 22, 1967, pp. 1, 4.

26. As quoted by B. J. Widick, in "Walter Reuther Breaks His Chains," *The Nation* (June 17, 1968), p. 782.

27. Hobart Rowen, "The Bone in Meany's Throat," *New Republic* (May 6, 1967), p. 9.

28. Msgr. George C. Higgins, "To Keep the Record Straight," *AFL-CIO News,* June 22, 1968, p. 7.

29. Widick, *op. cit.*

30. Peck, *op. cit.* See also Henry A. Landsberger and Charles L. Hulin, "Role versus Personality as Determinants of Union Officials' Attitudes toward Union Members" (New York State School of Industrial and Labor Relations, unpublished paper); Anon., "Labor's New Breed of Middle Managers," *Business Week* (June 22, 1968).

Part III

7

BLUE-COLLAR NEIGHBORHOODS

The natural role of twentieth-century man is anxiety.—Norman Mailer

In a nation as much on the go as this one, a nation of restless, frequent movers, blue-collarites stand out as people of little geographic mobility: Their rate of movement between labor market areas is lower than all other occupational blocs save that of land-bound farmers.[1] America's 21 million Caucasian male blue-collarites show a decided preference for remaining in or close to the neighborhood they knew as children, the neighborhood that probably remains the residence of their extended family relatives. At present, four types of blue-collar neighborhoods earn special loyalty and have much significance for the worker's style of life.[2] This chapter analyzes social and structural considerations peculiar to each, special attention being given to the values reinforced or challenged therein.

STABLE CITY NEIGHBORHOOD

A narrow majority of Caucasian male blue-collarites prob-ably live in urban ethnic, religious, and social class enclaves relatively untouched by time and emphatically personal in character. Especially valued in these enclaves is the old tradi-tion whereby neighbors feel free to drop in on one another for coffee and talk without prior announcement or invitation. Where such blue-collarites cluster, sociologist Scott Greer points out, "we see not the 'faceless world of megalopolis,' but men in shirt sleeves playing softball, groups of women gossip-ing on the porches, children swarming in the streets. . . ."[3]

Life, in general, is quite personalized, a search for primary affiliation characterizing both the "well-heeled young bucks" and the bocce-playing old-timers in the case of the Italian-American. A dense and vibrant street life combines with a wide network of personal affiliations to weave the whole to-gether. Too much change and too much ambition too rapidly realized are avoided—the powerless can concentrate instead on the various distractions (friends, family, possessions) that make life tenable and help time pass.

Especially strong is the perception of the neighborhood as a safe port, as a supportive refuge from a confusing, cold, and seemingly oppressive outside world. Regardless of how de-crepit, outmoded, or unsafe it may appear to middle-class ob-servers, the typical blue-collar neighborhood has an "old-shoe" comfort and reliability for many of its residents. Friendliness mixes in these areas with a value sociologist Edward Ryan labels "commonness." "There is the strong theme that the good man is the plain man, that the average citizen—which the (enclave) dweller considers himself to be—has in him the elements of strength and goodness. In short, there is virtue in being of the common clay."[4] Neighborhood patterns of friendly interacting, the tavern for the men and the coffee klatsch and church service for the women, are oriented to an involvement in and enjoyment of human relationships. Such patterns also have their economic side: Job-seeking blue-collarites rely on the neighborhood network of friends and relatives for leads. (Indeed, research suggests that the network is 50 to 75 percent more helpful than the State Employment Service and all other means of job-seeking).[5]

Ethnicity receives its special support in exactly this setting. "Ports of entry" for partially assimilated white foreign stock who prefer to live with their "own kind," the "Little Italys," and Hamtramck-like areas of the nation's major cities are both insular and proud. Sociologist Anselm L. Strauss points out that "Polish citizens of our cities live—quite literally—in local parishes, whether their Protestant neighbors recognize this or not . . . it is here that the outsider really knows he is an outsider." [6] Crisscrossed by church and nationalistic organizations (the Knights of Columbus, the Sons of Italy, and others), the ethnic enclaves look especially to the Catholic City of God and to homeland cities such as Dublin, Cracow, and Naples for standards by which to live. Contrary to the advocates of the "Melting Pot" hypothesis, the enclave dwellers are still acutely conscious of their old-country origins and are committed to cultural self-preservation. Contrary also to some of the proponents of the "mass society" interpretation, the enclave dwellers maintain vital separate traditions.

Equally important, if much less discussed, researched, and understood, is the matter of organized crime in the blue-collar neighborhood. Along with ethnicity, the "rackets" receive their special support in stable city neighborhoods. In many such areas, the conventional and the criminal worlds maintain an accommodative relationship: As blue-collar children generally know, certain local racketeers, businessmen, and policemen are closely and reciprocally joined for common profit. This is not an association of equals: The "manicured mobsters" usually exercise dominant power and have the greatest influence in the conventional structure of the neighborhood. Social work careerist Irving Spergel describes how, in a particular blue-collar neighborhood he studied, the local racketeer was accorded both high status and respect, his family being envied for its access to jobs, money, and prestige. A "standard-bearer of the neighborhood," the local racketeer was "an acknowledged source of norms and values." Elsewhere Spergel notes that "the extensive adult criminal activity in the area was not conducted blatantly. It was carefully shielded and could easily remain unnoticed by a newcomer or someone unfamiliar with the area." [7]

The blue-collar neighborhood's support of the numbers racket, the bookie system, the loan shark racket (where the lender's body and life are collateral), and the sale of stolen merchandise link up with a third characteristic of the area, namely, its apparent toughness. In this context sociologists Albert K. Cohen and Harold M. Hodges, Jr. speak of a "general posture of truculent self-assertiveness, defiance, 'don't-push-me-around' touchiness." [8] They note three variants of this posture: Most residents "play it cool," or comply in law-abiding ways but try to make it clear on occasion that their compliance is purely expedient. A much smaller number "con" the powers by appearing compliant and then exploiting the trust they have earned. And a few employ an openly belligerent posture, at once most dangerous and "heroic." These neighborhood "hard heads" regularly put up a show of resistance and allow themselves to be overcome only by a superior force. In what is probably the most common posture, area residents perform in the style of one role but speak in the manner of another: "Toughness" actually reduces to tough talk.

These three features—ethnicity, criminal support, and a "hard" posture—especially aid manual workers in their rejection of middle-class standards that would tend otherwise to devalue them: Ethnicity and the pose of toughness do this through their provision of alternatives to white-collar standards. The criminal "conspiracy" helps with its demonstration of universal human frailty ("inside" gossip among blue-collarites often focuses on allegedly "bought" officials). The criminal "conspiracy" also contributes to a sense of smugness among many blue-collarites who view the world as crooked and phony and who are amused to think the "know-it-all" white-collarites are oblivious to this basic fact of life.

It is hardly surprising then to find that stable neighborhood blue-collarites remain very suspicious of the few real, and the many imagined, efforts "outsiders" are thought to make to change their ways. Settlement houses and welfare agencies are shunned by most persons, many area residents considering them externally oriented threats to the status quo. Neighborhood parochial and public schools are molded over time in the area's image, as are also the local parish church and police station. Residents of these ethnically homogeneous communities identify strongly with one another, family networks combining with such linkages as common employer, old country, and corner gang to promote considerable in-group sentiment— that is, the "nuzzling herd" effect. Sociologist Arthur Wood, writing in 1955 of a Polish-American community with 72 percent blue-collar representation, explains:

> Were it not for this strong motive toward ethnic solidarity, the disorganization of the Polish community would be far greater than it is. After all, what has an industrial maelstrom like Hamtramck (the community), or even American Protestantism, to offer as a substitute for the stabilization influence of Polish traditions.[9]

Blue-collar stable neighborhoods, in short, clearly offer much in the way of attitude and aid that help sustain residents against both internal needs and depreciations experienced outside the area.

TRANSITIONAL NEIGHBORHOOD

Because the stable blue-collar section appears to be a blighted slum to certain land-hungry city authorities, the blue-collar residents are often forced to move by the building of parkways, the conversion of land use from residential to commercial, or the replacement of blue-collar dwellings with middle-income town houses or high-rise apartment houses. Even where the change process is not as deliberate, many stable enclaves depreciate over time in property value and upkeep as the sons and daughters of the blue-collar residents move out to the suburbs. Absentee landlords of the old tenement or brownstone houses of the blue-collarites begin to subdivide vacant units and close their eyes to the overcrowding (and rent-sharing) practices of new tenants. Appalachian and Southern white and Negro migrants to the city, along with urban renewal authorities, press in on declining stable city neighborhoods, albeit for different reasons, but with the same impact. The blue-collar enclave initially resists, but, in due course, either slowly disappears or is routed "overnight" by more powerful renewal authorities. The enclave loses its insularity and distinctiveness and, in the process, generates its own peculiar (downhill) blue-collar neighborhood style.

Not surprisingly, in the beginning of the renewal process, elements of the blue-collar community pull together to resist rapid change:

> To the politician, the storekeeper, the minister and others who had some stake in the slum neighborhood, its destruction was especially to be feared. For such people, the passing of the old neighborhood meant the loss of power and place that had been hard won. In some cases it meant also the loss of a valued cultural heritage: the dispersal of a Greek slum, for example, meant an end to the shadow plays which, to the deep satisfaction of the older men, portrayed Greek history, scenes of peasant life, and the glories of strife with the Turks.[10]

Relevant here is the explanation researchers now offer for Boston's "Hicks phenomenon," or the strong antibusing position taken by supporters of the elected school board head, people generally less educated, poorer, and older than most Bostonians:

> Pure racism is far too simple an explanation. It is not open bigotry, nor the never-proven "white backlash," nor even the simple, much proclaimed desire to support neighborhood schools that has won Mrs. Hicks' elections for her. It is something much deeper and more meaningful for our times—*the perception of a threat to familiar, secure, and comfortable ways*. The hard resistance to this perceived threat has formed not around *school* segregation, which is an outpost, but around *neighborhood* segregation, which is the inner citadel.[11]

So deep does this reach, the researchers conclude, that in the magic words "neighborhood schools" the emphasis is on the first, and not the second, word.

Characteristically, however, blue-collar efforts to counter the neighborhood's disintegration are weak, uninformed, and generally ineffective (even so-called Mafia protection has limitations and vulnerability if the intent of the "newcomers" is unwavering). As with a self-fulfilling prophecy, the neighborhood's rejection of the social services of the "caretakers" exacts a price in naivete in utilizing them and their services. Similarly, resort to church, ethnic, and criminal "contacts" soon demonstrate the very real limits on the power of all three vis-à-vis the declining neighborhood and the outside forces of change and renewal.

As the situation grows increasingly tense, the character of the neighborhood changes. Unemployment rates reach new levels—a March 1966 study revealed that for men in the prime working years (25 to 64) the rate in poverty areas was 6 percent, nearly triple the rate for men in this age group in nonpoverty areas (for teen-agers in the poverty areas it was nearly 25 percent).[12]

Linked to economic disintegration is a rising crime rate, the poor preying especially upon the poor. Transitional neighborhoods may cease being hospitable, friendly, and supportive to inhabitants. The known (and therefore underestimated) risks of victimization from forcible rape, robbery, and burglary may increase as the average income level of area dwellers decreases.[13] Antagonistic police surveillance increases, and instances of "unnecessary force" or brutality in police-citizen contacts become ever more frequent.[14]

The pace of social change quickens, old stabilities are shattered, and the neighborhood begins to complete its process of decline. New residents, particularly the hill people, remain focused elsewhere:

On weekends, from the mill towns of Indiana go hundreds of carloads of Kentuckians on quick visits to the "old country." Some arrive just in time for the morning milking, or to help patch up an old house, and they floorboard it back to Indiana just in time to punch in at the factory Monday morning. They send money and clothes back to the old country, and many I've talked to plan to return, once they are set up financially, which of course they rarely manage.[15]

In this disorganized setting of ersatz residents and mini-neighbors, even the area's local racketeer is apt to become just "another of many small independent entrepreneurs—succeeding one day, failing the next."[16] Lacking power in controlling his own illicit activities, the petty racketeer is accorded no special status or respect and has no real claim on local jobs, money, or prestige. Only the real estate or relocation agent grows in significance, the others (the school, church, ethnic associations, and so on) having proved impotent in their efforts to preserve the past.

In a short period the transitional area often loses both blue-collar kin-network members and valuable neighborhood institutions (such as late-hour, credit-granting local stores). Candy stores fade away, and the area gains sullen stoops, veritable cornucopias of garbage, and dented double-parked Cadillacs. A new tone develops: rude, inequitable, unkempt, and abrasive. Needy and apprehensive individuals, including voluntary indigents from the young "beatnik" and hippy crowd, move in, and intergroup hostility reaches new heights.

Social disorganization of the transitional-area variety leaves a deep impression on the urban blue-collarites involved. Their propensity to scapegoat hostilities is strengthened: The "invaders," whether new residents or renewal authorities, are cited at the time and for years thereafter as the cause of the "refugee" worker's ensuing problems. Typical is this commentary from a young white divorcee and mother of three who lives in a transitional California blue-collar community:

When we first moved here, people had hope. Pat used to work nights at Douglas. During the day he took care of the garden, or we would buy things for the house. Then *they* started pouring in, and he just gave up. I don't think it had anything to do with me. It had to do with them. He saw them taking over everything, and he got wild. He just wanted to get out. Well, I had the children to think about. I just couldn't run away. So he went off with her.[17]

This young woman, in her day job as a saleswoman, in her night job as a bar hostess, and in her role as neighbor and citizen, likely shares her scapegoating tale with many other blue-collar wives over and again. Folk analysis like this contributes much to blue-collar bitterness where residential integration with lower-class whites or Negroes is concerned.

Of greatest significance is the challenge presented to blue-collarites who, refusing to live alongside of the "undesirables," would relocate and re-create elsewhere the world they had so recently lost. The old neighborhood, albeit possibly a "gray area" or "slum" in the lexicon of the city fathers, helped before its decline to sustain the worker-resident's concept of his value as a person, his particular organization of reality, and his sense of the continuity of the self within that reality. All this requires reestablishment, a fact that helps to explain the propensity of the dislocated to take their culture with them if they can, to resettle elsewhere in the same city, and to undertake, even if unconsciously, a restoration-like task.

STABLE SUBURB

Probably the second most popular answer to the relocation challenge entails residence in a traditional blue-collar suburb. This relatively expensive option, however, is generally open only to better-off semiskilled and skilled workers. (A typical new $22,000 home, purchased with a $17,000 mortgage for 30 years, costs $107 a month, not including taxes and other expenses. Over the 30 years the blue-collar owner will pay $38,678 on the original $17,000; he will work 3½ years just to pay current rates of interest on his mortgage.)[18]

Suburbia, the destination of millions of Caucasian blue-collarites, is not a new habitat for manual workers. Under the paternalistic guidance of steel and other industries, blue-collarites preceded white-collarites into planned architectural suburbs such as Hershey, Pennsylvania, and Homestead, Illinois, over one hundred years ago. Within the last thirty years, the blue-collar exodus from cities to suburbs has intensified, large numbers following their suburban-bound factories, some fleeing from the superdomination and economic exploitation of landlords, and many escaping from the panic they have helped create in transitional and declining city neighborhoods. What with perhaps 70 percent of the nation's workers now employed in suburban workplaces, a near-majority of the nation's Caucasian urban blue-collarites may now—or will soon—live in suburbia.[19]

The stable blue-collar suburb, a collection of "new homes for old values," is very much like the old city neighborhood. Made up largely, if not entirely, of manual workers who have been raised in the city and have been shaped by this upbringing before becoming suburbanites, the stable working-class suburb represents a faithful transposition, rather than a fundamental alteration, of the basic blue-collar style. Indeed, this goes so far as to include the transportation of the big city crime syndicate out to the blue-collar suburb, where the old standbys, the bookies, numbers operators, and loan sharks, are joined by new criminal operators of suburban waste disposal, restaurant, bar, and nightclub operations.

The myth of suburbia is shattered by the intractability of suburban-bound blue-collarites. According to the myth, the move should produce a drastic change in behavior and personality: Previously individualistic blue-collarites become organization men, and their wives become hyperactive socializers and status seekers. Democrats become Republicans. The unchurched return to religion. All parents join the PTA, and everyone becomes middle class.

The facts are otherwise. Blue-collar men apparently view suburbia as a place in which to relax, rather than as a school for new social graces. While some of their wives adopt the trappings of middle-class life (including PTA membership, an interest in Dr. Spock's advice, and the like), the men remain comfortably proletarian. For example, sociologist Bennett Berger's 1957 study of suburban, home-owning California auto workers found no particular interest among the men in adopting the patterns of middle-class social life. Rather, the ex-city dwellers had not been profoundly affected in any statistically identifiable or sociologically meaningful way:

> They were still overwhelmingly Democrats; they attended church as infrequently as they ever did; like most working class people, their informal contacts were largely limited to kin; they neither gave nor went to parties; on the whole they had no great hopes of getting ahead in their jobs; and, instead of a transient psychology, most of them harbored a view of their new suburban homes as paradise permanently gained.[20]

Graduate student Samuel Kaplan, after replicating Berger's 1957 research in 1965, generally found his conclusions to hold up—even after the workers had lived seven additional years in the suburb.[21]

While sociologist William Spinrad's 1964 study of forty-six New Jersey urban and suburban dwellers did find certain life-style differences between the two, these were not great and were very uneven in their distribution. Not surprisingly, blue-collar suburbanites differed in their stronger emphasis on consumption and leisure, their concern over their psychic separation from the workplace and from the union meeting hall, their lack of interest in their own workmates, and their sense of new status achievement. Most, however, gave no evidence of a switch to general political conservatism, and some showed up among the most concerned and involved trade unionists in the entire sample.[22] Similarly, the study made in 1963 by sociologists Albert K. Cohen and Harold M. Hodges, Jr., of approximately 2,600 male family heads residing in the San Francisco Bay area, explored self-concepts, status concern, familial loyalties, and sex norms among workers; since *no* significant differences were found between blue-collar urban and suburban dwellers, the authors wound up treating all the respondents as a single sample.[23]

Berger suggests that the critical change in the shift from city to suburb is one of house type, rather than of neighborhood life style. The new twin, ranch-type, or split-level (mass-development) home is larger and more modern than anything the blue-collarites have previously known in the city. It offers more privacy than city dwellers normally experience and makes available both a yard to landscape as one chooses and a possession with which to tinker and putter. Blue-collar family style is here distinctive in the pride taken in home ownership and in the self-expression and creativity evidenced in unusual house-paint schemes and jerry-built house extensions. (Sociologists Arthur Vidich and Joseph Bensman note in this connection that the blue-collarite's "inability to cope with introspection and self-reflection is indicated by the intensity with which he pursues work outside of the job. His home is a place not just for living but, more important, requires maintenance and constant improvement.")[24]

If a triumvirate of parish priest, ethnic leader, and local racketeer can be thought to symbolize life in the stable city neighborhood, and if the real estate or relocation agent can be thought to serve this function for the change-racked declining section, the shopping-center merchant is an apt choice in the case of the stable blue-collar suburb. Residents are especially consumption-oriented. Relatively high wages and easy credit enable many to indulge in their media-stimulated, seemingly endless material desires. Fads sweep through the areas, patios giving way in better-off suburbs to barbecue pits, lawn mowers to sit-in power jobs, ping-pong sets to pool tables, toy models to real boats. Soon a consumption mania is unconsciously relied upon to provide relief from life's boredom, a new form of routinization (the regular Saturday shopping jaunt is now a suburban "institution") and a way of having some fun while one leads the "comfortable life."

Especially striking is the terminal character of this life led in traditional blue-collar suburbs. The neighborhood and its style represent the "end of the line." Berger's interviews suggest that the rationale probably goes something like this:

> Here I am, the son of a sharecropper, with a ninth grade education and no salable skills, and look at me: I'm paying off a nice new home, have a good car (often two), my kids and my wife

are decently dressed; she has a washing machine, I have some power tools; what more do I have a right to expect? [25]

Berger raises the provocative matter of the equity component involved in the expectations of working-class suburbanites— many of his respondents have achieved a level of material living beyond which they feel they have no further right to aspire. For such blue-collarites the suburb represents the ful- fillment of whatever they have felt they have ever had a right to expect from "America." In the sense of a dream achieved, the proletarian suburb has its assimilative function, but, over- all, the reinforcement of blue-collar ways available in enclave residence, albeit suburban, combines with blue-collar origins to preserve a distinctively blue-collar way of life.

TRANSITIONAL BLUE-COLLAR SUBURB

In due course jerry-built suburbs may become rundown and slumlike, but this is not a current problem. Rather, the suburban transition now involving blue-collarites casts them in the role of dispossessor, not dispossessed as in the city. Transi- tional suburbs are those with a mixture of blue- and white- collar residents (even the archetype of the junior executive suburbia, Park Forest, Illinois, now has a minority of more than 10 percent of blue-collar residents). In fact, the suburb is transitional precisely because the mixture fails: On being "in- vaded" by blue-collarites, the suburb passes from white-collar to blue-collar domination. Status-sensitive white-collarites ac- tually uproot their community and pass the physical shell and township name over to the "undesirables." (Two newspaper reporters note of one such transitional suburb: "In the more sylvan reaches of [the upper-class county], the suburb fre- quently is written off as a giant housing project, populated by white trash.")[26] As in the situation of the city neighborhoods the blue-collarites themselves are fleeing, higher-status natives flee from their new blue-collar neighbors. A social "Gresham's Law" holds sway.

Marked by flux and strain, the transitional suburb may no longer be hospitable, friendly, and supportive. Rather, as sociologist William Dobriner discovered in the transitional Long Island community of Levittown, the turbulent suburb can and often does split bitterly along class lines.[27] At these times class peerage is the first condition of genuine social intercourse, play groups of children as well as adult neighboring patterns reflecting class antagonisms. Blue-collar husbands find it difficult to understand the middle-class husband who hangs up diapers, wheels the baby, and boasts about the pleasure he finds joining as his wife's bridge partner. These husbands, in turn, find it difficult to understand the blue-collarite who, on hot summer evenings, takes his supper out on the front lawn and shouts friendly greetings to passersby and to friends across the way. Social strangeness separates the classes despite the fact that the blue-collarites are atypical: Sociologist Herbert J. Gans judges that 80 percent of those blue-collarites he studied in 1958–1960 in Levittown were more modern than traditional in their values and behavior. (Over two-thirds divided evenly between skilled craftsmen and foremen; the remaining third was made up of semiskilled and unskilled blue-collarites.)[28]

Class particulars remain, and the blue-collar wives differ considerably from their middle-class counterparts. The blue-collar women not only value housewifery in principle, but many actually find it a source of satisfaction. Time is not a scarce commodity for them, their narrow range of activities and interests explaining a relaxed, even monotonous rhythm. Such women are not especially self-conscious or introspective. They often cite their mothers' counsel in personal problems, and they prefer to consult only with other women on personal matters. In every such respect, blue-collar wives contradict common middle-class norms and practice.

John Brooks captures much of this quite accurately in his pen portraits below of two families, each consisting of a couple in their late twenties, each with two or three small children, living side by side in a transitional suburb:

> Mr. White is of course a white-collar man—an employee of a book publishing firm, say—and the Whites live in a rambling

old house from the 1920's that they picked up for practically nothing when it was on the verge of falling to pieces, and have diligently "done over," almost entirely with their own hands. Mr. Blue next door is a garage mechanic, and his house is a small, trim rancher less than five years old. Mrs. White buys her clothes in the city, scanning the sales and discount stores for copies of Paris fashions; the local dress shop is good enough for Mrs. Blue. The Blues' quarter acre of lawn looks like a putting green, and Mr. Blue manicures it with a sit-down power mower; the White's lawn is studded with gray spots and weeds, and when Mr. White cuts it, he does so with a hand-pushed machine (wearing Madras shorts, which Blue wouldn't be caught dead in). The Blue car is a three-year-old Chevrolet, the White car is a timeless Volkswagen.

Both families consume alcohol moderately but in totally different pattern: The Whites have a cocktail or two daily, with some ceremony, often outdoors in full view of the neighbors, and they discuss their drinking freely, while the Blues abstain through the week except for Mr. Blue's occasional beer for TV-watching, and on Saturday night they sometimes get moderately drunk on boilermakers, behind drawn blinds, with a certain furtiveness. The Blues flaunt their knowingness about TV-program characters; as for the Whites, TV-watching is the thing *they* do furtively.

The Blues shout to each other, from room to room of their house or from corner to corner of their lot, without self-consciousness; the Whites modulate their voices to the point where they sometimes can't hear each other. When her children were under two years old Mrs. White sometimes let them play naked in the backyard wading pool, a practice that moved the Blues to ill-suppressed titters, though not to outrage. The Whites, naturally enough, have many books, and indeed, use books as the main decorative motif of their living room; the Blues haven't a book in the house, and even the occasional ones that Mr. White presses on them as a gift soon disappear mysteriously. Once every two years the Whites pay off their social debts by having a fairly large outdoor cocktail party; the Blues, pretending with elaborate politeness to be otherwise engaged in their own backyard, watch over the hedge with tolerant amusement. Here, in sum, are two families with hardly anything in common except their citizenship —yet their respective family incomes are practically identical, in the neighborhood of $8,000 a year.[29]

Accordingly, life in this neighborhood situation encompasses special types of strain. Making new friends in the locale can prove difficult, particularly when class boundaries draw firm lines around the eligibles. (Gans' study of the matter leads him to conclude that such blue-collarites "do not suffer from pressures to conform, but from a shortage of like-minded people in their surroundings. Were they to live in communities with more compatible people, many of their problems would disappear.")[30]

Strain is also traceable to the frequent division inside transitional suburbs over local school policies, this division going as deep as only something related to "displaced aspirations" possibly can. School policy, the transitional suburb's most divisive controversy, separates the modernists (mostly white-collarites) from the fundamentalists (mostly blue-collarites). The area's blue-collarites, already struggling with the suburb's heavy tax burden, are often willing to settle for large classes, split sessions, comparatively low salary schedules, and a traditional, nonexperimental curriculum. Dobriner's report is illuminating:

> In the case of Levittown's working-class and still ethnically bound Catholic population, the values of education and the importance of education as an instrument of upward mobility and social status are not yet fully perceived. This . . . is then superimposed over the marginal economic position of Levittown's Catholic population (47 percent of all residents), and the answer to Catholic conservatism stands revealed.[31]

Dobriner suggests in conclusion that "if you are doubtful about the importance of schooling in the first place, you could not reasonably be expected to pay for other people's educative 'frills'—particularly when you can't afford them anyway."[32]

The local school board and the omnipresent real estate agent can be thought to symbolize this suburban neighborhood's particular variant on the stable city neighborhood style. The real estate agent is especially significant because the transitional suburb is very attractive to certain mobile blue-collarites. (Dobriner predicts, for example, that over the next four years, Levittown, Long Island, may gain many new blue-collarites and return to comparative class homogeneity—and blue-collar dominance.)[33]

SUMMARY

Four kinds of living environment are characteristic of the nation's 21 million Caucasian manual workers. Each is marked by varying degrees of provincialism and defensiveness. Each, however, is also attractively marked in varying degree by increasingly rare *gemeinshaft* elements, by a personalized search for primary affiliation, by a vibrant street life, by the idea of the neighborhood as a safe port, and by a high valuation of cultural distinctiveness. Indeed, those former residents who gravitate back on weekends to the pure ethnic enclaves of old are rewarded by more than the remembrance of things past.

For the most part, the blue-collar neighborhood style perseveres against contemporary change pressures: Contrary to certain of the "Melting Pot" proponents, many blue-collarites maintain their neighborhoods as insulated to "outsiders." These remnants of another era are not living on their past glory alone, but evidence remarkable staying power instead—if left unviolated by public and private real estate powers. Contrary also to those who believe that the blue-collarite is absorbed into class-mixed suburbs, many of the working-class families involved remain decidedly more "blue" than "white" in their life style. Raised as blue-collarites, the working-class suburbanites remain just that; socialized in the homes and neighborhoods of the working class, the nouveau suburbanites remain at heart "neighborhood boys"—and their children look more than a little like them.

Notes to Chapter Seven

1. Area Redevelopment Administration, *The Geographic Mobility of Labor: A Summary Report* (Washington, D.C.: Government Printing Office, 1964). See also Bureau of the Census, *Census of Population, 1960, Occupational Characteristics,* PC (2) 7A, Table 8; John B. Lansing, *et al., The Geographic Mobility of Labor: A First Report* (Ann Arbor, Mich.: Survey Research Center, 1963), pp. 13, 64.

2. This chapter is confined to urban and suburban subjects, as in the entire book. For a discussion of blue-collarites as small city dwellers, see Robert J. Havighurst, *et al., Growing Up in River City* (New York: Wiley, 1962); William Simon and John Gagnon, "The Decline and Fall of the Small Town," *Trans-Action* (April 1967), pp. 42–51. For a 1954 discussion of blue-collarites as village dwellers, see John L. Fischer and Ann Fischer, *The New Englanders of Orchard Town, U.S.A.* (New York: Wiley, 1966). On blue-collarites as rural dwellers see Art Gallager, Jr., *Plainville Fifteen Years Later* (New York: Columbia University Press, 1961), pp. 88–89, *passim;* Alicja Iwanska, *Good Fortune: Second Chance Community* (Pullman: State College of Washington, Institute of Agricultural Sciences, 1958). On blue-collarites as trailer park residents, see Robert Mills French and Jeffrey K. Hadden, "Mobile Homes: Instant Suburbia or Transportable Slums?," *Social Problems* (Fall 1968), pp. 219–226.

3. Scott Greer, *The Emerging City: Myth and Reality* (New York: Free Press, 1962), p. 127.

4. Edward J. Ryan, "Personal Identity in an Urban Slum," in Leonard J. Duhl (ed.), *The Urban Condition: People and Policy in the Metropolis* (New York: Basic Books, 1963), p. 144, *passim.*

5. Harold L. Sheppard and A. Harvey Belitsky, *The Job Hunt: Job Seeking Behavior of Unemployed Workers in a Local Economy* (Baltimore: Johns Hopkins Press, 1966).

6. Anselm L. Strauss, *Images of the American City* (New York: Free Press, 1961), p. 64.

7. Irving Spergel, *Racketville, Slumtown, and Haulburg: An Exploratory Study of Delinquent Subcultures* (Chicago: University of Chicago Press, 1964), p. 17, *passim.* See also Fred J. Cook, "Just Call 'The Doctor' for a Loan," *The New York Times Maga-*

zine, January 28, 1968; Charles Grutzner, "Crime in Westchester," *The New York Times*, July 13, 1967, pp. 1, 12.

8. Albert K. Cohen and Harold M. Hodges, Jr., "Characteristics of the Lower Blue-Collar Class," *Social Problems* (Spring 1963), p. 307.

9. Arthur Evans Wood, *Hamtramck: A Sociological Study of a Polish-American Community* (New Haven: College and University Press, 1955), p. 204. On the ethnic reinforcement role of the "old neighborhood," see Nicholas Pileggi, "Saturday Italians," *New York World Journal Tribune*, January 15, 1967.

10. Martin Meyerson and Edward C. Banfield, *Politics, Planning, and the Public Interest: The Case of Public Housing in Chicago* (New York: Free Press, 1955), p. 99. See also Patricia Cayo Sexton, *Spanish Harlem* (New York: Harper & Row, 1965); Richard Elman, *Ill-at-Ease in Compton* (New York: Pantheon, 1967). For evidence that ethnic group affiliation has a bearing on specific mental abilities, see Susan Stodolsky and Gerald Lesser, "Learning Patterns in the Disadvantaged," *The Public Interest* (Fall 1967).

11. J. Michael Ross, *et al.*, "Negro Neighbors—Banned in Boston," *Trans-Action* (September/October 1966), p. 13. "The neighborhood roots of the Hicks' supporters are deeper and stronger than those of her partial supporters, and especially of her detractors" (p. 16). See also Eleanor P. Wolf and Charles N. Lebeaux, "Class and Race in the Changing City," in L. F. Schnore and H. Fagin (eds.), *Urban Research and Policy Planning* (Beverly Hills, Calif.: Sage Publications, 1967), pp. 99–130; James Q. Wilson, "The Urban Unease," *The Public Interest* (Summer, 1968). On the psychological costs to residents of "losing" a neighborhood's way of life, see Marc Fried, "Grieving for a Lost Home," in Duhl (ed.), *op. cit.*, pp. 151–171.

12. James R. Wetzel and Susan S. Holland, "Poverty Areas of Our Major Cities," *Monthly Labor Report* (October 1966), p. 1106.

13. 1966 N.O.R.C. National Survey, as reported in The President's Commission on Law Enforcement and Administration of Justice, *The Challenge of Crime in a Free Society* (Washington, D.C.: Government Printing Office, 1967), p. 38. See also Paul Eberts and Kent Schwivian, "Crime Rates and Relative Deprivation," unpublished paper read at the 1966 meeting of the American Sociological Association (Cornell University).

14. See Albert J. Reiss, Jr., "Police Brutality—Answers to Key Questions," *Trans-Action* (July/August 1968), pp. 10–19; David

Burnham, "Misconduct Laid to 27% of Police in 3 Cities Slums," *The New York Times,* July 5, 1968, p. 1.

15. Robert Gover, " 'Culture' Comes to Indianapolis," *The New York Times Magazine,* December 24, 1967, p. 10.

16. Spergel, *op. cit.,* p. 20.

17. As quoted by journalist Richard M. Elman, "Near Watts: The American Dream in Compton, Cal.," *The Urban Review* (June 1967), p. 7.

18. Sidney Margolius, "Higher Prices, Mortgage Rates Trigger New Housing Crisis," *AFL-CIO News,* May 18, 1968, p. 8.

19. As quoted in Kristol, *op. cit.,* p. 67. See also Mary G. Powers, "Class, Ethnicity, and Residence in Metropolitan America," unpublished paper read at the 1967 Eastern Sociological Society meeting (Fordham University).

20. Bennett Berger, "Suburbia and the American Dream," *The Public Interest* (Winter 1966), p. 81. See also Berger, *Working-Class Suburb: A Study of Auto Workers in Suburbia* (Berkeley: University of California Press, 1960).

21. Personal correspondence, May 1966.

22. William Spinrad, "Blue-Collar Workers as City and Suburban Residents—Effects on Union Membership," in A. Shostak and W. Gomberg (eds.), *Blue-Collar World* (Englewood Cliffs, N.J.: Prentice-Hall, 1964), pp. 215–224.

23. Cohen and Hodges, *op. cit.*

24. Arthur J. Vidich and Joseph Bensman, *Small Town in Mass Society: Class, Power, and Religion in a Rural Community* (Princeton: Princeton University Press, 1958), p. 306. See also Frank Marquart, "The Auto Worker," in Irving Howe (ed.), *Voices of Dissent* (New York: Grove Press, 1958), pp. 148–150.

25. Berger, *Working-Class Suburb, op. cit.,* p. 25.

26. Peter H. Binzen and Fred Selby, "Levittown Revisited," *Philadelphia Evening Bulletin,* April 20, 1967, pp. 1, 31.

27. For discussion, see William M. Dobriner, *Class in Suburbia* (Englewood Cliffs, N.J.: Prentice-Hall, 1963).

28. Herbert J. Gans, *The Levittowners: Ways of Life and Politics in a New Suburban Community* (New York: Pantheon, 1967), p. 23. Some 26 percent of the first 3,000 families to move into the new Levittown suburb in Pennsylvania between its 1958 opening and 1960 were blue-collarites; no current figures are available.

29. John Brooks, *The Great Leap: The Past Twenty-Five Years in America* (New York: Harper & Row, 1966), pp. 154–155. Reprinted by permission of the publisher.

30. Herbert J. Gans, "Effects of the Move from City to Suburb," in Duhl (ed.), *op. cit.*, p. 190.

31. Dobriner, *op. cit.*, p. 121. See also A. Shostak, "Education and the Family," *Journal of Marriage and the Family* (February 1967), pp. 124–139; Christopher Jencks and David Riesman, "The Catholics and Their Colleges," *The Public Interest* (Spring 1967), pp. 79–101.

32. Dobriner, *op. cit.*, p. 121.

33. *Ibid.*, p. 122. Gans is not as confident of this development in the New Jersey Levittown as home purchase prices there have risen sharply in recent years. Gans, *The Levittowners, op. cit.*, p. 36. Berger, however, anticipates more and more blue-collar residence in suburbia. Berger, *Working-Class Suburb, op. cit.*, pp. 9, 13. *A Times* reporter quotes the 1967 president of the Levittown, Long Island, Chamber of Commerce as predicting Levittown "would remain a community of working-class people who use it as a stopping-off point to build up a down-payment for a bigger house in another community." Agis Salpukas, "Levittown, at 20, Has Changed Much, but Residents Look the Same," *The New York Times*, July 29, 1967, p. 11. See also Reynolds Farley, "Suburban Persistence," *American Sociological Review* (February 1964), pp. 38–47.

8

BLUE-COLLAR
FAMILIES

*Because they are Americans, and because they are not
rich, [common men] have already escaped from freedom
into obligations almost beyond their capacities.*
—ROBERT LANE, *Political Ideology*

A mixture of stability and change characterizes the nuclear
family of Caucasian urban blue-collarites. Stability, for example, is apparent in the persistence of far-reaching matri-
archal norms. Change is evident in the new effort a small
number of better-educated blue-collar couples are now making
to achieve more intimacy and sharing than blue-collarites generally know. Here, in family life, rivalry between the traditional past and the modern present is especially and strikingly
apparent. This rivalry helps to explain the existence of two
related, but distinct nuclear family subtypes—the traditional
and the modern, each discussed at length in this chapter.

TRADITIONAL NUCLEAR FAMILIES

Generally found in stable urban and suburban areas, particularly in low-cost ethnic enclaves, traditional families are most often headed by the poorest paid, least well-educated, least mobile, blue-collar husbands and fathers. Large numbers of laborers, assembly line semiskilled workers, and low-echelon service workers lead such families, at least normally, and they form these families while both partners are generally in their late teens or early twenties.[1] The dominant pattern here is early marriage followed by rapid childbearing.

Striking in such families, however, is the separateness and isolation of the marriage partners. Sociologist Elizabeth Botts, in her typology of conjugal role relationships, characterizes such "segregated" couples as having a clear delineation of tasks and a considerable number of separate interests and activities. They have a clearly defined division of labor into male and female tasks, one compromised only at great risk to self-esteem.[2] (Sociologist Herbert J. Gans, referring to Italian-American families in this context, adds: "It is not that [the husband] rejects the possibility of joint action; it is simply something outside of his experience.")[3] Indeed, each sex views the other in a highly stereotyped way: Men tend to think of women as timid, emotional, and inferior: women are apt to view men as arrogant, insensitive, and childish. The expectation of friendship in marriage is infrequent.

Oftentimes women run these families, though they go to great lengths to protect their husbands in the latters' belief that theirs is the good old-fashioned patriarchal household they remember from their childhood. Indeed, while the women prefer to think of their husbands as men who ought to be strong and good economic providers, they generally treat their husbands as children to be looked after, indulged, and kept in line. Women commonly handle the household finances, raise the children, manage relations with shopkeepers and neighbors, guide the affairs of the extended family, and so forth. Not surprisingly, their commitment to marriage is generally much greater than is that of their husbands.

Personal relations are often strained in the early years. Frequently the couples are dissatisfied with the boredom of their marriage, its overall meagerness of communication, its mutual misunderstandings, and the real or suspected indiscretions of the mate (almost always of the husband). Blue-collar wives are by far the more dissatisfied sex; many of them conveyed to sociologist Mirra Komarovsky and her interviewers their yearnings for reassurance, counsel, appreciation, encouragement, and sharing for its own sake. Contrary to their "passive" role, "it is the women who nag, demand, and complain. The husbands' action is largely a *reaction* to women's demands, and one which often takes the form of leaving the field of battle." [4] The ability of the husband to withdraw from the relationship means that he need not try to scrutinize or understand the motives of his wife. Instead, he can assert his will—while she has to "handle" him.

Family members are constrained from reaching out to one another by a host of taboos and folk prescriptions based on a common fear of loss of identity in the absence of role restrictions. Generally unequipped as yet with the psychological jargon of the Freudian "trickle-down," the blue-collarites can sense, but can hardly communicate a deep-seated fear that their urges and dreams will draw them into prohibited—if desired— forms of conduct. Inaccurately envied by others for their lack of inhibitions and their presumed closeness to nature, many of them are, in fact, thoroughly afraid of themselves. The blue-collarite knows a trained incapacity to relate to the opposite sex that takes a heavy toll.

Sex relations among blue-collarites are hardly what mass culture caricatures of virile blue-collarites lead one to expect. First, as sociologist Lee Rainwater's review of the data suggests, frequency of intercourse is probably about at the same rate in the various occupational strata, although the blue-collarite and the white-collarite is each apt to believe that the nature of his own work leaves him too worn out to keep up with the other's allegedly higher frequency of sex relations.

Second, there is an apparent decline in interest in erotic love as one goes down the "social class" scale. In the "segregated" role relationship of traditional blue-collar families, this aggravates an already sharp lack of communication and openness about interpersonal relations. Third, while some traditional couples may achieve the "naturalness" that all couples of this family type are unduly famed for, the sex relations of most couples are seriously affected by the strains of economic deprivation, fear of pregnancy, and a general and joyless estrangement between the sexes. Finally, as in so many other areas of living, the erotic repertoire of these blue-collar couples is severely limited. Despite their early start at coitus, and regardless of their corner-tavern boasting, many or perhaps most of the males are creatures of highly-tabooed, unimaginative, and routine love-making behavior. When found in combination with severe limits in the vocal expression of love, these behavior norms can make life as unfulfilling here as it is elsewhere for many of these people.[5]

Child-rearing is colored from the start by the major family-planning decision: namely, how many children? To be sure, some childbirths are encouraged by a desire to combat loneliness or by the high value placed on sons who presumably will help care for the parents in their old age. Other births are linked to the fact that "the working class woman tends to feel she has only her body, her energy, and her good conscience to offer as evidence of her worth—having children is the most dramatic and absorbing accomplishment she can offer to the world that she has done well." [6] On the other hand, an unknown, and possibly large number of births, particularly in large families, are unwelcome accidents. These births provide the parents with additional unsettling evidence of their own helplessness.

Child-rearing in these families is apt to be a narrow, repressive matter. Many blue-collar mothers regard the behavior of their children as mysterious and almost beyond understanding. Believing the child to be inherently mischievous, these mothers endlessly threaten or cajole, but seldom discuss or reason with, their offspring. Discipline tends to be impulsive, inconsistent, and sharp, though it rarely entails the threat to withdraw love, a practice more common among many white-collarites (a blue-collar mother is likely to explain: "I hit you because I love you."). As early as possible, the child is taught to behave much like a miniature adult. He is encouraged to pursue helpful ways pleasing to adults—and he is badgered into wanting to be a diligent, responsible, industrious, sober, and self-controlled citizen.[7] In school, at church, and especially at home, everywhere, that is, but in the unregulated street, childhood is sorely constrained. It is also a one-parent matter, the blue-collar male conspicuous by his absence from all but the discipline and athletic component.

Child-rearing, and everything else in the traditional nuclear family, is influenced by financial problems, which are often acute. Unfortunately, either they go undiscussed or they are used by each spouse to indict the other. Many wives attribute their major problems in life to their lack of sufficient money for the necessities of life as well as such "luxuries" as an occasional babysitter or a visit to the hairdresser. With several children commonly about, the $24,000 average cost of rearing a child to age eighteen (calculated on an annual family income of $6,600) leaves very little for other family interests.[8] Financial strain is heightened by the fact that the range from entry to retirement earnings is very small, perhaps a few hundred dollars, for laborers and service blue-collarites. A sense of continuing deprivation combines with a realistic fear that an unexpected financial accident could suddenly upset a precarious financial balance; unease thus preoccupies the entire family.

Some rather limited relief is provided by the second income of the many blue-collar wives in traditional families who are gainfully employed (a little over a third of the wives of laborers, operators, and craftsmen and nearly half of the wives of nonhousehold service workers were employed in 1965, the latest data year).[9] Traditional family secondary earners show up in the poorer-paying, less attractive categories for time-honored female employ. Such women are probably heavily represented in the bloc of one-third of the nation's 26 million working women who earn less than $3,000 a year. While their husbands earn an average of $6,497 annually, white employed women bring home only an additional $3,859.[10] A second income, in short, may bring some relief from the traditional family's financial strain, but it is likely much less than suggested by the impressive surface fact of two incomes.

Consumption patterns are consistent with a view of an unsafe world of fleeting pleasures. Two tacks are taken: "debt indulgence" and "debt conservatism." In the case of debt indulgence, sociologist David Caplovitz's research suggests that the lower-paid blue-collarite frequently engages in "conspicuous consumption" as a form of compensation for blocked social mobility. Certain traditional blue-collar families, encouraged by the mass media to affirm their worth through the possession of expensive material goods, turn to local merchants for the high-cost credit purchase of color television sets, home entertainment centers, and so forth. These seemingly improvident purchases fill a great void that would otherwise exist in the living room life of the family. They are, moreover, consistent with a short-time, hedonistic orientation to an uncertain world. If the "breaks" and "connections," rather than ability and savings, make the difference, then securing immediate enjoyment from a few expensive and highly visible objects makes reasonable sense.[11]

(Typical is the situation of a thirty-one-year-old New York truck driver whose eight-child family was profiled in 1967 in *The New York Times*. On a base pay of $134 for five days, the blue-collarite pays a monthly bill of $170 for rent, $23 for heat, and $25 for gas and electricity. Food costs over $200 a month, and the family is nevertheless paying $27 a month on a $900 color TV-plus-stereo combination. The teamster has two garnishments on his salary—$20 a week for a loan that he took out for a friend and "got stuck on," and $30 a week paying off the hospital bill on his youngest child. With his credit union loan he estimates his total debts at about $3,000; with overtime he may gross $10,000, a deceptively large figure equal actually to the Federal Poverty Line Standard of $1,000 per family member).[12]

Other traditional blue-collar families, generally those with a stronger credit position, manage a more conservative consumption pattern. Sociologist Bennett Berger, for example, found the living rooms in blue-collar homes in stable suburbs "crowded with overstuffed furniture; the mantle, a glass or plaster menagerie; the walls adorned not with Renoir reproductions but with F. W. Woolworth landscapes or else gilt-edged photographs of members of the family." [13] Gans also found little evidence of profligacy:

> West-Enders do not believe in living beyond their means, and installment buying is kept to an absolute minimum. They distrust the outside world, and therefore are skeptical about a method of buying which would put them in debt to that world for a long time . . . Whenever possible, then, they use cash; and, since households are long established, expensive items are rarely needed.[14]

The outside world's appeals both for savings and for installment buying fall on deaf ears. Money is spent easily and steadily, but conservatively. Life is thought too short either for savings accounts or for endless installment debt.

Overall, traditional families are characterized by an ingrained separation among members, a strained silence, and a superficial self-sufficiency. Living very much the way most blue-collarites did fifty years ago, this large segment of today's blue-collar strata is marked by poverty of spirit as well as means. Little wonder that research finds the women most commonly in traditional marriages, the wives of unskilled workers, to be "perhaps the most deprived of all women." [15] Even with the reluctance of many Catholic blue-collarites to seek divorce, the helplessness of many traditional blue-collar marriages makes understandable the fact that the divorce rate is higher on the lower rungs of the economic and status ladder, and marriage is less stable among working-class than among middle-class couples.[16] Blue-collar tradition-holding families pursue a course increasingly uncommon in a society as dynamic and fluid as our own. Their family type may well have outrun its adaptive purpose, leaving traditional family members with outlived and outworn values.

MODERN NUCLEAR FAMILIES

In every case where the data permit differentiation among traditional or modern families, the key element distinguishing the latter appears to be that of "last year of school completed." [17] Where the couple has had no high school, or where neither has graduated from high school, the likelihood is that they will evolve a traditional marriage. Where the marriage partners have both graduated from high school, or where the wife has had considerably more education than the husband, the likelihood is that a relatively modern marriage may evolve. The occupational success, greater earning power, and heightened self-esteem that frequently accompany educational attainment play a large part, as do also the improved powers of personal reasoning and the improved ability to communicate that hopefully go along with a high school or junior college diploma.

Generally found in transitional suburbs, modern blue-collar families are most often led by well-paid, mobile, and young manual workers. Large numbers of bench-assembly semiskilled workers, skilled craftsmen, and upper-echelon service workers nominally head up such families, power in family decision-making actually being divided between the spouses according to merit (for example, the husband will choose which car to buy after the wife, as budget-tender, agrees that an installment purchase is feasible).

Modern blue-collar families are marked by a high degree of integration and closeness between husbands and wives. While household tasks are not entirely interchangeable, little that needs to be done is viewed as beneath masculine dignity (these blue-collar men have a somewhat relaxed norm of masculinity). Spouses in these marriages are less traditional in their thinking about sex-linked behavior and join in more social activities together. Repudiating the characteristic awkwardness of the blue-collarite in emotional matters, the couple explores new avenues of communication. They seek intimacy where others settle for accommodation.

Men and women share the running of these families, patriarchal authority and masculine privilege being much less prevalent here than in traditional marriages. The wives in modern marriages generally match their blue-collar husbands in educational attainment. They are more self-assured and competent, and they receive more respect from their husbands than do wives in traditional families. While the wives defer to their husbands, they openly and unapologetically share in the management of the family and join their husbands in a deep emotional involvement in family life. This does not go so far as to make the marriage truly equalitarian; the heritage of a patriarchal blue-collar upbringing and the customs of the day combine to assure acknowledgment of male leadership. Emotional involvement, however, does deepen commitment and it helps the marriage partners to balance power and responsibility within the marriage.

It appears that slightly more of the wives in modern than in traditional marriages are working women. The former apparently have a greater need to alleviate the boredom of housewifery and to gain a respite from their own child-rearing obligations. Many also enjoy the security available in providing a second income for the family, as well as sharing in the camaraderie of working with like-minded women. Research by sociologist Robert Blood, Jr. suggests that the autonomy of the working wife in household tasks may decrease somewhat, while her power in major economic decisions may increase. Overall, however, neither shift means that one partner comes to dominate the other. Rather, working-wife marriages seem stronger than ever before, the couples now sharing household tasks, sharing problems related to their common employment status, and sharing the fruits of extra income.[18] Understandably, while many blue-collar men strongly condemn working women as a competitive menace, as a rate-cutting and job-stealing threat to the male labor force, individual blue-collarites generally exclude their own wives from this indictment.[19]

In these modern blue-collar marriages, personal relations are likely to be much less strained in the early than in the later years. When the marriage is still young, expectations are high and considerable effort is made to insure achievement. Husbands demonstrate unusual sensitivity to what is going on in the world of their wives. The women, in turn, play a large role in the emotional sustenance of their husbands. Marriage conflicts are "talked out"; husbands avoid contemptuous dismissal of their wives even though many of the men tend to avoid sore subjects and to withdraw in the face of demands they cannot meet.

Over time, however, disenchantment frequently takes over. Komarovsky's data suggest that "older educated husbands disclose themselves less fully and have a slightly lower degree of empathy than do the younger men." [20] Both spouses come to complain that the other does not really listen, and only talks about boring things. It is as if the demanding effort at modernity eventually exhausts the partners as they age, assuming, that is, that the disillusionment reported is a function of age and not of some other variable (such as the quality and character of childhood socialization received a half-century ago).

Sex relations are more relaxed in response to birth-control mastery, more intimate in response to greater emotional rapport, and more varied in response to the fewer inhibitions of "emancipated" women. Housewives in modern blue-collar marriages endorse the ideal of sexual fulfillment for women and the ideal of frank discussion of sex preferences between marriage partners. Rainwater's rare data in the matter suggest that these women find sex relations "highly gratifying" twice as often as do women in more traditional (more segregated and conflict-marked) marriages. This pattern holds for husbands as well, though within a narrower range of responses.[21] Rainwater adds here:

Their sexuality is an intimate oasis to which they can retreat from daily problems and in which they can find a renewed sense of aliveness and of support and closeness with another human being. Such, of course, is a function of intercourse in all social classes, but sexual relations acquire a particular significance in the contrast they provide with some of the less rewarding aspects of the working class world.[22]

On the other hand, unlike some traditional blue-collar couples who can achieve a modicum of sexual adjustment despite unhappiness in their marriages, most modern blue-collar couples link their sexual adjustment to their overall satisfaction with the marriage. This all-or-nothing connection is the counterpart of the jeopardy that permeates traditional concerns with the husband's unreliability. While a key issue, it is thought by many modern couples to be not only a problem, but also an opportunity to improve the marital relationship by working through the couple's difficulties in this area.

Child-rearing is colored from the start by the ability to control the number of children in the family. The "modern" blue-collar husbands explain to researchers that more can be accomplished for their children if family size is kept small. (Middle-class family planners, in contrast, stress likely gains for the adults themselves in goods, time, and reduced responsibilities.) These blue-collar couples, including the many Catholics among them, use contraceptive devices regularly, and do not appear to be in conflict about this aspect of their sexual relationship.

Child-rearing is a focal activity, possibly the most important in the maintenance of the entire marriage relationship. Together the couple struggle to combine the concern of the wife with the child's self-actualization and the husband's more traditional interest in making "men of boys." Revealing is the fact that more blue-collar women than men express feelings of inadequacy in raising their children.[23] This in turn relates to the finding that the pattern of child-rearing, even in modern blue-collar marriages, remains basically conservative. Children are respected as individuals—but as individuals for whom self-control and respectability, rather than creativity or achievement, remain the dominant child-rearing goals. Sociologist

Melvin Kohn explains that "parents are most likely to accord high priority to those values which seem both important, in the sense that failure to achieve them would affect the child's future adversely, and problematic, in the sense that they are difficult to achieve." [24]

Financial problems are omnipresent. Their negative effects, however, are mitigated considerably by the effort these couples make to develop rational, commonly understood, and mutually acceptable ways of resolving family problems. While worries over absolute need are few, worries increase over relative deprivation (as measured against successful kinfolk or, possibly, against standards set by suburban neighbors). Budgets, debt consolidation schemes, installment buying, credit-line checking accounts, and other intricate ventures receive attention as part of a lifelong effort to accommodate a narrow income range and a small retirement figure. A sense of struggle, one imbued with pride in past achievement and guarded confidence in the likelihood of securing present gains, preoccupies the family.

Consumption patterns are consistent with a view of a world rich in material offerings, especially in a never-ending variety of seemingly indispensable products (these run the gamut from a showy, leather-bound encyclopedia set the children "must have" to a finished basement without which a home is "positively incomplete"). While bargain-hunting is a popular sport, major durables and many food staples are generally purchased on a top-of-the-line basis ("You get what you pay for"). Unlike the situation among traditional families, modern blue-collar couples frequently regard their homes as a major investment. Many dollars are spent on home improvements, home additions, and property landscaping (all in a style "modern—but homey"). Equal care is given to major household appliances and, in many cases, members of extended kin networks will call on one another for help in machine repair and house painting, carpentry, laying linoleum, and the like. Consumption mania is common in keeping with the modernity of these families. [25]

In short, then, modern blue-collar families, a distinct minority among all blue-collar units, are characterized by a demanding companionship, a challenging notion of the ideal and a substantial reservoir of happiness and love. Following living patterns which are quite different from those of an overwhelming majority of blue-collarites, this small segment of the nation's 21 million Caucasian manual workers expect much from marriage, worry more about it, and are more conscious of disappointment. On the other hand, when things go right, as they often do, the returns seem greater than in traditional families, the satisfaction appears deeper, and the love of family members for one another is presumably richer.[26]

SUMMARY

Constrained by respect for the traditional roles, by a reaction that invests family life with hard-to-achieve goals, and by behavior that masks the consequences of family life inadequacy, many or most blue-collarites find family life a neverending challenge. Large numbers of blue-collarites take the family (nuclear and extended) as the most significant of all reference groups. In reaction to their own contradictory feelings and beliefs, these men prefer to think that a life spent tending a machine (or console board) is somehow sanctified by its being a "sacrifice" for the good of the family. The contradiction between this and the actual stringency of life in the family of the *typical* manual worker is either denied or only dimly perceived. It is apparently sufficient that the family, like the neighborhood, remains a safe (if only a barely sustaining) port. In the entire system of rationalizations that blue-collar men derive for life as it is lived (or, better yet, tolerated), the working-class family remains the key factor, the "beginning and end of all things"—a heavy burden it falters under.

Notes to Chapter Eight

1. Robert N. Rapaport, "The Male's Occupation in Relation to His Decision to Marry," *Acta Sociologica* (1964), pp. 68–82. See also Robert F. Winch and Scott A. Greer, "The Uncertain Relation

between Early Marriage and Marital Stability. A Quest for Relevant Data," *Acta Sociologica* (1964), pp. 83–96; Ronald Freeman and Lolagene Coombs, "Childspacing and Family Economic Position," *American Sociological Review* (October 1966), pp. 631–648.

2. Elizabeth Bott, *Family and Social Network* (London: Tavistock Publications, 1957), pp. 53–55. See also John Scanzoni, "Occupation and Family Differentiation," *The Sociological Quarterly* (Spring 1967), pp. 187–198.

3. Herbert J. Gans, *The Urban Villagers* (New York: Free Press, 1962), p. 51. See also Robert D. Blood, Jr., and Donald M. Wolfe, *Husbands and Wives: The Dynamics of Married Living* (New York: Free Press, 1960).

4. Mirra Komarovsky, *Blue-Collar Marriage* (New York: Random House, 1964), p. 199. Rainwater adds: "No matter how much 'husband managing' may be required in the adult household role, the working class wife is uneasy about her assertiveness, and unsure how far she can go and still retain her own husband who is, after all, one of his sex." Lee Rainwater, *et al.*, *Working-Class Wife* (Chicago, Ill.: Oceana, 1959), p. 84.

5. Lee Rainwater, *Family Design: Marital Sexuality, Family Size, and Contraception* (Chicago: Aldine, 1965), pp. 68, 100–101. "Half of the men and of the women indicate a frequency of once or twice a week and the balance split more or less evenly between greater and lesser frequencies" (p. 100). See also Lee Rainwater and Karol Kane Weinstein, *And the Poor Get Children: Sex, Contraception, and Family Planning in the Working Class* (Chicago: Quadrangle Books, 1960).

6. Rainwater, *et al.*, *Working Class Wife, op. cit.*, p. 97.

7. See in this connection, Leonard I. Pearlin and Melvin L. Kohn, "Social Class, Occupation, and Parental Values: A Cross-National Study," *American Sociological Review* (August 1966), pp. 466–479. See also Eleanor Pavenstedt (ed.), *The Drifters: Children of Disorganized Lower-Class Families* (Boston: Little, Brown & Co., 1967); Daniel Miller and Guy E. Swanson, *Inner Conflict and Defense* (New York: Holt, 1960).

8. "Census-Eye View of Sales in the '70s," *Business Week* (June 10, 1967), p. 124.

9. Derived from V. C. Perrella and E. Waldman, "Marital and Family Characteristics of Workers in March 1965," *Monthly Labor Review* (March 1966), p. A-19, Table P; pp. A-20, A-21, Table Q. Note that rough percentages of other occupational types include professionals, one-third; managers, one-third; clerical, nearly one-

half; and sales, one-third. See also E. Waldman, "Marital and Family Characteristics of Workers, March 1966," *Monthly Labor Review* (April 1967), pp. 29–36.

10. Harry Ferguson, "Firms Are Unfair to the Fair Sex: The Woman Who Works Is Getting a Raw Deal," *Philadelphia Evening Bulletin,* January 12, 1967. Note that nearly a third of all married women work outside the home, and their number equals half the total of all working women. See Carolyn Bird, *Born Free: The High Cost of Keeping Women Down* (New York: McKay, 1968); Esther Peterson, "Working Women," *Daedalus* (Spring 1964), pp. 671–696; F. Ivan Nye and L. W. Hoffman, *The Employed Mother in America* (Chicago: Rand McNally, 1963).

11. David Caplovitz, "The Problems of Blue-Collar Consumers," in A. Shostak and W. Gomberg (eds.), *Blue-Collar World* (Englewood Cliffs, N.J.: Prentice-Hall, 1964), pp. 110–121. See also David Caplovitz, *The Poor Pay More* (New York: Free Press, 1963).

12. Nan Ickeringill, "New York: 'Plenty of Companionship,'" *The New York Times,* February 24, 1967, p. 38.

13. Bennett M. Berger, *Working-Class Suburb: A Study of Auto Workers in Suburbia* (Berkeley: University of California Press, 1960), p. 78. "The deviants, that is, those with 'good taste,' tend toward chintz and colonial maple" (p. 78).

14. Gans, *op. cit.,* p. 186.

15. Gerald Gurin, *et al., Americans View Their Mental Health: A Nationwide Interview Survey* (New York: Basic Books, 1960), p. 227. Cf. Komarovsky, *op. cit.,* pp. 331, 341–342.

16. Anon., "Till Death Us Do Part," *Trans-Action* (April 1967), p. 2. See also J. Richard Udry, "Marital Instability by Race, Sex, Education, and Occupation Using 1960 Census Data," *American Journal of Sociology* (March 1966), pp. 203–209. A 1962 N.O.R.C. study of residents of four small communities in Illinois found marital unhappiness occurring more frequently among men of lower socioeconomic status. Norman M. Bradburn and David Caplovitz, *Reports on Happiness: A Pilot Study of Behavior Related to Mental Health* (Chicago: Aldine, 1965), p. 39. See also Anon., "Home Life, Social Rank Found Tied," *The New York Times,* May 9, 1964, p. 17.

17. On the characteristics of modern blue-collar marriages, see Komarovsky, *op. cit.,* pp. 119, 171, 180, 196, 201. See also Herbert J. Gans, *The Levittowners: How People Live and Politic in Suburbia* (New York: Pantheon, 1967); Patricia Cayo Sexton, "Wife

of the 'Happy Worker,'" in A. Shostak and W. Gomberg (eds.), *op. cit.*, pp. 81–85.

18. Robert O. Blood, Jr., "The Husband-Wife Relationship," in Nye and Hoffman, *op. cit.*, pp. 282–308.

19. See Sidney W. Peck, Chapter Seven, "A Woman's Place Is with Her Kids," *The Rank-and-File Leader* (New Haven, Conn.: College and University Press, 1963), pp. 180–223.

20. Komarovsky, *op. cit.*, p. 203.

21. Rainwater, *Family Design, op. cit.*, pp. 64, 66.

22. Rainwater and Weinstein, *op. cit.*, p. 101.

23. Komarovsky, *op. cit.*, p. 80. On the significance for an adult's child-rearing preferences of his own childhood, see Ray E. Helfer and C. Henry Kempe (eds.), *The Battered Child* (Chicago: University of Chicago Press, 1968).

24. Melvin L. Kohn, "Social Class and Parental Authority," *American Sociological Review* (June 1959), p. 364. See also Donald G. McKinley, *Social Class and Family Life* (New York: Free Press, 1964); Melvin L. Kohn, "Social Class and Parent-Child Relationships," *American Journal of Sociology* (January 1963), pp. 471–480; Melvin L. Kohn, *Class and Conformity: A Study in Values* (Homewood, Ill.: Dorsey Press, 1969).

25. For discussion, see Rainwater, *et al.*, *Workingman's Wife*, *op. cit.*, p. 197, *passim*.

26. See in this connection, Nathan Hurvitz, "Marital Strain in the Blue-Collar Family," in A. Shostak and W. Gomberg (eds.), *op. cit.*, pp. 92–109.

9

BLUE-COLLAR
SONS

Diogenes struck the father when the son swore.—BURTON

Sixteen-to-twenty-one-year-old sons of Caucasian manual workers differ considerably among themselves: One can profitably distinguish among blue-collar Rebels, Accommodators, and Achievers. Rebels include both nondelinquent and delinquent school dropouts. Accommodators include high school graduates both of vocational and of general academic programs, while the achievers are generally college-bound blue-collar youngsters. Each of the three types struggles to meet the various challenges of adolescence and young adulthood in its own way, and the mosaic which is adult blue-collar life accurately reflects the differences thereafter.

THE REBELS

Generally found in transitional blue-collar neighborhoods, especially in worn, low-cost ethnic enclaves, blue-collar rebels frequently attend notoriously inadequate neighborhood public schools. Buildings are often dilapidated, classes are crowded, textbooks are outdated or inadequate, teachers are weary and demoralized, administrators are inept and fearful, and parents are apathetic or fatalistic and trusting. The emphasis in school is placed on quietism and punitive constraint.[1] Teachers who are drawn from "better" sections of the city (though often from blue-collar origins) frequently move through the lives of the white working-class youngsters with chilling condescension—"ready to cut them down in a minute for daring to speak with the natural slang and style of their neighborhood, or for failing to parrot back coy answers to dull questions."[2]

The Caucasian rebel in such a school is commonly a low-level achiever, usually below grade standards for his age—as measured, that is, on culturally biased national achievement tests. With blue-collar parents who themselves have low educational attainment, the rebel may receive only awkward, if unrelenting and often punitive pressure to "do well." Uncomfortable with the better-adjusted blue-collar accommodators favored by school authorities, the rebel generally avoids involvement in the extracurricular school life of his student peers and flees the place at the earliest opportunity.

After school hours, however, the young rebel is strongly attracted to an impulsive, independent, undisciplined, unsupervised, rebellious, and peer-oriented style of life. The particular "youth culture" of these youngsters is largely independent of parental control and is antagonistic toward the adult culture of the "squares." The rebels themselves are disdainful of the "deferred-gratification" pattern of those blue-collar boys intent on graduation and class mobility. Rather, the rebels retain the generally more promiscuous pattern of the hard-core working-class poor and remain sexually alert and indulgent.

Not surprisingly, many blue-collar rebels become high school dropouts. In 1965, for example, some 252,000 young men, or 13 percent of all sixteen-to-seventeen-year-old sons of Caucasian blue-collarites, were dropouts as contrasted with only 4 percent or 39,000 of the sixteen-to-seventeen-year-old sons of Caucasian white-collarites.[3] A very few of the rebel dropouts may have been pulled out of school by economic pressures on the family. Many more have been pushed out of school by disgruntled school authorities (as in the aftermath of a classroom fight or a series of course failures). A large number may have been drawn out by the lure of the money and prestige inherent in gainful employment. And a few may have starkly walked out on their own, young men no longer willing to endure the grievous insult of education that does not, in their view, educate—and may actually dull one.

Accordingly, dropouts are only selectively responsive to remedial efforts aimed at them. Research by sociologists Robert A. Dentler and Mary Ellen Warshauer suggests that school and welfare programs that do attempt to deal *directly* with dropout prevention are "irrelevant, if not futile." Rather, the state of the local labor market appears the really critical variable: If there is substantial economic opportunity in the area, boys now hopeful of job advancement may elect to remain in school. Some may even return to school after dropping out (a Syracuse study found 25 percent seeking more schooling within two years of quitting).[4] If times are bad outside, few rebels can muster up enough patience to endure long years of drudgery in pursuit of the diploma they know they should have. Believing themselves at the mercy of external circumstances or their own impulses, many rebel dropouts come finally to experience their dropping out of school as something in which they do not have any real part.

Related to this situation is that of the youngster who "drops out" of conventional behavior as well as out of formal schooling. It is estimated that about 95 percent of all seventeen-year-old delinquents are not attending school, while 85 percent of the sixteen-year-old and 50 percent of the fifteen-year-old delinquents are not in school.[5] Such youngsters are often aware they are violating the law, but rely for protection on the fact that most juvenile cases are casually dismissed, the already heavy probation caseload discouraging any large number of new referrals.[6] Interesting here is sociologist Delbert S. Elliott's finding that low-status boys have a higher delinquency rate while *in* school, where they may be under pressure to compete for middle-class goals, than as dropouts who, no longer frustrated by unequal competition at school, have little or no need to attack the school or the normative system it represents.[7]

The blue-collar rebel as a "delinquent" is most commonly found in areas that combine low economic status and high ethnic concern. That is to say, police arrests and public awareness of delinquency are highest in such areas. New research, however, suggests that aspects of the association between status and delinquency may be due more to differentials in arrest and in conviction than to any absolute class differences in the amount of certain kinds of delinquent behavior. Indeed, when official delinquency reports were compared by researchers to subjective reports of actual kinds of delinquent behavior committed, certain "class" differences vanished. Nevertheless, the 1967 Report of the President's Commission on Law Enforcement and Administration of Justice concludes on this score that "there is still no reason to doubt that delinquency, and especially the most serious delinquency, is committed disproportionately by slum and lower-class youth." [8]

Some of the blue-collar rebels are encouraged to enter into delinquent careers by a community and family milieu conducive to law violation (the thesis of Walter B. Miller, and of Richard Cloward and Lloyd Ohlin, and endorsed by a gang-reforming priest, Father C. Kilmer Myers, who comments on how "really difficult it is to be a Christian on [New York's] Lower East Side—especially if one is young"). Other blue-collar delinquents may be in revolt against the imposition of middle-class values by "caretakers"—school, church, and others —and may retaliate by setting these values on their head (Albert K. Cohen's thesis). A few probably aspire to careers in the rackets (Irving Spergel's thesis), and some may seek in delinquency a counterbalance to their own failure to develop motivation to achieve along conventional lines (Jackson Toby's thesis—adapted from Bennett Berger's analysis of the emphasis in "youth culture" on irresponsibility, hedonism, and expressive behavior).[9]

From still another perspective, blue-collar delinquency appears a means of affirming masculine prowess. A restless search for excitement, "thrills," or "kicks" substitutes for more mundane and routine patterns of behavior. A sort of aimless drifting or grandiose dream of quick success takes the place of a commitment to security, routine, and methodism. And a readiness for aggression, for the use of violence in support of honor, or "rep," and as proof of courage, or "heart," substitutes for less adventuresome activities. Above all, the delinquents seem provoked by the sense of fatalism that challenges one inside blue-collar culture. Sociologist David Matza comments here:

> For subcultural delinquents to be "pushed around" and be thrust into the mood of fatalism is tantamount to temporarily losing their prematurely and thus precariously gained manhood . . . Some dramatic reassurance that they can still make things happen is necessary. . . . The mood of fatalism neutralizes the bind to law, elicits the situation of company, and fosters a sense of desperation which in turn provides the will or thrust to commit a new infraction.[10]

The delinquent is jolted back to the humanistic mood, is rejoined to the moral order, by the commission of crime: An infraction is among the few acts that can immediately and demonstrably make things happen. Even as it invokes the criminal process, a delinquent act can more significantly serve as a symbol of restored potency and virility.

Whatever his delinquent style, though especially as a narcotic addict, the blue-collar rebel is not especially responsive to remedial efforts. Few take seriously the common call by blue-collar fathers for the use of the "old man's belt" to discipline youthful irresponsibility. And hardly more are effectively reached by the state's various efforts. Continuation schools, for example—although designed to help youngsters work while completing a high school diploma, especially youngsters on probation or on dropout-returnee status—generally do a very poor job. Many such schools fail to maintain an employment program, are deficient in their educational offerings, and generally warrant their poor reputation in the community.[11]

Once a convicted law violator, the rebel confronts a host of inadequate state responses to the challenge of reform. For example, while strict discipline and severe punishment no longer characterize most correctional schools, overcrowding, inadequate facilities, and an underpaid, undertrained staff combine to reduce the rehabilitative value of the average nine-month stay. The more widely used probation system suffers the same shortcomings, excessive case loads especially undermining the system. Experimental centers, like Highfields, New Jersey, with its group therapy orientation, remain highly praised, though little emulated. Most successful are the many thousand street-gang workers employed by Youth Boards to win the confidence of gang members and to steer them into constructive group activity, jobs, individual counseling, and the like. (Or, as one ex-worker puts it: "Turn their youthful thoughts to the joys of basketball over rumbles, picnics over cigar-store heists, and a job over income gained from rolling homosexuals.")[12] Even here, however, bureaucratic red tape, the ineffectiveness of many social workers, the sadism of some policemen, and the callousness of some public officials combine to prevent realization of the full potential of the program.

The Job Corps, the labor market, and the military draft are sometimes thought promising answers to the nation's delinquency problem. Ironically, however, delinquents are frequently screened out of all three. That is, eligibility standards operate to exclude youngsters with certain kinds of police records, with little or no consideration of the needs of the individual case. While situational pressure to find and to keep white teen-agers in the now-defunct Job Corps (to protect racial "balance"), along with the willingness of "patriotic" judges to permit Vietnam military service to substitute for probation or confinement, may "help" some few delinquent sons of manual workers, these remain short-term and small-scale advances.

So ineffective is much that passes itself off as remedial that a small but significant number of adolescent blue-collar rebels aggressively carry their rebellion on into young adulthood, and are disproportionately represented among the inmates of state and federal prisons.[13] Typical here are blue-collar members of California's notorious native-fascist motorcycle gangs—Hell's Angels, and such related groups as Satan's Slaves, Coffin Cheaters, Devil's Henchmen, Outlaws, El Diablos, Hangmen, Misfits, and the Gypsy Jokers. Made up largely of undereducated and job-switching sons of blue-collarites in their twenties, the "outlaw" motorcycle clubs are unpredictable, dangerous, and defiantly alone. "We're bastards to the world and they're bastards to us," one member explains, adding that the Nazi paraphernalia frequently worn is chosen because of its association with the license to band together, to push people around, and thereby to be somebody.[14]

The outlaw motorcycle gangs celebrate the cynical blue-collar version of American ideals of virility and behavior: Anything goes as long as you don't get caught. Crude, dirty, unkempt, reckless, brutal, arrogant, racist, and nihilistic, the outlaw cyclists are all-time losers:

> For this group of lower-class white high-school dropouts the symbols, trappings, mutual loyalties, initiation rites, drugs, hypersexuality and authoritarianism of the gang obscure for the first time the essential boredom and barrenness of their lives, unfit for a technical-bureaucratic society where everyone who is second-best is only subhuman.[15]

Writer Hunter S. Thompson warns that the Angels and others —dropouts, failures, and malcontents—may be the forerunners of a fast-growing legion of young dispossessed unemployables. And their untapped energy may inevitably find the same kind of destructive outlet that "outlaws" like the Hell's Angels have been finding for years.[16]

Whether as Angels or otherwise, few blue-collar rebels are going to be changed by explicit reform efforts to this effect. Rather, in the last analysis, and with reference now to the largest number, the concomitants of aging (marriage, family, maturity) will probably continue to have more positive and lasting impact than society's antidelinquent efforts. Small bad blue-collar boys grow up; most become big and better blue-collar men. Company bowling teams and soft-ball clubs replace both the corner group and the bopping gang for many. In the process, blue-collar sons file away memories of brighter, bolder times—memories to warm one's hands in front of when chilled in later years working the assembly line, or "red-balling" it down the pike.

THE ACCOMMODATORS

Generally found in traditional blue-collar neighborhoods, especially in sections preferred by better paid semi-skilled workers, the blue-collar accommodator makes up the bulk of the nation's blue-collar young. Unlike blue-collar rebels, accommodators accept school as an unavoidable evil. They dimly recognize the challenge of making things happen, but will go no further than maintaining an illegal muffler on a custom rebuilt hot-rod, acting rowdy after a winning football game, or, in other like ways, conventionalizing their mischief-making. And they considerably downgrade the need the rebels feel to confirm sex role identification. Accommodators dilute blue-collar admiration for toughness and physical prowess. For all of this they receive assurance and rewards both from admiring parents and relieved middle-class "caretakers."

An appreciable number of accommodators seek out or are routed by school authorities into vocational high schools of varying quality. A 1967 evaluation study of such schools in nine Northeastern areas found them offering reasonably good courses in certain traditional areas but failing to keep abreast of technological innovations through new courses and new training advances. The research team concluded overall that the vo-ed schools "have not been able to serve the needs of either the students or the communities." [17]

The largest number of accommodators attend public high schools with significant blue-collar blocs. Sociologist Edgar Z.

Friedenberg's rare study of a typical school of this sort leads him to criticize its grim prisonlike atmosphere and its relentless attack on independence of spirit and mind. Many of those who do not drop out, he contends, are forced to relinquish their own powers of critical observation, their integrity, and their ability to form their own vision of the world. Of equal significance is Friedenberg's finding that this exhausting acquiescence is accompanied by a deep-seated class rivalry, one that separates as antagonists the relatively crude accommodators, with their limited occupational horizons, and the more ambitious of the middle-class crowd, with their college or white-collar goals. In the language of the high-schoolers themselves, the accommodators are not simply "cooled out" by the authorities, but they are also "put down" by their middle-class high school peers—a development rich in its implication for the later behavior of blue-collar adults.[18]

Almost regardless of whether they attend a vocational or a public high school, the blue-collar accommodators characteristically move to protect themselves by endorsing their own special variant of "youth culture":

> . . . an emphasis on fun and adventure; a disdain for scholarly effort; the more or less persistent involvement in "tolerated" status offenses like drinking, gambling, occasional truancy, "making out" in the sense of sexual conquest, driving cars before the appropriate age, smoking, swearing, and staying out late.[19]

Aggression is considerably tempered from that endorsed by the rebels, and crimes that victimize others are avoided. In the manner of William F. Whyte's "Corner Boys," the young blue-collar supporters of their own brand of youth culture avoid serious delinquency by a certain wariness and make a special effort to coexist with middle-class institutions.[20] They use their youth culture as an equalizing mechanism, one that helps erase the distinctions of socioeconomic background among its devotees, even as it discourages high ambition and academic values with its irresponsibility and mediocrity.

Linked more to the problems youngsters have in relation to one another than out of opposition to adults, youth culture, particularly among the blue-collar accommodators, cushions youngsters against the damage to their self-esteem that might otherwise accompany their declaration against success in high-status endeavors—and their estrangement from white-collar youngsters, blue-collar rebels and achievers, and most adults.

The blue-collar boy, as an accommodator, persists in his high school attendance for several mutually reinforcing reasons: His parents are convinced that a high school diploma is a grim necessity for him in the evolving labor market. Because he accepts a dependent role and is inwardly and outwardly conformist, his teachers find his demeanor unthreatening, and they are inclined to move him smoothly along. Finally, his friends among his peers are low-status youngsters who reinforce his own modest economic aspirations. All in all, the accommodator may see no real alternative to school. Delinquency is frightening, and street-corner idleness is a bore. With resignation perhaps, the accommodator settles in (some 60 percent of all blue-collar boys graduate from high school, a third of whom actually go on to enter college).[21]

Not surprisingly, college attendance is severely downgraded by young accommodators. Research finds blue-collar youngsters indifferent in the choice between four-year college and other possibilities in the immediate post-high school period.[22] A disproportionate number of accommodators fail to attend college even when they possess high academic aptitude, but it is not a lack of finances that explains this fact—it is more often a lack of interest. Four-year college may be regarded as nothing more than a difficult struggle by the typical blue-collarite who believes he has reason to doubt both his academic skills and his ability to pay the $12,000 required for higher education in the average four-year private college programs. The boy is also likely to be aware that skilled workers can earn more than many college graduates and that blue-collarites much like himself are disproportionately represented among the nongraduating college dropouts. Finally, he may know that most blue-collar college graduates enter the salaried, or less lucrative, professions (such as teaching, social work, and engineering). Some accommodators may conclude that the gain in prestige from going to college will hardly compensate them for the delay in securing material benefits. Many of these youngsters redirect their ambitions and join the 67 percent of all youngsters who do not go to college and the 50 percent of all high school graduates who regularly terminate their formal schooling with high school graduation.

On graduating, the accommodator confronts both the draft and the employment office. While publicity has focused primarily on the sons of the poor, the rejection rate of such youngsters makes it likely that their group ranks second to that made up of Caucasian sons of blue-collarites. (Relevant here is the fact that 57 percent of male high school graduates enter military service, as compared with only 40 percent of college graduates, 50 percent of non-high school graduates, and 60 percent of college dropouts.)[23] Accommodators might especially be drawn to enlist by the well-publicized availability of job training: In fiscal 1966, for example, 750,000 servicemen completed specialized training programs in 2,000 courses ranging from auto repair to aerospace technology.[24] Lacking any clear-cut data, it does not seem unreasonable to speculate that accommodators probably do moderately well in the armed services: In a very special way, military life represents no great change from the order-taking, other-directed existence that blue-collar sons have always known.

Similarly, an unknown number of accommodators do moderately well in Associate Degree programs in the nation's 900-odd two-year junior colleges. More and more blue-collar boys are among over 1,600,000 students taking advantage of the low-cost vocational education available in new two-year community or junior colleges. Programs in aeronautics, automotive trades, building and construction, drafting, electrical technology, and machine technology are well-subscribed, the blue-collar students avoiding the four-year duration and liberal arts emphasis of conventional colleges even while preparing themselves for the upgrading of skill-level common to much blue-collar employ. With the reputation some of the junior college vocational programs already have for blandness, practicality, and ease of completion, blue-collar accommodators likely feel themselves well served.[25]

The largest number of accommodators probably choose job-seeking over all other alternatives. The accommodator's record is here an uneven one, the possession of a high school diploma no necessary guarantee of a job. Rather, the unemployment rate for white male teen-agers (dropouts and graduates) has remained about 2.3 times the national unemployment rate throughout the 1960s, this fact leading experts in 1966 to label it "shockingly high" and to conclude it has "undergone some structural worsening in recent years." [26]

Between unemployment and a job, the blue-collar accommodator had two further alternatives, the 40,000-member Job Corps and the 150,000-member Neighborhood Youth Corps. While data are not available, it is likely that many accommodators sought extra schooling in the now-defunct Corps and are among its 50,000 graduates, even as other accommodators have been among the 900,000 teen-agers who have used the part-time work of the ill-fated NYC to help them stay in school and get some on-the-job training at the same time.

In due course most accommodators find some sort of full-time blue-collar employ. Their knowledge of the labor market, however, is characteristically uneven and unreliable, the more so because well-meaning parents, friends, and the mass media transmit only incidental (and potentially stereotyped) ideas about the world of work. Accommodators are often under financial and psychological pressure to speedily secure work, and many take the first job available. The importance of this entry post is underlined by the fact that blue-collarites generally remain in the bracket they begin in: In 1962, for example, some 41 percent of all male craftsmen, 28 percent of the male operatives, 22 percent of the male service workers, and 15 percent of the male laborers had begun working years before in the very same occupational bracket, something otherwise true of only 24 percent of all employed men.[27] To be sure, there is considerable job-switching by some accommodators in the early years, but government specialists judge much of this "uninformed (or misinformed) and wasteful." [28] However this may be, the accommodator is launched, and the youthful phase of his life (whatever his years) is at a decisive end.

Relevant in evaluating the accommodator's record are findings from an exceedingly rare longitudinal study (1959–1963) on post-high school youth. The majority of noncollege-goers expressed dissatisfaction with their lives and livelihood. Most of the men were limited to factory jobs, and while not preferring them, had not changed or improved them. Few could find in their work the options and opportunities for exploration necessary for adequate vocational and personal development. Little or no discernible personality development was apparent in these young men over time, and a great many of them expressed regret that they had not entered college.[29]

If the rebel pays a price in social marginality and personal loneliness for his style of life, the accommodator pays much for denying his own need as a youngster and young adult for diversity of experience and for some modicum of self-realization. His rejection of the goal of ascent into the ranks of the white-collarites seems petty and insignificant alongside of his premature attitude of acquiescence and resignation. The accommodator grows old too soon; he does not mature through the trial of trying new roles and experimenting with new causes. Indeed, he may have no cause beyond his own welfare, no self-enlarging concept of what human dignity might entail —if nurtured and continuously clarified and redefined. The passive and "realistic" accommodator defers to one prosaic set of given "facts," accepts his traditional responsibilities, and disregards his own sense of self-authority. Such a young adult, Friedenberg warns, fails to realize that life has more to offer than is entirely envisioned in a blue-collar existence.[30] Never experiencing the kind of scouting appropriate to and an integral part of adolescence and young adulthood, the accommodator runs the extraordinary risk of never becoming fully the man he might have.

THE ACHIEVERS

Originating especially in success-oriented transitional suburbs (those heterogenous areas passing slowly from white-collar to blue-collar domination), the blue-collar achiever apparently qualifies for the role of "popular hero." Emblematic of the American Dream realized, the achiever is distinguished by his victory over his humble origins, his willingness to separate from his "modern" blue-collar family and friends, and his eagerness to assume a new personal and public identity as a white-collarite.

Blue-collar achievers are likely to have in common the experience of having been reared in families where the father is in a high-status (skilled) occupation, where a "strong" mother has married "down" or is presently in a white-collar job herself, where a grandfather was in nonmanual work, and where other family members or friends of the family have had some favorable college experience.[31] Sociologist Ely Chinoy suggests that the parents of the achievers transfer their own frustrated mobility aspirations to the youngsters.[32] (Critic Stanley Kauffmann adds, however, that the seeming self-sacrifice involved may actually have meant: "The hell with struggling. I'll float. Let someone else—my children, for example—fight the currents.")[33] In any case, like the accommodator, the achiever knows early what life is "all about," though for him life is about striving rather than settling in.

Many of the achievers are directed by their ambitious parents into the nation's parochial school system (30 percent of all school children participate in this system). Classes are sometimes crowded; discipline is very firm; and religious precepts guide the entire curriculum. Rebels are quickly uncovered and transferred to the public school system, while accommodators are treated with quiet respect. The achievers, on the other hand, are especially honored, the parochial high school offering access to both parochial and secular colleges and universities. Sociologist Father Joseph H. Fichter sums up the appeal of the parochial schools with a list of adjectives especially relevant to a discussion of blue-collar achievers: The schools win attendance for the "virtues of respectability, cleanliness, conformity, ambition, and patriotism." [34]

The largest number of blue-collar achievers probably attend cosmopolitan public high schools. Recognizing this kind of school as a critical sorting mechanism, many achievers early dissociate themselves from their blue-collar peers and identify with the college-oriented, middle-class reference model usually dominant in suburban schools. Engaged in "anticipatory socialization," they form close clique ties with their middle-class peers, involve themselves in the extracurricular world of high school life, and otherwise pursue the kind of leisure-time activities that middle-class youth normally enjoy. Taking their schoolwork seriously, they are found to be both receptive and responsive by their teachers. Believing in the consistency between the high school curriculum and their own career plans and accepting without strong protest the doctrine of adolescent inferiority that underlies the school's use of *in loco parentis,* the achievers are encouraged by their early taste of (academic) success. A "good boy" like the accommodator, the achiever emulates and surpasses him.

A large proportion of blue-collar achievers terminate their formal education with high school graduation and secure white-collar employ. These youngsters appear especially drawn to the well-paying and challenging posts opening up for key-punch operators, computer programmers, and other space age types of employment, even as many others are drawn to more traditional posts as uniformed airline clerks, retail store "management trainees," civil service career candidates, and the well-established like. Regardless of the job title and specifications, the simple fact of its being a white-collar post (albeit one that may pay less than skilled craft jobs earned by some accommodators) probably provides a deep feeling of accomplishment for both the achiever and his proud parents.

More significant for involving greater strain on class and reference group ties is the situation of the smaller, but growing number of blue-collar achievers who go on to college. Admission nowadays to public institutions is increasingly easy to secure. With a steadily rising standard of living, the extension of scholarship and loan programs, and the growth of the junior college and the inexpensive state college or university, there would seem today to be a college or university to fit many blue-collar budgets. Moreover, with over half of all college students working their way through school, blue-collar achievers have this additional alternative open, along with that of a part-time school program, work between terms, or some combination of these.

College for many achievers is far different from the popular stereotype of "collegiate culture," which includes football, fraternities, dates, cars, drinking, and campus fun. Where blue-collar sons dominate a campus, as at many state colleges, they replace the collegiate culture with another one that is less time- and dollar-consuming—the "vocational culture." To the blue-collar achievers (some of whom are married and many of whom work from twenty to forty hours a week) college is largely off-the-job training, a place that helps one insure a job advance and permits one to buy a diploma somewhat as one buys groceries. The faculty at such schools often teach taxing fifteen-hour course loads in a mechanical, prosaic way, and faculty research is neither expected nor common. The library is understocked and out-of-date, the facilities pedestrian, and the parking lot overcrowded. Not surprisingly, like participants in the better-known collegiate culture, many blue-collar achievers are also resistant to intellectual demands on them beyond what is required to pass. To many, "ideas and scholarship are as much a luxury and distraction as are sports and fraternities" —this despite the fact that many in the ranks of the achievers have graduated near the top of their high school class.[35]

Where blue-collar achievers find themselves at a high-status university as scholarship winners rather than at a "vocational culture" school, college may also prove a far cry from the stereotype of gay times and good friends. Research suggests that the achievers at such a school do not easily adapt and gain acceptance—despite the fact that many had enjoyed friendships with college-oriented peers in high school, most had long before adopted a middle-class reference group and its attendant norms and values, and almost all had acquired awards and offices in the past that would stamp them as likely leaders in the student culture. Nevertheless, the blue-collar achievers are quickly identified as marginal individuals, limited in manners and money, and nearly half do not succeed over their college years in overcoming the social barriers initially encountered. They are excluded from the fraternities, go through long periods of not dating, and are perceived as "social isolates and/or unpopular" by their peers. For many such "strangers," although not for all, the price of social mobility is social isolation.[36]

One common reaction to this extended period of estrangement is a drop in grade performance in the freshman year, the only time most achievers fail to maintain the relatively superior academic record realized in both high school and in later undergraduate years. Another more serious reaction, because of its permanent consequences, is withdrawal from college. Not all the achievers are superior performers, and, especially at the "vocational culture" schools, an unknown but possibly significant number of potential blue-collar achievers are "cut down" early in the college advancement process. Critical here is what has been called the "psychocultural dimension of stratification," with its various motivation components. A blue-collar background does not especially motivate one toward college; ambivalences in motivation linked to family origins do not cease to exist after youngsters enter college. On the contrary, sociologist Bruce Eckland concludes, "the motivational element is the primary contribution that social class makes to performance in college." [37]

A large majority of blue-collar achievers apparently do make it through, however, their experience of academic success in high school helping to sustain their motivation. College admission and attendance in their case apparently aid the process of dissociation by which these achievers move forward. Data from a 1958 study of college freshmen from blue-collar families provide some insight into how far achievers drift from blue-collar orientations. In sharp contrast to the rebels and to the accommodators, the upwardly mobile college-going sons of manual workers had fairly well-defined occupational goals. They attached high importance to being in an occupation that would provide them with a sense of self-fulfillment. They considered it as important as did other college students to have the job give them an "opportunity to be helpful to others." And they deemphasized the importance of having a job that provided them with adventure. Overall, these achievers believed that the opportunity for securing the middle-class goal of success was wide open to them.[38]

Nevertheless, even as the other two blue-collar adolescent types pay a price for adoption of their particular substyles, so also does the achiever confront a "bill" uniquely his own. He expects, of course, to be rewarded by an appreciative society with increased lifetime earnings, job security, and higher status than that of his parents. The achiever, however, as an adolescent and young adult, may not easily free himself of nagging doubts about social separation and self-worth. As sociologist Pitirim A. Sorokin pointed out over forty years ago, upward social mobility comes at a psychological cost to the individual. Part of this cost is an experience of rootlessness, of psychosocial isolation and loneliness.[39] Related is a feeling of esteem confusion. Confronted with the necessity of being disloyal to his earlier values, the achiever may experience both adjustment pains and uncertainty in his new basis of self-evaluation—an uncertainty that may prove permanent.

As a marginal man involved in two different reference groups, the achiever may never be comfortable in either. The California study of college freshmen as blue-collarites referred to above found considerable evidence that their anticipatory socialization was somewhat partial: In sharp contrast to middle-class freshmen the upwardly mobile blue-collarites

set lower limits on the occupational goals they consider acceptable

did not as often expect to be "outstanding" and pegged their anticipated earnings lower than do other freshmen

had not yet acquired the middle-class regard for the interpersonal satisfaction that work may provide (that is, high regard for "working with people rather than things")

had not come to value personal autonomy in the work situation (as with a job that would leave them "relatively free of supervision by others" and give them a "chance to exercise leadership") de-emphasized the extrinsic rewards of the job (money, security, and social status and prestige)

were less likely to contemplate those careers which are the mainstay of the upper and upper-middle classes (such as careers in law, medicine, or architecture).[40]

This last point has special importance, because it helps explain an ironic development: In spite of their previous divorce from the blue-collar class (with attendant psychic costs), the achievers do not seem to go very far.

Turner notes in a related context that the stratification of destination may provide a better clue to stratification in the larger society than the stratification of origin.[41] It would seem that the incompleteness of the achiever's internalization of middle-class values often dominates the achiever's career planning. Specifically, like their blue-collar fathers, many college-going achievers believe the hardest part of a job is getting hired. These students fix their academic objectives on easily obtainable vocational targets, often without noting the lack of second or third steps in a specific occupational ladder. Their example corresponds with the idea that it is difficult to take more than one step up the social ladder without special advantages (financial, intellectual, or personality). One step up for the achievers is apparently equivalent to becoming a teacher or engineer rather than a physician or a lawyer.

Under pressure to convince the "old crowd" that a college education leads quickly to practical financial benefits, the upwardly mobile, job-anxious blue-collarites finally learn less (and earn less) than was suggested by their early "promise" of achievement. Fixated on low-level vocational aims, many achievers cannot comprehend—either in high school or later at college—those values of higher education which lie in something other than the job for which it may be a prerequisite. A sociology instructor of many such students comments: "Such goals as the development of a capacity to appreciate and create, a willingness to accept responsibility for the direction in which society is moving or might be induced to move—these are only dimly recognized by most students." Here, concludes the instructor, "is prudent, working-class morality . . . with a vengeance." [42]

SUMMARY

Three kinds of substyle presently divide the sons of white urban blue-collarites, each substyle a response to the challenge of career planning, of personal autonomy, and of sex role identification. Significantly, each of the three kinds of young man approaches the prospect of manhood as a blue-collarite from a very different perspective: Rebels often view it as an unavoidable hardship—against which one fights until subdued (as in a teen-age marriage) or until a real alternative is secured (such as a career in the rackets or in the Army). The accommodators generally view blue-collar employment as right and natural, a tradition in the family, and rather deserving of respect. Finally, the achievers reject the notion of a blue-collar destiny in its entirety.

Each substyle contains a disturbing surprise of its own: Some of us are easily cheered by unexamined Horatio Alger life histories. But the situation of upwardly mobile blue-collar sons suggests that many such climbers appear never fully to leave or to arrive anywhere. Some of us are also inclined to romanticize juvenile delinquency in the spirit of *West Side Story*. But the situation of many blue-collar rebels makes it clear that the boys suffer much and profit little for their self-centered revolt.

Above all, some of us are inclined to applaud the fidelity of those who stay close to home and to the old ways. But we do this too easily, and with little recognition of the jeopardy involved therein to ourselves. The fact that the largest number of blue-collar sons accommodate themselves early to a blue-collar destiny is fraught with significance. As Friedenberg points out, an enormous loss of imagination, energy, and talent is involved in this premature surrender to "fate." Even more, having previously dared little as play-it-safe accommodators, many adult blue-collarites remain unwilling thereafter to risk or dare very much at all. Few qualify for the ranks of those on whom an adventurous and inventive society must depend. Few boast the energy and challenge necessary, if they are to exercise the historical role of young adults as initiators of change and as architects of progress.

Notes to Chapter Nine

---

1. On the inferiority of education received by the poor and the blue-collar bloc, see Robert Rosenthal, *Pygmalion in the Classroom*, (New York: Holt, Rinehart and Winston, 1968); Robert E. Herriott and Nancy H. St. John, *Social Class and the Urban School: The Impact of Pupil Background on Teachers and Principals* (New York: Wiley, 1966); Patricia Cayo Sexton, *Education and Income: Inequalities in Our Public Schools* (New York: Viking, 1961).

2. Jonathan Kozol, "Department of Lower Learning," *New Republic* (May 20, 1967), p. 34. On the hostility of teachers from blue-collar origins to blue-collar matters, see Robert E. Doherty, "Attitudes Toward Labor: When Blue-Collar Children Become Teachers," *The School Review* (1963), pp. 87–96. On the preference of blue-collar mothers for authoritarian styles of teacher and of middle-class mothers for discovery-styles, see Sam D. Sieber and David E. Wilder, "Teaching Styles: Parental Preferences and Professional Role Definitions," *Sociology of Education* (Fall 1967), pp. 302–315.

3. Data are from the October 1967 Current Population Survey of the Bureau of the Census, as reported in Harold Howe II, *Equality of Educational Opportunity* (Washington, D.C.: Government Printing Office, 1966), pp. 27–30. Overall, about 35 percent of all high-schoolers do not graduate.

4. Robert A. Dentler and Mary Ellen Warshauer, *Big City Dropouts* (New York: Center for Urban Education, 1965). "In the aggregate, withdrawal is associated more relevantly with the growth prospects present not in the student but in the city he inhabits." *Ibid.*, p. 59. Duncan, however, contends that "when jobs are scarce young men seem to defer leaving school; when jobs are plentiful, the dropout rate accelerates." Beverly Duncan, "Dropouts and the Unemployed," *The Journal of Political Economy* (April 1965), p.

134. See also Daniel Schreiber (ed.), *Profile of the School Drop-out: A Reader on America's Major Educational Problem* (New York: Vintage Books, 1968); S. M. Miller, *et al.*, *School Dropouts: A Commentary and Annotated Bibliography* (Syracuse: Syracuse University, Youth Development Center, 1964); Arthur L. Stinch-combe, *Rebellion in a High School* (Chicago: Quadrangle, 1964).

5. Manpower Research Bulletin No. 3, *Young Workers: Their Special Training Needs* (Washington, D.C.: Department of Labor, May 1963), p. 10.

6. On the care with which such well-founded calculations of small-risk are based, see David Matza, *Delinquency and Drift* (New York: Wiley, 1964), pp. 101–152. "Delinquents in fact do evade apprehension the vast majority of the time. Since the theory of police incompetence and delinquent potency is tenable, it may be of service. It serves as a major means of discounting apprehen-siveness, and thus is part of the preparation underlying the will to crime." *Ibid.*, p. 187.

7. Delbert S. Elliott, "Delinquency, School Attendance, and Dropout," *Social Problems* (Winter 1966), pp. 306–314. On the frustration and failure experienced by working-class boys at school, see Albert K. Cohen, *Delinquent Boys* (Glencoe, Ill.: Free Press, 1956).

8. President's Commission on Law Enforcement and Adminis-tration of Justice, *The Challenge of Crime in a Free Society* (Wash-ington, D.C.: Government Printing Office, 1967), pp. 56–57. Note, however, this caution: "To date, no significant or reliable data on the occupations of the parents of delinquents are available in the United States." Walter A. Lunden, *Statistics on Delinquents and Delinquency* (Springfield, Ill.: Thomas, 1964), p. 92. See also La Mar T. Empey and Maynard L. Erickson, "Hidden Delinquency and Social Status," *Social Forces* (June 1966), pp. 546–554.

9. Walter B. Miller, "Lower Class Culture as a Generating Milieu of Gang Delinquency," *Journal of Social Issues* (Summer 1958), pp. 5–19; Richard A. Cloward and Lloyd E. Ohlin, *Delinquency and Opportunity* (Glencoe, Ill.: Free Press, 1960); C. Kilmer Myers, *Light the Dark Streets* (New York: The Seabury Press, 1957); Cohen, *op. cit.*; Irving Spergel, *Racketville, Slumtown, Haul-burg: An Exploratory Study of Delinquent Subcultures* (Chicago: University of Chicago Press, 1964); Larry Karacki and Jackson Toby, "The Uncommitted Adolescent: Candidate for Gang Social-ization," in A. Shostak and W. Gomberg (eds.), *Blue-Collar World*

(Englewood Cliffs, N.J.: Prentice-Hall, 1964), pp. 165–176. See also T. N. Ferdinand, Chapter 4, "A Social Typology of Delinquency," *Typologies of Delinquency* (New York: Random House, 1966), pp. 80–151.

10. Matza, *op. cit.*, pp. 189, 191. "Even if they are caught, the mood of humanism may be restored. By committing an infraction, they have themselves made the counteraction of adult officials happen—no mean accomplishment." *Ibid.*, p. 190.

11. Glen H. Elder, Jr., "The Schooling of Outsiders" (Berkeley: University of California, unpublished paper, 1965).

12. Vincent Riccio and Bill Slocum, *All the Way Down: The Violent Underworld of Street Gangs* (New York: Ballantine, 1962), p. 16. For a constructively critical discussion of delinquent reform efforts, see Chapter 3, "Juvenile Delinquency and Youth Crime," *The Challenge of Crime in a Free Society, op. cit.*, pp. 55–90.

13. *The Challenge of Crime in a Free Society, op. cit.*, p. 161. See also Paul H. Gebhard, *et al.*, *Sex Offenders: An Analysis of Types* (New York: Bantam Books, 1967 ed.), p. 51.

14. William Murray, "Hell's Angels," *Saturday Evening Post* (November 20, 1965), pp. 33–39.

15. Joel Fort, "FTW: A Motto for Our Times," *Psychiatry and Social Science Review* (June 1968), p. 18.

16. Hunter S. Thompson, *Hell's Angels* (New York: Random House, 1966), pp. 260, 266.

> . . . they are acting out the daydreams of millions of losers who don't wear any defiant insignia and who don't know how to be outlaws. The streets of every city are thronged with men who would pay all the money they could get their hands on to be transformed—even for a day—into hairy hard-fisted brutes who walk over cops, extort free drinks from terrified bartenders and thunder out of town on big motorcycles after raping the banker's daughter."

Cf. ". . . But the fascination rubs off the more you know about them. You are left with just the greasy, scurvy ugliness of it." Thompson, as quoted in "Hell's Angels: Sleazy Cowboys Ride the Existential Range," *The Village Voice*, February 23, 1967, p. 17. See also Frank Reynolds, *Freewheelin Frank: Secretary of the Angels, as Told to Michael McClure* (New York: Grove Press, 1967).

17. Jacob J. Kaufman and Carl J. Schaefer, *The Role of the Secondary Schools in the Preparation of Youth for Employment* (University Park: Institute for Research on Human Resources, Pennsylvania State University, 1967), p. 7. See also L. J. Barnett, "Does Education for Work, Work?," *The Urban Review* (May 1966), unpaged.

18. Edgar Z. Friedenberg, *Coming of Age in America: Growth and Acquiescence* (New York: Random House, 1965). See also Carl Nordstrom, *et al.*, *Society's Children: A Study of Resentment in the Secondary School* (New York: Random House, 1967); "The Teen-Agers," *Time* (March 21, 1966), p. 59.

19. David Matza, "Subterranean Traditions of Youth," *The Annals* (November 1961), p. 116. See also Ralph Turner, *The Social Context of Ambition* (San Francisco: Chandler, 1964), pp. 138–170.

20. William F. Whyte, *Street Corner Society* (Chicago: University of Chicago Press, 1954 ed.). See also Edmund W. Vaz (ed.), *Middle-Class Juvenile Delinquency* (New York: Harper & Row, 1967); G. Marwell, "Adolescent Powerlessness and Delinquency," *Social Problems* (Summer 1966), pp. 35–47; Walter Reckless, *et al.*, "The 'Good' Boy in a High Delinquency Area," *Journal of Criminal Law, Criminology, and Police Science* (August 1955), pp. 18–26; Herbert Gans, *The Urban Villagers* (New York: Free Press, 1962), pp. 28–31.

21. S. M. Miller, "The Outlook of Working Class Youth," in A. Shostak and W. Gomberg (eds.), *op. cit.*, pp. 122–134.

22. Francis G. Caro, "Social Class and Attitudes of Youth Relevant for the Realization of Adult Goals," *Social Forces* (June 1966), pp. 495, 497.

23. John C. Esty, Jr., "The Future of the Draft," *The Nation* (September 12, 1966), pp. 209–213. On differential casualty rates for different social groupings, see Albert J. Mayer and Thomas F. Hoult, "Social Stratification and Combat Survival," *Social Forces* (December 1965), pp. 155–159.

24. *Manpower Report of the President, 1967*, U.S. Department of Labor (Washington, D.C.: Government Printing Office, 1968), p. VII.

25. For rare confirmatory data, see James W. Trent and Leland L. Medsker, *Beyond High School* (San Francisco: Jossey-Bass, 1968), p. 68, *passim*. Many of the data presented on the non-

college-going accommodator in this book are unique in the literature in the field.

26. Joseph D. Mooney, "Teenage Labor Problems and the Neighborhood Youth Corps," in F. H. Harbinson and J. D. Mooney (eds.), *Critical Issues in Employment Policy* (Princeton: Industrial Relations Section, 1966), pp. 96, 98. Some 11 percent of all whites between sixteen and nineteen years of age were unemployed in 1966. *Manpower Report of the President, 1967, op. cit.*, p. 39.

27. Walter L. Slocum, *Occupational Careers* (Chicago: Aldine, 1966), pp. 174–175. Comparative percentages for others: Professionals, 44; managers, six; sales, 21; clerical, 31; farmers, 22; farm laborers, 62. ". . . first job, alone, is more important than education and father's occupational status combined." S. M. Lipset and F. T. Malm, "First Jobs and Career Patterns," *The American Journal of Economics and Sociology* (1953), pp. 247–261. See also J. Kenneth Little, "The Occupations of Non-College Youth," *American Educational Research Journal* (March 1967), pp. 147–153.

28. *Manpower Report of the President, 1966*, U.S. Department of Labor (Washington, D.C.: Government Printing Office, 1967), p. 91.

29. Trent and Medsker, *op. cit.*, pp. 36–37, *passim*. "Limited ability, limited education, a constricted socioeconomic background, overdependence on a dogmatic or fundamentalist religion, and an unenlightened, unstimulating, and autocratic family background seem to be prominent factors associated with regression in social maturity" (p. 212).

30. Edgar Z. Friedenberg, "The Education of James Conant and Paul Goodman," *The New York Review of Books* (November 19, 1964), pp. 10–12; A. Shostak, "Education and the Family," *Journal of Marriage and the Family* (February 1967), pp. 124–139; Trent and Medsker, *op. cit.*, p. 265.

31. E. G. Cohen, "Parental Factors in Educational Mobility," (Cambridge, Mass.: Radcliffe College, unpub. Ph.D. dissertation, 1958). See also E. H. Mizruchi, *Success and Opportunity: A Study of Anomie* (New York: Free Press, 1964); S. Keller and M. Zavalloni, "Ambition and Social Class: A Respecification," *Social Forces* (October 1964), pp. 58–70.

32. Ely Chinoy, *Automobile Workers and the American Dream* (Boston: Beacon, 1965 ed.). See also R. A. Ellis and W. Clayton Lane, "Structural Supports for Upward Mobility," *American Sociological Review* (October 1963), p. 756.

33. Stanley Kauffmann, "The Young in Head," *New Republic* (January 28, 1967), p. 26.

34. Joseph H. Fichter, S.J., *Parochial School: A Sociological Study* (Garden City: Anchor Books, 1964 ed.), p. 498. See also A. M. Greeley and P. H. Rossi, *The Education of Catholic Americans* (Chicago: Aldine, 1966).

35. R. J. Potter, "Portrait of a Working-Class College," *Dissent* (Winter 1964), p. 48. See also Joseph Scimecca and Roland Damiano, *Crisis at St. John's: Strike and Revolution on the Catholic Campus* (New York: Random House, 1967).

36. R. A. Ellis and W. C. Lane, "Social Mobility and Social Isolation: A Test of Sorokin's Dissociative Hypothesis," *American Sociological Review* (April 1967), pp. 237–252. The subjects consist of twenty-two Caucasian freshmen who entered Stanford as first-year freshmen in the fall of 1958; all were blue-collar achievers. ". . . the evidence bears out Sorokin's dissociative hypothesis that upward mobility is itself a disruptive social experience which leaves the individual for an appreciable period without roots or effective social support." *Ibid.,* p. 237.

37. Bruce K. Eckland, "Social Class and College Graduation," *American Journal of Sociology* (March 1964), p. 40. See also James A. Davis, *Great Aspirations: The Graduate Student Plans of America's College Seniors* (Chicago: Aldine, 1964).

37. R. A. Ellis and W. Clayton Lane, "Social Mobility and Career Orientation," *Sociology and Social Research* (April 1966), pp. 287–290. See also Robert J. Havighurst, "Youth in Exploration and Man Emergent," in Henry Borow (ed.), *Man in a World of Work* (Boston: Houghton Mifflin, 1964).

39. Pitirim A. Sorokin, *Social Mobility* (New York: Harper & Bros., 1957), pp. 522–525, *passim.* See footnote 1 in Ellis and Lane, "Social Mobility and Social Isolation," *op. cit.,* p. 237 for references to more current statements.

40. Ellis and Lane, "Social Mobility and Career Orientation," *op. cit.* See also Joel Gerstl, "Education and the Sociology of Work," in Donald A. Hansen and Joel E. Gerstl (eds.), *On Education—Sociological Perspectives* (New York: Wiley, 1967), pp. 224–261.

41. Turner, *op. cit.,* p. 212. See also Robert Perrucci, "Education, Stratification, and Mobility" in Hansen and Gerstl (eds.), *op. cit.,* pp. 105–155; B. K. Eckland, "Academic Ability, Higher Education, and Occupational Mobility," *American Sociological Review* (October, 1965), pp. 735–746.

42. Potter, *op. cit.*, p. 48. On the blue-collar impact on college culture, see Burton R. Clark and Martin Trow, "Determinants of College Student Subculture," *The Study of College Peer Groups: Problems and Prospects for Research* (Ann Arbor, Mich.: Social Science Research Council, 1960).

10

BLUE-COLLAR
DAUGHTERS

There will never be a generation of great men until there has been a generation of free women—of free mothers.
— ROBERT G. INGERSOLL

Five interrelated challenges—accommodating puberty, moderating sexual behavior, forming a feminine self-identity, molding new relations with authority figures, and framing an adult future—confront all adolescent girls, but they have special significance for the daughters of blue-collarites. These girls meet the five key challenges of adolescence and young adulthood with the principal styles of the rebel, the accommodator, and the achiever. Each type is discussed below, particular attention being paid to the vast bulk of white urban daughters of blue-collarites who appear to be accommodators —now and forevermore.

THE REBELS

A provocative portrait of a blue-collar rebel was gathered recently by Chicago radio interviewer Studs Terkel. He includes among the seventy first-person life stories published in his book, *Division Street: America*, the record and thoughts of a sixteen-year-old white blue-collar girl, Lily Lowell:

> A black heart is tattooed on her pale arm: "Somebody told me, 'You ain't got no heart,' so I put one on my arm." (Laughs) . . . She has been drinking since she was twelve. "I don't drink to to make myself drunk but to free myself. Sniffing glue makes you high, but it deadens your brain. Grass (marijuana) is a lot better than glue."

She quit high school after three months:

> "I was involved in some kind of trouble." She now acts as a "governess" for four small children, whose middle-class parents travel a great deal . . . When she is not "away" in other quarters of the city (she associates with "way-out" people older than herself) or in state institutions, she lives with her thirty-nine-year-old mother, stepfather, and ten brothers and sisters. Among her peers, in a lower-middle-class white neighborhood on the West Side of the city, she is a leader. Often she draws, writes poetry and long letters to friends.

Later in the interview Lily shares with Terkel a long letter she had just written to a troubled fifteen-year-old girl friend. In it Lily recounts her own youth as a runaway and "swinger":

> Believe me, I was a good girl once, and at times still am. I was trying to put the cork in the bottle, so to speak. But every time I do, someone from the past pops up and it starts all over again . . . So here I sit, smoke in one hand, bottle in the other, regrets, and pain in my heart . . . Don't go on like you do, or you will end up like me, a big fat Zero in the eyes of God . . .

When Terkel suggests to the sixteen-year-old girl that all the kids in the neighborhood respect and look up to her, Lily retorts: "Because they don't know me. They know the *outside* of me, they don't know me." [1]

What, then, are the blue-collar rebels like? Many are Lily Lowells; many others resemble her but vary in significant ways. By and large, blue-collar girls who warrant the label "rebel" appear to come especially from low-income, highly disorganized households of undereducated laborers living in criminogenic slum sections of the city. Common to these families are many deep-seated and corrosive frustrations that build on ignorance, fear, and disappointment. The girls in such families often feel unprotected and friendless, many growing up in homes where, if there is anyone, the generally inadequate mother is the only source of strength and stability.

In keeping with a Victorian backwardness about sex (see Chapter 8 on the blue-collar family), the young rebel is often left totally unprepared by her mother and sisters for the biological changes of young adulthood. A researcher relates how "over and over the girls talked about the beginning of puberty as something unexpected, frightening, unexplained. Information was usually gained from other youngsters, and sometimes in school, but the damage was done: fear had become part of growing up." [2] In his turn the father, though frequently not part of the family, may compound the harm done by forcing or encouraging incestuous relations or nonphysical, but highly emotional entanglements. Such relations are a phenomenon much more frequent than is generally assumed in a society like ours that makes their discussion taboo. Little wonder that "facing life" for many comes to mean a hard-bitten, distrustful cynicism directed toward almost all adults.

Sexual experiences are probably begun earlier, are probably more frequent, and are probably more uneven than is true in the situation of the other two types of blue-collar female adolescent.[3] Though many of the blue-collar rebels may be unwillingly initiated into sexual relations, large numbers learn quickly to traffic in sexual wiles. At odds with society on various fronts, the girls "act out" their problems by flouting prohibitions against heavy petting or premarital relations. In keeping, however, with their pathetic endorsement of Hollywood-based notions of romantic or true love, the girls are not especially promiscuous, and many try to confine their attention to one blue-collar boy at a time.

Throughout their youth the girl rebels generally fail to secure rewarding relationships with adult authority figures. Many go through childhood without knowing the meaning of personal or social success. Teachers, in particular, make demands the girls often find foreign: demands for orderliness, attentiveness, achievement in verbal skills, and grade-oriented competitiveness. (In 1965 the percentage of blue-collar girls who were dropouts was four times as high as that of white-collar girls: 12 percent versus 3 percent, with 238,000 blue-collar dropouts involved.) [4] Similarly, the girls often feel themselves pressured by social workers, psychologists, judges, and others who seek trust, measure response, or mete out judgments. Blue-collar rebels find many such authority figures uninformed about the lives the girls themselves actually live.

As rebels, the girls often see little future ahead. In the words of sociologist Gisela Konopka: "The touchstone of our understanding of the adolescent girl in conflict is not just loneliness, it is loneliness which sees no way out, an inner helplessness confronted with an enveloping 'anonymous' world." [5] While most appear to be of average intelligence, the largest number have had severe school problems. Few complete school, and, as school failures, the rebels find themselves barred from the new employment opportunities now opening up to women with diplomas and degrees.[6] While standard blue-collar jobs as waitress and countergirl are always available, many of the girls share society's view of these positions as dreary, temporary, poorly rewarding, physically demanding, and personally degrading. A few rely dreamily on occupational "magic" (Barbra Streisand, they point out, began as a cashier in a Chinese restaurant). Most turn their hopes toward a youthful, romantic marriage. Vague about the responsibilities involved, many rebels do not value marriage as such, but view it instead as the only legitimate way out of having to support themselves at dreary conventional jobs or at self-defeating illegal pursuits (prostitution, theft, and the like).

The rebel, more than any other blue-collar type, may choose violation of the law as an alternative in seeking solutions to her life problems. While there is no consensus among academic students of the subject, the origin of the delinquency of many young rebels appears related to their sense of the injustice done them and to their desire to somehow affirm their new adulthood. These girls often perceive their own law violations as simple variations on behavior strictly prohibited to juveniles but casually permitted to adults—such as drinking, leaving home, or "making out." (Relevant here is the fact that Children's Bureau statistics based on large-city court reports reveal that more than half of the girls referred to juvenile court are referred for conduct that would not be criminal if committed by adults.)[7] The girls seek to affirm their adulthood with a demonstration of control over their social environment (for example, many rebels shoplift goods they feel unjustly deprived of and deeply desire). Very few are full-time, regular law-breakers; most only drift into intermittent delinquency, sexual and otherwise.[8]

Those who escape incarceration find little effective guidance away from continued difficulties with the law. Rather, the weight of the neighborhood, the family milieu, the school's inadequacies, and the girl's own low self-esteem and evaluation of her prospects seem to dominate events. A four-year study of girls with potential problems enrolled in a New York City vocational high school established recently that the impact of a caseworker's preventive effort, "If any, was minor." On all the indices employed—dropping out of school, academic performance, truancy, getting pregnant, and others— the valiant efforts of the social workers had no noticeable effect.[9]

When indicted for an offense, the rebel is routinely and poorly treated. In nearly three out of four of the nation's juvenile courts, youngsters are never referred to community welfare agencies. Few probation officers see their wards more than once every six weeks, and probation case loads are so heavy that officers often terminate probation after only a month.[10] While a 1967 Supreme Court ruling requiring certain reforms may lead to changes in these 1966 research findings, the girl rebels who have been hurt in the past—and in the interim—are more numerous than statistics will ever tell.

For those arrested and convicted of criminal behavior, the future is especially uncertain. In reformatories the prospects of rehabilitation are very uneven: Little or no vocational training, short of cottage-cleaning and beauty culture, is generally undertaken. Institutional programs still include practices like solitary confinement which humiliate and decrease self-esteem. At the same time these same programs almost always exclude the use of group therapy and the creative arts so successful otherwise in isolated demonstration projects. Better off are the all-too-few rebels who manage to secure a place in the all-too-small women's division of the Job Corps.[11] Overall, what hope exists for rehabilitation rests largely with the blue-collar girl rebels themselves. Many desperately wish to be part of the "good" world, and most struggle in their own awkward way to join or to rejoin that world—as blue-collar accommodators.

THE ACCOMMODATORS

Conventional blue-collar daughters frequently come from commonplace, tradition-endorsing homes such as those maintained by semiskilled workers living in stable ethnic enclaves.[12] The girls are often overprotected and closely supervised: Their adolescent rebellion reduces to a mild and conventional one (hysteria at Beatle concerts, necking with a steady date, or illicit smoking in the high school locker room). A major motivation of these girls is their fervid desire to retain membership in the blue-collar community they have known since birth, the only community they can imagine for themselves.

Overall, the vast majority of accommodators meet the challenge of puberty with less difficulty than in the case of the rebels, and the additional challenge of moderating their own sexual behavior poses no special problem. Knowledge as an antidote to fear and confusion can frequently be had from mothers and older sisters in the warm and tight-knit families of the accommodators. Similarly, the stable blue-collar neighborhood endorses a sex code that helps to regulate conduct and set limits. (Vincent Riccio, a Youth Board worker, writes in this connection: "I have heard a million whistles, a hundred pretty uncouth questions—almost always from a drunken kid, but never have I seen a girl touched who didn't want to be touched.")[13]

Like the rebels, the accommodators are also intrigued by an unrealistic, highly romanticized version of male-female relations. This helps explain their early interest in steady dating (a safe way to "practice" marriage), their preoccupation with faddish clothes and makeup styles, and their endless stream of gossip about local boy-girl affairs and distant Hollywood romances. Unlike the rebels, the accommodators are the "good girls" of the neighborhood, and, as they view themselves as appropriate mates for eligible young blue-collarites in the area, they have a valued reputation to protect. Oriented toward early marriage, the blue-collar accommodators are heavily represented among the half-million or more seventeen-year-old young women who marry before their eighteenth birthday, a bloc equal to 25 percent of all seventeen-year-old females. They are also disproportionately found among the half of all young women who marry before they are twenty years of age.

Courtship has a special flavor where accommodators are concerned. As marriage rather than career or college is the focus for the immediate post-high school period, a number of blue-collar girls try to use sex and even pregnancy to move neighborhood boys into marriage. Premarital relations are common, though carefully screened to protect the girl's reputation as a "one-man woman." The girls remain traditional in their disbelief in the sexual rights of the woman and frequently do not get personal satisfaction from male-centered coitus bereft of foreplay or variations in technique or procedure (such sexual expressions, including heavy and extended petting, are often condemned as animalistic perversions by traditional blue-collarites). The girls accept the double standard because "men are that way," and they take their chances on drawing their teen-age steadies into a sex-and-marriage relationship. Sociologist Robert R. Bell estimates that "when all unmarried pregnancies are taken into account, it may be that over half of all white lower-class women are pregnant at some time· prior to marriage." [14] The manipulation skills entailed in learning "how to get around the men," in learning how to lead partners from bed to altar to nursery, undoubtedly stand the girl accommodators in good stead in their young marriages.

Looking closely at their high school experience, it appears that many girl accommodators may profit considerably from secondary school. A significant minority, oriented exclusively toward marriage, are free of the pressure boys feel to secure a good grade record, an impressive school transcript, and possibly even college admission. These blue-collar girls are oriented instead to the school's complex informal social system. They glide through their academic exercises while struggling instead with the problem of learning the appropriate feminine role and attracting the attention of members of the opposite sex. Their challenge to the school, or their claim of the right to make a dating and a marriage decision, is one the high school takes little official notice of, as it is generally not acted on until after graduation.[15]

Other blue-collar accommodators, particularly those few who seek an education in a vocational high school for girls, are not as fortunate. Rather, new research suggests these blue-collar girls chose their high school courses not out of interest, but out of grim resolve to prepare for a short-term, semibearable traditional job that will occupy them before a quick marriage (file clerk, pool typist, and others). Girls who want to obtain vocational preparation have very few options available to them. The explanation here revolves about "culture stereotypes" that condition the girls themselves (as well as school administrators) to believe the blue-collar girls are not capable of getting or holding any but traditional female posts. Neither trained to plan nor prepare for new employment possibilities, many accommodators of high natural ability underachieve the whole of their workplace lives.[16]

Indeed, blue-collar accommodators as a whole go nowhere in the labor market. Sociologist Ethelyn Davis' study of careers as concerns of blue-collar girls found 41 percent expect marriage to prevent them from securing jobs they most desire. Even more dismaying is the fact that 75 percent never expect to obtain the job they would most like to have.[17]

The situation improves slightly for the bulk of accommodators who secure high school diplomas, but improvement is confined here to the matter of the distribution of traditional female jobs. As might be expected, diploma-earners secure comparatively desirable clerical jobs and avoid factory and waitress-like service employ with more success than do high school dropouts.[18] Blue-collar accommodators in general also seem to work earlier outside the home, longer before marriage, longer before becoming pregnant, and longer before giving birth than was true of their blue-collar mothers. Many accommodators work at cleaner, more demanding, and better-paying work than their mothers ever knew, and a large number of such budget-pressured and restless girls return to work at the first possible opportunity. This particular variable especially sets the daughters off against the *"kirche, kinder und küche* (church, children, and kitchen) orientation of their home-bound grandmothers—and mothers.

In the main, the feminine identity and adult future of the accommodators are intimately linked to the general blue-collar endorsement of home and family as opposed to a family-less pursuit of a career or a college education. Of greatest significance is the role of the accommodators as carrier and protector of the local culture; much more than either the rebels or the achievers, the accommodators encompass in their example, and expect to inculcate in their husbands and children, the standard blue-collar values.[19] Riccio notes from his Youth Board experience that the "good girls" are "the only ones who really effect dramatic changes . . . love, and then marriage, have saved more potential bums than all the clergy, police, social workers, and Youth Board people combined. Far, far more." [20]

THE ACHIEVERS

Possibly the smallest of the three subtypes, the blue-collar girl achievers are also the least often discussed in the literature.[21] Typical of such girls are the two female winners of the six four-year $6,000 scholarships awarded in 1967 under the AFL-CIO College Merit Scholarships Program:

> Patricia A. Kennedy, 17, is the daughter of a Louisiana Post Office employee, and is a graduate of a local parochial high school. Looking to a career as a research biologist she expects to major in biological sciences at Rice University. At high school she belonged to the National Honorary Math Club, edited the school yearbook, worked part-time as a saleslady and a babysitter, and made practically all her own clothing.
>
> Rita Diane Jensen, 17, is the daughter of a California hotel cook, and is the top grad of a class of 454 at a local public high school. Looking to a career in teaching art and fashion design, she will major in art at Humboldt State College. Her greatest interests lie in art, but she also plays the guitar, sings, belongs to a modern dance club, and does creative writing.

Significant is the fact that the avowed career interests of the four male winners involve three of the four in the pursuit of the Ph.D., while only one of the two girls may attempt to go as far.[22]

Many blue-collar girls who persevere through to college degrees and to full-time careers probably spent their youth in the comparatively affluent suburban homes of better-educated skilled workers (such as postal clerks, chefs, and others). In such a setting the girl is likely to be well prepared for the physiological and personality changes that bring her into young adulthood. More troublesome may be the challenge of moderating sexual behavior, for the achiever, unlike the other two subtypes, rejects early marriage as an alternative to school or career and seeks to have as wide a choice as possible in the marriage "market." Concerned to guard her reputation and to protect her hope of marrying into college-bred, white-collar circles, the achiever must curb her desire to join the socially oriented high school crowd of blue-collar accommodators, even as she seeks to avoid a romantic attachment to a blue-collar friend that might result in crib-rocking rather than matriculation.[23]

Achievers engage here in a type of anticipatory socialization that can be very restricting. To attract men from a higher sociocultural level the girls strive to achieve behavior they imagine prevalent in middle-class circles. Their definitions of "lady" often become narrower and more conventional than is true of many born into the middle class. When the blue-collar achievers, or their ambitious parents, cannot measure up to what they wish to attain, considerable psychological discomfort ensues.[24]

To buttress the drive for achievement, high school is taken in grim earnest and is turned to every possible advantage. In high school the achiever probably seeks out the company of college-oriented peers, and may find such friends in selected extracurricular activities (the school newspaper, language or science clubs, the debate society, and others). However, while popular with her teachers, the achiever may never find comfort in her isolation from blue-collar accommodators and in her intermittent contact with students from high-status origins.

Overall, the achiever contends with serious problems in defining a feminine identity. In addition to the general cultural problems involved in the "feminine mystique" the blue-collar achiever has to wrestle with a background hostile to careers for women. Often part of the first generation in her family's history to have delayed her marriage and childbearing and to have become part of the college world, the achiever is regarded both with pride and skepticism by family members and blue-collar friends. Pride in accomplishment combines with fear and suspicion of the unfamiliar world the girl has entered. Furthermore, because ambition is so characteristically masculine, the achiever is obliged to take on some values from across the sex line, to acquire in certain respects a less feminine constellation of values than other girls. Few developments are as likely to disturb blue-collar families as the phenomenon of a daughter appearing to "put on pants"; few developments threaten the already-uncertain status of male manual workers as directly.

These strains, in combination, cannot help but take a heavy toll in peace of mind. They may well explain why so few girls take this particular route, and they may also explain the apparent disinclination of blue-collar girls to pursue college much beyond the associate or bachelor's degree. Most of the girl achievers seem to choose short-preparation, quick-employ careers, such as those available in fashion design, school teaching, nursing, or the like. Their willingness to accept low-paying occupations probably links up with the fact that they are not expected to achieve economic success, but instead to come to value the respectability and proper style of life encouraged by their college attendance. Earning then often only as much as experienced clericals from the ranks of blue-collar accommodators, the girl achievers are obliged to believe their extra effort and difficulties amply rewarded by the prestige of a white-collar post and the chance at a white-collar husband.[25]

SUMMARY

The daughters of the men with whom this book is concerned, the Caucasian daughters of 21 million male blue-collarites, divide into three types, each of which reacts differently to the key constraints of adolescence and young adulthood. Accordingly, each approaches the prospects of a lifetime of womanhood as a blue-collar woman from a very different perspective, and this summary fact carries important implications for blue-collar marriage, family, neighborhood life, and so forth. Accommodators, the majority type, place a high value on traditionalism, sentimentality, and routinization. Their situation leads observers of working-class life to conclude that "for the girls, the high point of life is adolescence—especially the courting period—and that they age quickly after marriage and childbearing, becoming old and passive much earlier than do middle-class women." [26]

While occasional job-holding marks these girls off from the generation of their blue-collar mothers, the similarities between them far outweigh their differences. Like their mothers, accommodators are committed to their own sense of inadequacy where change and reform are concerned. What was "good enough for mother" remains the preferred way—almost regardless of cost. A familiar penalty is preferred to an unknown risk, all to the effect of helping the young blue-collar woman achieve some (desperate) sense of control over the otherwise hurly-burly character of her life and our modern times.

Notes to Chapter Ten

1. Studs Terkel, *Division Street: America* (New York: Pantheon, 1967), © 1967 Pantheon, pp. 368–375. Reprinted by permission of the publisher.

2. Gisela Konopka, *The Adolescent Girl in Conflict* (Englewood Cliffs, N.J.: Prentice-Hall, 1966), p. 41. The entire section on the rebel draws most heavily on this source. See also Lillian C. Kovar, *Faces of the Adolescent Girl* (Englewood Cliffs, N.J.: Prentice-Hall, 1968).

3. Research suggests lower-class females start their petting and kissing behavior earlier than those in other classes who marry later, and are more likely to marry their teen-age steadies. See Ira L. Reiss, "Sexual Codes in Teen-Age Culture," *The Annals* (November 1961), p. 55; Ira L. Reiss, "America's Sex Standards—How & Why They're Changing," *Trans-Action* (March 1968), pp. 26–32.

4. Harold Howe II, *Equality of Educational Opportunity* (Washington, D.C.: Government Printing Office, 1966), pp. 27–30.

5. Konopka, *op. cit.*, p. 41.

6. Harvey R. Hamel, "Employment of High School Graduates and Dropouts in 1965," *Monthly Labor Review* (June 1966), pp. 643–649.

7. President's Commission on Law Enforcement and Administra-

tion of Justice, *The Challenge of Crime in a Free Society* (Washington, D.C.: Government Printing Office, 1967), p. 56.

8. "Boys and girls commit different types of offenses. About 50 percent of male delinquents are involved in some type of theft, while only about 10 percent of female delinquents are thieves. On the other hand, over 50 percent of female delinquents are charged with sex offenses, family offenses, or sex connected offenses; only about 25 percent of boys are charged with these kinds of offenses." Ruth Morris, "Female Delinquency and Relational Problems," *Social Forces* (October 1964), p. 82. Grosser contends that offenses are expressions of sex roles. For example, girls' involvement in illicit sexual relationships is an expression of the "relational" goals of their role whereas boys' stealing and destruction of property is a reflection of the "status" goals of wealth, power, and prestige. George H. Grosser, *Juvenile Delinquency and Contemporary American Sex Codes* (Harvard University, unpublished Ph.D. dissertation).

9. Henry J. Meyer, *et al.*, *Girls at Vocational High* (New York: Russell Sage Foundation, 1966). The authors suggest that perhaps "the diagnosis and management of environment might produce better results than the diagnosis and management of individuals through the prevalent case work method."

10. J. W. Anderson, "A Survey of Juvenile Courts Shows Failure to Aid Young," *World Journal Tribune*, January 22, 1967, p. 16. See also President's Commission on Law Enforcement and Administration of Justice, *The Challenge of Crime in a Free Society, op. cit.*

11. See in this connection, Marjorie Hunter, "Job Corps Helps Slum Girls Shed 'Mud of Gutters,' " *The New York Times*, December 18, 1966, p. 32.

12. "Routine Seekers" is the expressive concept formulated by Herbert Gans to designate the group I call accommodators. For discussion, see Gans, *The Urban Villagers: Group and Class in the Life of Italian-Americans* (New York: Free Press, 1962), pp. 28–73.

13. Vincent Riccio and Bill Slocum, *All the Way Down: The Violent Underworld of Street Gangs* (New York: Ballantine, 1962), p. 88.

14. Robert R. Bell, *Premarital Sex in a Changing Society* (Englewood Cliffs, N.J.: Spectrum, 1967), p. 144, *passim.* For research which suggests that girls with illegitimate pregnancy have no personality traits that distinguish them from girls in general, see Starke R. Hathaway and Elio D. Monachesi, *Adolescent Personality*

and Behavior: MMPI Patterns of Normal, Delinquent, Dropout, and Other Outcomes (Minneapolis: The University of Minnesota Press, 1963), p. 53.

15. For related discussion, see Arthur L. Stinchcombe, *Rebellion in a High School* (Chicago: Quadrangle, 1964), p. 129, *passim*.

16. Jacob J. Kaufman, *et al.*, *The Role of the Secondary Schools in the Preparation of Youth for Employment* (University Park, Pa.: Institute for Research on Human Resources, 1966), pp. 10–11. See also Meyer, *et al.*, *op. cit.*; James Ridgeway, "The Girls in White," *New Republic* (February 19, 1966), pp. 10–12.

17. Ethelyn Davis, "Careers as Concerns of Blue-Collar Girls," in A. Shostak and W. Gomberg (eds.), *Blue-Collar World* (Englewood Cliffs, N.J.: Prentice-Hall, 1964), p. 155.

18. For confirmatory data, see *The Negroes in the United States: Their Economic and Social Situation*, Department of Labor (Washington, D.C.: Government Printing Office, 1966), pp. 128, 115–116.

19. Turner's data lead him to suggest adolescent girls are "less weaned from their strata of origin than men are at this stage of life . . . the girls continue to believe in the values which their backgrounds have forced on them while the men do not." Ralph Turner, *The Social Context of Ambition: A Study of High School Seniors in Los Angeles* (San Francisco: Chandler, 1964), pp. 217–218.

20. Riccio and Slocum, *op. cit.*

21. A rare study of high school seniors (706 in the San Francisco Bay area) found working-class students' post-high school plans, for boys and girls respectively, were: college, 43 and 37 percent; technical school, 31 and 29 percent; and no further education, 25 and 34 percent. For middle-class students these percentages were 66 and 61, 20 and 20, and 14 and 19. Irving Krauss, "Sources of Educational Aspirations Among Working-Class Youth," *American Sociological Review* (December 1964), p. 867.

22. *AFL-CIO News*, May 6, 1967, p. 12. The awards have been made for the past nine years and include fifty-four winners; a study of their post-award records might reveal much about blue-collar achievers.

23. On the reluctance of upward mobile women from lower-class backgrounds to risk sexual behavior that might interfere with their mobility, see Ira L. Reiss, "Social Class and Premarital Sexual Permissiveness: A Re-Examination," *American Sociological Review* (October 1965), p. 753. See also Bell, *op. cit.*, p. 116.

24. For discussion, see Moore and Holtzman, *op. cit.*, p. 265; Bell, *op. cit.*, p. 117. Cf. William Foote Whyte, "A Slum Sex Love," *American Journal of Sociology* (1943), pp. 24–31.

25. On the occasional success of achievers, see Ronald M. Pavalko and Norma Noger, "Contingencies of Marriage to High-Status Men," *Social Forces* (June 1968), pp. 523–531.

26. Gans, *op. cit.*, p. 73. For confirmatory data, see James W. Trent and Leland L. Medsker, *Beyond High School* (San Francisco: Jossey-Bass, 1968), pp. 210–212, 257, 261, 266, *passim.*

Part IV

11

BLUE-COLLAR
LEISURE

This civilization is not going to depend on what we do while we work but on what we do in our time off.—HERBERT HOOVER

Free-time behavior is fully as revealing as worktime behavior where the style and prospects of blue-collar men are concerned. With the equivalent of a four-month paid holiday available annually, today's blue-collarites enjoy about 1,200 hours per year more free time than did their grandfathers in 1890.[1] In their free time, blue-collar men do what they want to do, things they believe they have earned the right to do through their investment in work. Contemporary blue-collar leisure preferences and goals are analyzed in this chapter, the discussion revolving about the fundamental question: How well is the worker served, and how well does he serve himself through his increased and increasing leisure?

LEISURE PREFERENCES

To judge from 1960 survey results there is impressive uniformity in the choices that blue-collar men make from available leisure options.[2] Indeed, the 1960 survey suggests that most Americans, whether blue- or white-collar, have remarkably similar leisure preferences. Where blue-collar men stand out is in the slightly greater emphasis they place on home workshop and repair activities and the much greater emphasis they place on fishing, hunting, observing sports, and picnicking. Also striking is the failure of photography or swimming to make the "top 12" list of the blue-collarites polled. The expense of the former and the limited availability of the latter may account for much of this.

LEISURE PROFILES

In keeping with the professed choices of the workers themselves special attention is paid below to the significance for male Caucasian blue-collarites of television, visiting, gardening, reading, and so forth. The character of the discussion is influenced both by the availability of data and by the unique attributes of the leisure option itself.

Television.   Making very heavy use of the medium, the blue-collar viewer adopts a casual and relaxed attitude toward it. Television, instead of demanding anything from the viewer, actually helps drain off emotion and strain produced during the day. An avenue of escape from all that is or may be burdensome, TV is pursued primarily for pleasure and for enjoyment.

In a very important way TV is essentially a confirmatory exercise. By exercising discrimination at channel-switching, blue-collarites are able to expose themselves only, or especially, to a particular brand of TV fare (a phenomenon much in effect like visiting only with members of one's extended family or old neighborhood). By exercising discrimination, blue-collar men are able to minimize the lure of middle-class manners as they are stressed in certain TV shows. Defensively, and deliberately, blue-collarites confine themselves to a mixture of soap operas, situation comedies, Westerns, sports, and suspense-mystery shows that promotes a *weltanschauung,* or philosophy of life, warmly held by many workers.

Blue-collar men as TV fans demonstrate a decided preference for traditional Westerns, with their predictability and rugged morality. Many blue-collar men quietly identify with the virile and handsome hero, an epitome of maleness. The Western hero is thought a moral man who defeats the immorality of the outside world (such as the world outside the "old neighborhood"). While almost never a blue-collarite, the Western hero is regarded by workers as one who employs blue-collar attitudes and techniques:

> For example, he is loyal to his buddies, and will not desert them for a woman. His tools are cunning, physical strength, and courage; and the *deus ex machina* that arrives just in time at the end proves that fate and luck are on his side.[3]

Few Western fans among blue-collarites appear sensitive to the criticism that violence in their TV shows may be excessive, even in a moral cause, or that there may be undue glorification of a very questionable era of conquest and hardship.

Television sports coverage is another fast-rising and exceedingly popular interest of blue-collar viewers (among many others), the men far outnumbering the women in the matter. Vying with it in violence, drama, and action (if only verbal) is a new TV attraction, the Joe Pyne–Alan Burke format interview shows. Faith healers, flying saucer cultists, promoters of a rock-and-roll religion, a man who plans to fly over the Grand Canyon on a jet-powered motorcycle—these guests tend to excite and hold the interests of jaded blue-collarites who delight in watching an interviewer exploit weakness and devastate his guests.[4] Still more popular is Johnny Carson's

Tonight Show, wherein the interviewer's "pose of sophisticated nonchalance reduces all human experience to a wisecrack and a giggle." [5]

Unlike the real world, the TV dream construct of many blue-collarites never affects that part of the mind where the inner agonies of men may be located. In response to real world pressures, the choices of TV shows of blue-collarites offer easy answers to difficult questions, hide the sordid and squalid aspects of real life, and comfort viewers who are often baffled, frightened, and in need of a sanctuary.

Conspicuous by their absence from blue-collar TV fare are current events programs, dramas, and particular suspense-mystery shows that imply that effective social control can be exercised by poised, adept, civilized, and clever men, or by the kind of man many blue-collarites do not believe themselves to be. Preferred, in short, are TV shows that do not tax the intellect or emotions, but provide only pleasure and enjoyment. Undesired themes and values are screened out, the blue-collarite gaining only resonance of cultural commonplaces from a media that seems itself intent at times on deserting its own potential to challenge, stir, and inform.

Visiting.   Consistent with observations made in earlier chapters on strong blue-collar family ties and on the gulf that separates the sexes, a great amount of the visiting done by manual workers involves seeing relatives of the same sex. Much rarer is joint social life whereby a blue-collar couple will join one or more other couples (nonrelatives) for an evening out.

Blue-collar visiting has its own particular standards. For one, a woman generally does not visit another when the latter's husband is at home. This reflects both the notion that a husband has first call on his wife's companionship and that such a visit might be interpreted as a sexual interest in the husband (a blue-collar norm holds that people of the opposite sex do not generally come together except for sexual reasons). [6] Another typical standard holds that visiting is best done only among "one's own kind." In a mixed-class suburb, for example, blue- and middle-class families do not socialize with each other. Although workers expect to treat neighbors as equals and to be treated in the same way, a blue-collar norm regards middle-class acceptance as problematic.

Increasingly, visits among extended family members seem to focus on bargain-hunting. Family shopping is a major, and quite possibly the major leisure activity of a good many blue-collarites. Week-night, Saturday, and, in many locales, Sunday-afternoon shopping at late-hour supermarkets and department stores frequently occupies three-generation and extended family parties. Hours are nonchalantly, even eagerly, given to browsing, comparing, and bargain-seeking, the shopping trip commonly including at least one away-from-home meal. Both a manifestation of and a major prop to the blue-collarite's consumption "mania," the ritual of the family weekly shopping trip can affirm worthiness of self and life style in making meaningful acquisitions immediately possible. It can also motivate further work-role effort by tantalizing with still-out-of-reach rewards. Credit-card purchasing, late and off-hour shopping, and blue-collar materialism complement one another here in a most emphatic way.

Close to the living room and shopping center as a locus of blue-collar visiting is the "friendly" neighborhood tavern. The typical blue-collar bar differs considerably from middle-class drinking lounges: Free-lance writer Joe Flaherty describes an Irish "male bar" in Brooklyn in these terms:

> It was strictly a no-nonsense joint, no frills, no extras, you came here to drink (and place bets with a regular bookie). A long mahogany bar dominated the room. Workmanlike whiskey bottles, without pouring spouts, formed a shape-up on the back bar. John Fitzgerald Kennedy's memory was encased on the wall between Irish and American flags. A shuffleboard stood against the side window like a low, sleek schooner in a bottle. The white marble floor gave a regimental click to every footstep. The only feminine-appearing thing in the place was a garishly made-up jukebox, but even that was denied: it was not plugged in.[7]

In many such places blue-collar men congregate regularly, this being part of a pattern of "corner-boy" camaraderie encouraged in the "old neighborhood" from one's earliest years forward. Indeed, much of what is left today of the old "bosom-buddy" style of relationship is concentrated in such neighborhood bars—even as blue-collar couples especially preserve much of what is left of strong family relationships. Blue-collar patterns and frequency of visiting serve both causes well.

Gardening, Fishing, Hunting, and Camping. Certain outdoor-participative activities have much appeal to male blue-collar-ites.

For example, urban dwellers with strong ethnic attachments sometimes keep up small backyard gardens that replicate those once tended in Greece or Italy. More characteristic, however, is the abandonment of vegetable plots and ambitious, if small, vineyards in favor of bush-and-lawn tending by blue-collar suburbanites. Herbert Gans reports that in one mixed-class suburb blue-collarites believed that yard-tending cost them more in spare time than it did their white-collar neighbors, and that it may be more of a chore for them than for anyone else.[8]

Deep-sea fishing and large and small game hunting have related roots: They draw support with their potential for providing an immediate and practical reward (edible produce). They also excite blue-collar interest as a summons to adventure. Both provide an opportunity to struggle with the elements, to escape from the artificialities of urban civilization. The daring, hardy, and manly character of a day spent bobbing like a cork on a small boat out on rough seas, or hoisting a deadly shotgun through miles of wild (and hunter-infested) wilderness is not unattractive to drama-starved, order-taking, and boredom-fighting blue-collarites. Finally, not insignificant are the side benefits of unrestrained drinking, card playing, and male camaraderie that accompany "good" fishing and hunting trips.

All three back-to-nature activities gain support from what sociologist Arnold W. Green calls "the ancient rural bias."[9]

As shared by many blue-collarites, this particular bias inclines certain urban dwellers, with or without rural origins, to look to nature activities rather than to city-based human relationships for clues to the "good life" and to the meaning of existence. The rural bias also links up with a widespread public dislike and distrust of the "cosmopolitan" city. Holders of this bias desire accordingly to counter the alleged ill effects of city life through "return-to-nature" personal renewal exercises. For blue-collarites this has come to mean mostly gardening, fishing, and hunting.

Interestingly enough, camping does not seem to attract much blue-collar support. Expense is probably a factor here, as well as the fact that blue-collar families seek to make ease, convenience, and comfort a way of life. A husband may cheerfully endure a smoke-filled, beer-stocked hunting cabin stay with his drinking buddies, but may decline to share tight quarters with his citified wife and demanding children. The blue-collar wife, in turn, may be characteristically reluctant to "face isolation from the buzz of her sisters, and deprivation in what she had been trained to regard as an irreducible standard of comfort." [10] Blue-collarites make up a disproportionately large share of trailer-camp dwellers, but this appears to be a matter of economy and convenience, and has little bearing on the general blue-collar disinterest in family camping.

Reading. While probably sharply underrepresented among book-club members and library users, blue-collarites are often avid newspaper and pocketbook readers. Here, as elsewhere in the matter of leisure activities, blue-collarites choose particular items that uniquely complement their general style of life—and preferred values.

For example, blue-collarites do not read just any newspaper. Very few seem willing to wrestle with papers such as *The New York Times*. Besides being put off by its complexity and profundity, many workers are inclined to dismiss the *Times* and *Times*-like newsmakers as a bunch of "nice Nellies" ("The News That's Fit to Print").

Accordingly, a significant minority among the nation's 21

million Caucasian male blue-collarites support one or two national tabloids, and, many local tabloids stand out among the nation's 10,000 newspapers as custom-tailored blue-collar fare. The table of contents of a typical tabloid, the *National Enquirer* (issue of January 21, 1968), caters to blue-collar curiosity about exotic Arab child weddings, Hollywood marital and sexual difficulties, the "covered-up" health menace in milk, the ability all men may have to "think" an object into motion by using electrical muscle power, first photos of the luxury-priced Continental Mark III, and photos and crime details concerning new additions to the FBI's "Most Wanted List."

A competitor is the *Confidential Flash*, "The Nation's Most Exciting Tabloid: No Fear—No Favor, the People's Paper." An issue of June 21, 1969 carries features comparable to those of the *Enquirer* and equally bizarre ads. These advertisements offer such unusual items as "guaranteed" aphrodisiacs, bennies and pep pills, erotic novelties, and pornographic movies and stills (some featuring racially integrated couples, oriental girls, or sexual deviates). Also unique to these tabloids is a full page or more of personal box-numbered messages from "nonprudes" of both sexes anxious to hear from open-minded "swingers" interested in "good times," "modern pleasures," and "private fun and games."

Local tabloids, like the *New York Daily News* (the world's largest circulation daily), place somewhat less emphasis on sex and sensationalism and much more emphasis on a "family paper" staple, the tabloid's sports section. The many sports fans among the paper's blue-collar (and white-collar) readers demand readable, stimulating, and thoroughgoing sports coverage. Stories are painstakingly accurate and quite lively. The story writers are well-known columnists and personalities whose articles and opinions are argued about for hours in the local bars (many blue-collarites are self-schooled experts in sports statistics and hold passionately to personal sports judgments). As blue-collar fans generally know for themselves what happened on the field, they press sports writers for behind-the-scenes details, for gossip about clubhouse doings. Accordingly, much homey wisdom, folksy moralism, and "trickle-down" psychoanalytic commentary mix inside the modern tabloid's sports section.

Close behind sports in apparent popularity with blue-collar tabloid customers are stories of crime and violence (judging, that is, from headlines, placement, pictures, and other means of emphasis). Mirroring the grosser attitudes of their readers, the tabloids slant their crime reporting to suggest the defendants are guilty as charged and, in the spirit of "trial by fury," to demand the execution of those convicted of murder and rape. Competing for blue-collar attention with a score or more of monthly magazines devoted entirely to "true crime" tales of sex, sadism, and punishment, the tabloid crime writers press their every advantage: The same story will skillfully weave contradictory material so as to hold the reader who seeks to escape from daily dullness by identifying himself with a law violator, even as it also holds the reader who has a need for a scapegoat on whom he can vent his own aggressions.

With comparable deliberation the tabloid crime coverage will stress the race of the accused (if Negro), the power of the defendant (if a politician or Mafia type), and the inadequacy of watered-down penalties (the "pinko" Supreme Court is regularly castigated). While good "plain folk" police and law-enforcement personnel may win occasional praise, greater attention is paid to scandals that expose the bribing of police by organized criminal elements or the actual participation in crime of law agents. White-collar crime gets more than passing mention, but the star attraction is the sensational trial that mixes sex and mayhem.

In a more conventional and constructive vein, several million do-it-yourself fans among the nation's blue-collarites support a raft of home workshop and home and car repair magazines (a literary magazine satirist alleges "they tell you how to solve home problems you did not know you had, with special tools, materials, and skills you do not possess").[11] A leading example of the do-it-yourself monthlies, *Popular Mechanics*, boasts that its readers are not "beatniks, potheads, or playboys." It goes on to characterize them by applying these now-familiar blue-collar images:

They'd rather look at a picture of auto racing champion Dan Gurney in a G.T. than go shopping for a dress with their wives. They'd rather buy a boat than take a cruise. They'd rather build a summer home than spend a month at the Greenbrier. They'd rather paint the house than the town. They'd rather have a new outboard than wall-to-wall carpeting.[12]

To hold its rugged and talented blue-collar following, the homecraft magazine features picture-essays like these:

12 Weekend Projects for Your Home
Which Glue Is Best?
How to Stay Alive on the Turnpikes
Shortcuts for Saturday Mechanics
Be Lazy about Lawn-Sprinkling
10 Record-Changer Troubles You Can Cure

Judging from rising circulation statistics and subscriber characteristic analysis, the homecraft and workshop publications have refined a formula of lasting appeal to male blue-collarites anxious to hold their own with the gadgetry and mechanical aspects of modern life.

Finally, and in a related fashion, there is reason to believe that both blue-collar men and women pay particular attention to exposé publications. A leading example, *Confidential,* was so strong in newsstand sales in the late 1950s as to be at the time "the most successful magazine ever published in America." [13] A typical issue might include articles exposing some aspect of a celebrity's life (such as a Senator's boyhood arrest record for car theft, the impotence of a virile cowboy hero, or the lesbian proclivities of a famous actress) and an article or two on some health topic (such as the possible toxic effects of a well-known patent medicine, or a possible cure for a major disease).

A readership study by Charles Winick suggests blue-collar fans especially value getting the "inside story." It seems to provide "almost a kind of magical control over the famous, perhaps a vehicle for hostility against them, concealed behind expressions of morality and surprise." [14] New gossip provides readers with spectacular material with which to initiate conversations. A need to identify with the illicit and sinful to fan latent feelings of sinfulness is undoubtedly also a factor here.

Critical as well is the reader's cynical belief that until *Confidential* came along the more conventional media were protecting the godlike celebrities, and that now, via successors to the defunct *Confidential,* the blue-collar reader can know the world as it really is—and drain off some of the hatreds and hostilities the world provokes by focusing them on the sorry spectacle of the exposed celebrity. The blue-collarite senses new personal power through his inside knowledge of the once-secret shortcomings of the proud: He stands taller in his new-found moral superiority or, at the very least, feels less guilt-ridden for having discovered celebrities with whom he shares some indiscretion or personal failing. Exposé serves Americans of many strata, but blue-collarites especially seem to benefit from it.

Auto Sport.   For many blue-collar men an auto is the biggest play toy of them all. Innumerable hours, much hard work, and perhaps 10 percent of one's annual income support a serious effort to keep up or improve on the mechanics, power, comfort, and style of the family car (or cars).

Blue-collar men monopolize auto matters somewhat as their wives determine daytime and children's TV fare. Most working-class women take no part in choosing the family's car, or in related decisions thereafter that are thought the "husband's department." Interesting in this connection is the legacy of discontent involved here: When asked by researchers to name the family's "unwisest purchase," the nod was most often given by blue-collar wives to one of the husband's automotive "lemons." [15] Overall, the women almost invariably felt that it was their husbands who secured the family's major pleasure in automobile ownership.

Beyond pleasure driving, an increasing number of blue-collar men are employing autos as racing vehicles—and thereby, as a major leisure interest. Drag racing, once the preserve of adolescent blue-collar rebels (and certain middle-class youngsters), is increasingly popular with adult blue-collarites. Over

500 specially-constructed drag strips annually attract over 250,000 racers and 4 million spectators. Lay and professional drivers join with fans in celebrating style and power: All are bound together by jargon (a "deuce" is a 1932 Ford; a "tube steak" a frankfurter) and fetishes (iron crosses, WW I German helmets) common to the auto cult. T-shirts with inscriptions such as "Pabst—breakfast of champions" are the order of the day at meets, which combine everything from jazzed-up jalopies to sleek $30,000 custom cars. Consistent with the mechanical prowess and power concern of many blue-collarites, the drag-racing cult continues to grow.

The practice of tourism—whether by car or otherwise—appears to attract little blue-collar interest. While there is much visiting of close relatives in other states (and even an infrequent visit back to "the old country"), blue-collarites are underrepresented as visitors to state and national parks, historic shrines, and other such tourist attractions.[16] Economics may play a role here, but more important may be the intra-personal and interpersonal demands inherent in tourism: One must relate to strangers, adroitly take and step out of roles, and competently meet unexpected developments of high-stress character. Fears of "being taken" or "suckered" combine here also with provincial ignorance of where one might go, smugness in concluding little elsewhere is really worth visiting, and preference for the hometown version of things.

Do-It-Yourself Hobbies.   Home-workshop and repair activities are very extensive. These range from puttering with the family car to large-scale alterations of the family residence ("finishing" the basement or building a patio are typical). Consistent with their mode of work and their status as urbanites, many blue-collar men have a heightened appreciation of, and a dependence upon, gadgetry. Tools proliferate and home workshops swell with "never-can-tell-when-you-will-need-it" miscellanea, or the blue-collarites' version of the white-collarites' (unread) home library or ever-growing record library. Provocative in this connection is the contention of some social scientists that the do-it-yourself movement has partly grown

out of the hobbyist's yearning to exercise the skill of a craftsman, a skill long since surrendered to machines and left underemployed in most blue-collar work. In combination with utility
and economy, this "instinct for craftsmanship" promises many
future years of blue-collar do-it-yourself concern.

Fraternal Organizations.   Leaving aside labor unions, which
are discussed elsewhere, it appears that the Knights of Columbus, various ethnic societies, veterans groups, the Masonic order, and the Ku Klux Klan are especially popular with manual
workers (middle-class organizations like the Kiwanis, Elks, Odd
Fellows, and others have far fewer blue-collar supporters).

Blue-collar joiners may be markedly energetic and single-
purpose in their orientation. For example, Herbert Gans notes
that in a mixed-class suburb, blue-collarites were the first to
organize a men's group (in this case, a VFW chapter). From
the start the blue-collarites wanted a primarily social organization, while the chapter's few middle-class members struggled
unsuccessfully to introduce a community-service orientation.
The VFW chapter leaders also included several active Democrats, and the blue-collar veteran's group, while ostensibly
nonpolitical, gave covert support to party activities. The VFW
chapter in turn enjoyed support for its fraternal projects from
the reciprocating political party.[17]

Writer Steward Alsop, focusing on the KKK, notes elements
that help explain a general blue-collar interest in fraternal
groups: "The Klan has everything that makes a boys' secret
club so satisfactory for 12-year-olds—oaths, rituals, costumes, a
sense of belonging, no girls, and an enemy." [18] By awarding
rank and insignia the Klan, and its fraternal counterparts, permit "little men" to realize dreams of office, to indulge other
pet romantic fantasies, and to act out some of their dreams.
With strength of this sort, fraternal groups understandably
have a strong call on the support of a small, but important
bloc of blue-collarites.

Spectator Sports.   Large numbers of blue-collarites are drawn
to the partisanship, violence, detail, and drama possible in

attendance at football, baseball, hockey, boxing, wrestling, racing, the roller derby, and other such activities. Though the worker cannot or will not comprehend much of the mystery of his contemporary world, the blue-collar sports fan can and will immerse himself emotionally and viscerally in his favorite spectator sport.

To spend a season identifying with a superior team that eventually wins a world championship title, or even clowns itself into "the cellar," is to heighten one's own existence and personal identity in a very special way. To vicariously crash through the line, or break up a possible double play, or win a grueling car race, or survive a destruction-derby contest is somehow to feel one's own manhood confirmed. To join with one's ethnic bloc in raucous ethnic partisanship during a wild wrestling night at the local arena, a night that just might end in a good old-fashioned chair-and-head-smashing arena riot, is valued by many as high living. To have coworkers turn to one to settle exceedingly refined points about baseball statistics, racehorse form, or prizefight records is to enjoy a very special boost to the ego. And to know with surety that the "good guys" will win a wrestling team-touch match, that the newcomer is being "moved along" by the "fight mob," and that the "big money" players on a professional football team are going to come out ahead in a predictable scenario is flattering and comforting in a world otherwise unpredictable and discomforting.

Considerable romanticism is involved in blue-collar admiration of certain professional athletes. Manual workers often perceive the athlete as someone really like themselves—only more handsome, better conditioned, and far more gifted. Many a middle-aged Italian blue-collarite, for example, takes personal pride in the DiMaggio saga:

> The great Joe DiMaggio (his feat of hitting safely in 56 straight games is considered the one unbreakable baseball record) not only filled the gargantuan shoes of Babe Ruth, but married the sex goddess of the civilized world—a parlay of fantasies not even Horatio Alger would have dared imagine.[19]

Fans, however, are not reluctant to turn harshly on fallen idols, as this description of roller-derby antics makes clear:

> . . . they often attack the skaters as they leave the ring. They boo them on the street, hiss at them in supermarkets, and write them obscene letters. In their more devilish moods they have been known to shoot at the skaters during the games with BB guns and throw objects of art ranging from beer cans to heavy chunks of metal.[20]

Many blue-collarites do not go as far, but do get a special "kick" from booing an $82,000-a-year celebrity like the sometimes unpopular Phillies baseball star, Richie Allen.

Frequently the game and its teams are generously thought to involve such admirable features as collaboration, rivalry, supreme skill in the craft, joy and pride in the skill, and innocence. Goose Goslin, one of baseball's earlier stars, put it this way: "It was just a game, that's all it was. They didn't have to pay me. I'd have paid *them* to let me play. Listen, the truth is it was *more* than fun. It was heaven." [21] Blue-collarites understand this sentiment and often envy its holders in a nonhostile way. Professional athletes are romantically believed really to *like* to do what they they are doing, and to like to do it supremely well. As few blue-collarites feel the same way about their own work, they are all the more inclined to admire this in their favorite athletes. They are also inclined to expect the very best—almost regardless of cost or complication ("Remember high school, when the football team scored a moral victory? It meant you lost the game.").[22]

Related to this last matter is a factor sometimes lost sight of in explaining the relationship of blue-collarites and spectator sports, or the support gained here by the worker's characteristic cynicism. Blue-collarites are resigned to professional boxing as a mob-controlled racket. They are also resigned to wrestling as a substitute for medieval morality plays and old-fashioned vaudeville. Many such workers let their cynicism influence their appraisal of amateur sports, including collegiate play. These men, for example, take pride in appearing nonplussed when college basketball players are exposed from time to time for having "shaved points" at the hire of professional gamblers. Believing that everyone has his price and that "the world is a racket," a number of blue-collarites lean on the seamier aspects of commercial leisure-time sports for support of such a jaundiced world view.

Blue-collarites also pay very close attention to the earnings of professional athletes, particularly when the player is a former blue-collarite or is a product of a blue-collar background. A good number of sports fans agree that the name of the game is money: One needn't be a football fan to know about the $400,000 paid to Joe Namath for signing with the New York Jets or the $15,000 earned by each of the Green Bay Packers for a day's work in 1967 against the Kansas City Chiefs. Blue-collarites have such financial data memorized for the vast comfort they give: The data support both a sports variation on the Horatio Alger fantasy of sudden wealth for late-discovered self-worth, and a set of "playboy" fantasies about the secret well-heeled love lives of virile professional athletes.[23]

Participative Sports.   Blue-collarites engage in a wide range of athletic endeavors, including such less-well-known sports as bocce, curling, schoolyard handball and stickball, and motorcycle racing. Three additional interests, pool, soccer, and bowling, are briefly discussed below.

The playing of pool has long been a leading blue-collar interest. Historically, workers have especially valued the male sanctuary aspect of the poolroom. In their "secular monastaries" rough-hewn men have long enjoyed the casual use of profanity and the occasional use of violence. Even now men thrill at the chance to watch or, more rarely, dare a game with such notable contemporary "hustlers" as Handsome Danny, Detroit Whitey, Cicero, Cornbred Red, Peter Rabbit, The Red Raider, or the immortal Minnesota Fats.[24] There is also much appeal in the ability a poolroom *aficionado* has to mingle with big-name gamblers, racketeers, hoodlums, prostitutes, and specialists in "hot goods" and pornography.

Long since stigmatized and opposed by "middle-class morality," blue-collar poolrooms were once the keystone of a now-declining all-male subculture. This cultural world demanded a no-woman's-land that catered to internal refugees from the larger "outside" world of female-imposed gentility. The blue-collar poolroom continues even today to serve as a male escape-hatch from effete and "feminized" cultural pressures. Few workers show any interest in the newfangled "high-falutin" billiard parlors currently being promoted as "safe and pleasant for women and children": Pool for blue-collarites remains an attraction precisely for the opposite reason—and as such, may long draw a regular and devoted, if limited, number of blue-collar fans.[25]

Soccer has a small, but rabid and growing following among both blue-collar fans and participants. The game is still very much a European and Latin-American import. Sunday afternoon matches in public parks in this country are attended by foreign-language-speaking working-class crowds, and the ethnic flavor of the event could not be stronger. Indeed, journalist David Cort finds it a "gloomy prospect" that many of the Old Country teams involved are "fighting out and perpetuating their imported national antagonisms on the field and in the stands." [26] However this may be, the game has long since established its claim to blue-collar allegiance in 131 countries abroad —and America may not always remain a comparative exception in the matter.

Bowling has a large blue-collar following, one aided especially by the popularity of company (and to a lesser degree, union) bowling teams. The comparative ease with which thousands of blue-collar bowlers have worked up to an average of 180 or better helps explain some of the game's popularity, as does also the important excuse it offers to help one get away from "the girls" and have an evening out with "the boys."

Finally, an underrecognized participative sports concern of blue-collarites has them managing and coaching the athletic teams of their youngsters. In one recent situation analyzed by Gans, the blue-collar fathers differed sharply in attitude from middle-class fathers in the same softball association. The middle-class men only wanted to enable all their children to play, including the less skillful among them. The blue-collarites, in contrast, preferred Little League membership, with its emphasis on competition, winning, and the sidelining of the poorer players. Not insignificant was the additional fact that success in a national athletic program might put the community, the team, and its adult sponsors "on the map." With such strong motivation it is not surprising that a small but significant number of blue-collar men invest considerable time and effort in the after-school athletics of their (impressionable) children.

Gambling. Blue-collarites bet on various sporting events, card games, crap games, pinball machines, cockfights, political elections, and the policy or numbers game (the "poor man's racetrack"). None of these is a new interest, many having strong ethnic connections (the Italian numbers game, for example, is "an enterprise so ethnically parochial that its slips are printed in Italian and its winning number is based on the last three figures in a day's total sales on the Milanese stock exchange").[27] Overall, illegal operations are preferred by many blue-collar clients because credit is readily available, one's wife and creditors are kept in the dark, and the bookie, runner, or gambler generally maintains a friendly relationship with the blue-collar bettors, players, or "sports."

While the policy or numbers game is frequently played on the basis of a dream or hunch, considerable study and skill is often involved in other forms of blue-collar gambling. During the 250 days of the racing season, for example, workers in the factory and in the neighborhood bar critically evaluate the choices of handicappers, tips of friends, time charts, breeding patterns, the relative ability of trainers and jockeys, the weather, the extra weight the horse is assigned to carry, and the competition. With a record number of 40,000 horses racing today the serious bettor's scholarly pursuit gets more demanding all the time. Proficiency is awarded by much admiration from fellow blue-collarites. Extreme sanctions, however, follow violation of certain precise norms, such as a ban on "betting the red board"—or claiming to have picked the winner only after the race is over.[28]

Sociologist Irving K. Zola suggests much of the fundamental attraction of gambling involves the chance to "beat the system": By outsmarting "the system" through rational means (handicapping their bets), wagerers demonstrate they *can* exercise control, and, for a brief moment, *can* control their own fate. Off-track betting and related forms of gambling appear to be a kind of escape from fate, an escape from the ultimate futility of direct effort toward a goal. Ironically, gambling seems to operate to deny the vagaries of life and to give its blue-collar followers a chance to regulate life.[29]

Gambling has the additional power to help men harness or channel their otherwise destructive frustrations: Instead of lashing out at society the losers lash out at "the system." Gambling also provides an alternative reward system to that uncomplimentary one of the larger society. Wagerers *can* "achieve" and *can* gain recognition for their accomplishments by exercising skill and knowledge in the selection of winners. Finally, through gambling, men can purchase thrills and even desirable letdowns, a welcomed change of pace. This is probably what the legendary Nick the Greek had in mind when he explained: "The next best thing to winning—is losing." [30]

Radio.   Long a blue-collar favorite, radio-listening may be gaining in popularity, so great is the appeal of its ethnic programs, its sportscasts, and its hit-tune and country-style disk-jockey shows.

Foreign-language radio shows have a strong following among middle-aged and older workers nostalgic for news of the "old sod" and for the sound of music from yesteryear. Also growing in popularity among blue-collarites are the phone-in talk shows that have proved a boon to people whose literacy level makes writing letters-to-the-editor impractical. Strong opinions about every conceivable subject are phoned in daily by blue-collar men and women, among others, the participants often disagreeing sharply with one another. Blue-collar teen-agers prefer and follow local disk jockeys. Many delight in phoning in dedications to one another, the pleasure possible in hearing one's own name over the air apparently considered a fair price to pay for the quantity and quality of commercials exacted by adult businessmen as their price for "free" radio fare.

Adult blue-collarites show their own strong interest in a different type of disk-jockey show: Reflecting the rural origins of many first-generation blue-collar urbanites, the listeners support the friendly warmth of nostalgic cowboy and country music, with its strong flavor of poor white Southern culture. Their support is estimable: Close to 40 percent of all commercial records produced today are country records. Blue-collarites apparently enjoy the fact that most country songs are in effect two-and-a-half-minute soap operas set to music. The lyrics reveal much about life as it is being lived today in beer joints, diners, gas stations, truck stops, bus depots, and, of course, in the bedrooms of trailer camps, unhappy homes, and seedy hotels. It is rich in "the frank coarseness of its rough humor, the unapologetic syrupyness of its sentiment and, most of all, in the basically honest rhythm of words that come from the gut by way of the heart." [31] Blue-collar support into the indefinite future seems assured.

LEISURE ISSUES

In coming back now to the fundamental question of the chapter—How well is the worker served and how well does he serve himself through his increased and increasing leisure?—it is appropriate in closing to confront the matter of the worker's susceptibility to the influence of his leisure choices.

"High culture" critics of the blue-collar leisure record often contend that the impact of leisure on blue-collarites is both clear and one-way: The worker is nothing more than putty in the hands of the nefarious media masters. This charge, however, has elicited far more affirmation than research. What evidence there is challenges this puppet image in a very telling way.

The impact of specific leisure choices appears restricted to the power to intensify patterns of behavior that are already established. Leisure choices do not seem to have the power to change behavior. Blue-collar attitudes and ideas may be modified, but conversion is unlikely. In effect, blue-collarites appear to make their own leisure profile rather than to be "made" by it. Blue-collarites appear more as selective consumers than as will-less pawns. Leisure's impact seems both secondary and segmental, far more in the nature of confirmatory than manipulative matter.

Similarly, blue-collarites appear more detached from the "message" of their leisure pursuits than is suggested by the "invidious influence" hypothesis. Distrusting much of the outside world, blue-collarites distrust its mass leisure components as well. Sports fans, for example, generally recognize that sports announcers are paid to promote the sport with sugar-coated and saccharine superlatives, rather than to report it—and many blue-collar fans accordingly discount much of the broadcast superlatives. Workers also accuse each other in a teasing way of being taken in by the Madison Avenue propaganda, and with this joshing help protect each other from too close an involvement in the fantasy.

Blue-collarites, in sum, remain responsible for their own leisure record. It is of small profit to scapegoat the mercenary and nefarious media masters: They serve up what the market (in this case, the blue-collar consumer) demands. Far more useful is recognition of the complementarity between the worker's leisure record and his total way of life. In such recognition, rather than in the easier practice of blaming the anonymous masters of the media, one can begin to understand the enormity of the reform task ahead—and the necessity of reform along all fronts simultaneously.

SUMMARY

Blue-collarites choose leisure pursuits that have the power to affirm acquired wisdom rather than provide any confrontation with novel and possibly taxing matters. They choose leisure pursuits that have an ability to "massage" rather than for any message the medium might contain. They also use their leisure as a source of relief from strain, a response to the enervating character of much of their work. And, finally, they see to it that leisure helps resonate the general blue-collar culture.

In their accommodative approach to leisure, in their passive and lighthearted way, the nation's blue-collarites may sell themselves short—and leave undeveloped a potential for personal growth through leisure that none can really afford to ignore. Blue-collarites use—and are used—by their leisure, but the social gain in every direction is far less than it could be.

Notes to Chapter Eleven

---

1. For a full discussion of the history and economics of work hours and leisure hours, see Juanita M. Kreps and J. J. Spengler, "The Leisure Component of Economic Growth," in National Commission on Technology, Automation, and Economic Progress, *The Employment Impact on Technological Change* (Washington, D.C.: Government Printing Office, 1966), pp. 363–397. See also Erwin O. Smigel (ed.), *Work and Leisure: A Contemporary Social Problem* (New Haven, Conn.: College and University Press, 1963).

2. The data are from George Fisk, "Personal Disposable Time: The Psychology of Occupational Differences in the Use of Leisure," in G. Fisk (ed.), *The Frontiers of Management Psychology* (New York: Harper & Row, 1964), pp. 251–268. Fisk employs Survey Research Center Study 685, November 1959, and Study 694, May 1960, of the Omnibus Surveys available at the University of Michigan in Ann Arbor.

3. Herbert J. Gans, "The Alienated Audience: Boston's West End Society Makes Selective Use of Middle Class Media to Uphold Its Own Values," *Comment* (December 1962), p. 17. See also K.

L. Steckmesser, *The Western Hero: In History and Legend* (Oklahoma City: University of Oklahoma Press, 1966).

4. John G. Dumme, "The Hate Hour," *Saturday Evening Post* (December 2, 1967), pp. 24–25.

5. Neil Compton, "TV While the Sun Shines," *Commentary* (October 1966), p. 96.

6. Herbert J. Gans, *The Levittowners* (New York: Pantheon, 1967), p. 183. See also Herbert J. Gans, *The Urban Villagers* (New York: Free Press, 1962).

7. Joe Flaherty, "Frankie Carlin, the Bookie," *The New York Times Magazine,* April 2, 1967, p. 28. See also Sherri Cavan, *Liquor License: An Ethnography of Bar Behavior* (Chicago: Aldine, 1966).

8. Gans, *The Levittowners,* p. 268.

9. Arnold W. Green, *Recreation, Leisure, and Politics* (New York: McGraw-Hill, 1964).

10. *Ibid.,* p. 13.

11. Derek Williamson, "Do-It-Yourself Indeed," *Saturday Review of Literature* (July 30, 1966), p. 8.

12. Anon., *"Popular Mechanics* Is Part of Today!," *The New York Times,* August 18, 1966, p. 60 (full-page advertisement by and for the magazine).

13. Charles Winick, "Celebrities' Errancy as a Subject for Journalism: A Study of *Confidential,*" *Gazette* (1962), p. 329.

14. *Ibid.,* p. 331.

15. See in this connection, Lee Rainwater, *et al., Workingman's Wife* (New York: Oceana, 1959), p. 192.

16. Green, *op. cit.,* p. 26.

17. Gans, *The Levittowners,* pp. 55, 67.

18. Steward Alsop, "The Loaded Pistol," *Saturday Evening Post* (April 23, 1966), p. 22. See also Gerald George, "Fraternally Yours, in Ferment," *National Observer,* February 21, 1966, p. 22.

19. Mario Puzo, "The Italians, American Style," *The New York Times Magazine,* August 6, 1967, p. 7.

20. Bernard McCormick, "Porky Pig's Chicken: There's Something About the Roller Game That Brings Out Blood Lust in the Fans," *Philadelphia Magazine* (June 1968), p. 15.

21. Lawrence S. Ritter, *The Glory of Their Times* (New York: Macmillan, 1966), p. 287.

22. Allen Woode, "The March on the Pentagon," *Ramparts* (February 1968), p. 51. See also Arnold R. Beisser, M.D., *The Madness in Sports* (New York: Appleton-Century-Crofts, 1967).

23. Robert H. Boyle, *Sport: Mirror of American Life* (Boston:

Little, Brown, 1963). See also Edward L. Rousseau, "The Great American Ritual," *The Nation* (October 4, 1958), pp. 188–191.

24. John Paterson, "Peter Rabbit Adlibs When He Enters Town," *National Observer*, November 21, 1966, pp. 1, 11.

25. Ned Polsky, "Poolrooms: End of the Male Sanctuary," *Trans-Action* (March 1967), pp. 33–40. See also Ned Polsky, *Hustlers, Beats, and Others* (Chicago: Aldine, 1967).

26. David Cort, "Soccer: The Rabble Game," *The Nation* (August 30, 1965), p. 101.

27. Murray Kempton, "Che Cosa? Means 'What's That?'," *The New Republic* (October 12, 1963), p. 6.

28. Marvin B. Scott, *The Racing Game* (Chicago: Aldine, 1967).

29. Irving Kenneth Zola, "Observations on Gambling in a Lower-Class Setting," in A. Shostak and W. Gomberg (eds.), *Blue-Collar World* (Englewood Cliffs, N.J.: Prentice-Hall, 1964), p. 360.

30. Flaherty, *op. cit.*, p. 124.

31. Bernard McCormick, "Dial M for Money," *Greater Philadelphia* (June 1966), p. 108.

12

BLUE-COLLAR
POLITICS

In our age there is no such thing as "keeping out of politics." All issues are political issues . . .
—GEORGE ORWELL

Politics, the poet John Ciardi suggests, "is the moral man's compromise, the swindler's method, and the fool's hope." [1] To America's blue-collarites it is clearly all three and still more, its full measure here being the weighty task of this brief chapter.

Six interrelated questions are considered:

1. What is the general outline of the worker's political philosophy?
2. How does the blue-collarite commonly vote (and why does he not vote at times)?

3. What sorts of demographic variables influence his political record?
4. How do "working-class authoritarianism" and race prejudice affect the blue-collarite's political attitudes and action?
5. What role do labor and class identity play?
6. What are blue-collar politics likely to resemble in the foreseeable future?

Unfortunately, data will not sustain a comparison of skill-bloc differences, and the heterogeneous amalgam of blue-collarites is treated of necessity as a single construct. This limitation combines with the crude state of development of such critical concepts as "authoritarianism" to limit sharply the progress that can presently be made in understanding blue-collar politics. Within these restrictions an attempt is finally made to appraise the gains and cost of the blue-collarite's distinct style of politics both to the worker himself and to the nation as a whole.

POLITICAL PHILOSOPHY

Perhaps the best single short introduction to the general political philosophy of America's blue-collarites is available in the writing of Eric Hoffer, the sixty-eight-year-old "blue-collar Montaigne" and "dockside Plato." Popular today with several hundred thousand readers and with millions of television viewers, Hoffer, a retired West Coast longshoreman-turned-author, captures much of the essence of the blue-collar political stance.

Hoffer places two goals at the center of his political philosophy: He would have men celebrate both conventional patriotism and patriotic conventionality. A first-generation American, Hoffer prides himself on being a staunch defender of the country. Hoffer also prides himself on his defense of the status quo in national affairs, and he insists there is really little wrong therein. Above all, Hoffer warns that social conventions must be vigorously defended against the intellectuals ("pet them, but do not give them power") and the youth (whose "penchant for self-dramatization prompts them to extremist poses and gestures").[2] America must be turned anew to the old pieties and homey virtues; it must be protected from the harebrained schemes of power-hungry intellectuals ("Who are they, these little piglets, to tell us how to run the country?").[3]

Like many other blue-collarites, Hoffer rails against the strongest tides of modernity: He remains

. . . of and for the masses while intellectuals exert ever greater influence over events; against revolution as expectations rise and explode in the underdeveloped world; against youth as the median age of the American voter sinks below 30; for individualism in the epoch of collectivization; for honest, sweat-making labor as automation and technology destroy jobs; for "patience" and "reason" as absurdist America is rocked by riots, LSD, happenings, war, and the Disneyland politics of Maddox, Wallace, and Reagan.[4]

To help keep America on the right track, Hoffer urges a restoration to prominence of blue-collar "horse sense," much as in President Andrew Jackson's day.

Like many other blue-collarites, Hoffer remains reluctant to recognize that injustices may have structural sources that require social change (Hoffer blames the failure of Negroes to create community self-help efforts, rather than white-directed discrimination, for the Negro's plight). And, like many who still remember with anger the machinations of left and right during the Depression and World War II years, Hoffer rejects the idea that one can usefully distinguish among the champions of alternative calls for social change (Hoffer condemns all calls for change as coming from "slogan-slingers").[5]

This "sock-it-to-them" philosophy re-creates several major blue-collar political dispositions. It especially captures both the "them versus us" feeling and the nostalgia for times past when common sense and the common man were allegedly in the saddle. It also makes plain both the workingman's intolerance of dissent and his distrust of patriotic and moralistic nonconformity. Above all, Eric Hoffer's variations on blue-collar political philosophy are consistent with the tight-laced, backward-glancing, and phobic character of blue-collar politics.[6]

POLITICAL RECORD

How do blue-collarites vote? For the past twenty years that the forty-three-year-old worker has been voting he has regularly supported candidates of the Democratic party.[7] Indeed, perhaps the most common finding in the field of political behavior is that the lower the socioeconomic status, whether measured by "objective" standards or by the respondent's self-rating, the more Democratic the voter in America.[8] Accordingly, it is not surprising that an early 1968 Gallup Poll found 52 percent of its manual-worker respondents identifying themselves as Democrats, in contrast with 43 percent of the white-collarites and 35 percent of the professionals and businessmen (46 percent of all adults identified themselves as Democrats, the others dividing equally between Republicans and Independents).[9]

The blue-collar vote is not a monolithic Democratic vote, however, as sizeable defections to the Eisenhower candidacy in 1952 and 1956 (and current—1968—support of George Wallace) makes plain. More specifically, only those blue-collarites whose parents have been white-collarites, those who work in the cleaner and more modern service industries, and those who pursue careers as highly-skilled, well-paid craftsmen are likely to show pro-Republican tendencies.[10] There are also controversial data that show a correlation between pro-Republican sentiment and both rural origins and Protestant affiliation among blue-collarites.[11] Overall, however, political analysts do not hesitate to link-up "blue-collar" with "Democratic."

In addition to support of the Democratic party, blue-collarites have four other distinguishing voting characteristics: Many can be rallied behind a job-linked political issue by organized labor. A few can be counted on to oppose any political endorsement of social change (such as fluoridation). A very few regularly vote the parties of the radical left, and, even more, the radical right. Finally, large numbers prefer political platforms of fiscal and governmental economy: School-bond issues, for example, often run into opposition from tax- and inflation-aggrieved blue-collarites, even as many workers resent "give-away programs" for potential competitors for jobs. According to many workers, that government is best which taxes least— and governs even less.

Whether or not proportionately more blue-collarites than others are preoccupied by these four political matters is by no means clear. It is certain, however, that the worker's political profile conspicuously includes a prolabor, anti-change, anti-Establishment, and anti-expenditure vote. While limited and often unpredictable, all four kinds of vote persist inside of, and on occasion even dominate, blue-collar politics.

Discussion here is incomplete without at least passing mention of the fact that many blue-collarites do not vote at all (possibly 35 percent of all unionists stay home from the polls). These men, and others in the blue-collar ranks, also monopolize the "no opinion" or "do not know" column in polls of political attitudes and knowledge.

The roots of blue-collar political withdrawal go far back: Childhood socialization, both at home and in school, explains more of the worker's political apathy than is sometimes realized. At home, for example, various blue-collar child-rearing practices may lead to beliefs in one's own personal inadequacy, to the possession of deferential tendencies, and to the handicap of a constricted imagination, among other regressive political mechanisms. In primary school blue-collar youngsters show a greater deference toward political leadership and a lesser sense that political choices are theirs to make—that *their* judgments are worth acting upon—than do upper-status children.[12] One recent study has found that citizenship education in secondary schools actually trains blue-collar youngsters to be docile political followers. Civic education courses of this variety leave blue-collar pupils oblivious to opportunities for political participation and possibly even leadership.[13]

In explaining blue-collar political apathy, the high correlation between blue-collar status and the notion of anomie, or utter hopelessness, demoralization, and discouragement, should be noted.[14] Relevant as well is the primitive nature of blue-collar life, with its almost overwhelming personal hardships, its sense of obligations without end, obligations that leave no time or energy for anything else.[15] Also playing a part in the creation of apathy is a host of disheartening political and mechanical barriers to voting, including red-tape registration and residence requirements, ancient literacy tests, and long lines on (workday) elections.[16] Snobbishness and intrigue in middle-class-dominated local political clubs has a similarly discouraging impact.[17]

In short, it is not surprising that some blue-collarites stay home on Election Day; it *is* surprising that so many more come out to vote.

VOTING CORRELATIONS

Why do the blue-collarites who vote vote as they do? What sorts of things explain their political behavior?

1. As is true outside of blue-collar ranks, childhood socialization patterns are perhaps the critical variable in understanding adult political preferences. Blue-collarites learn their politics in the homes of their fathers and tend to remain politically faithful thereafter (as do also two-thirds to three-quarters of the general population).[18]

Inclined as many workers are to socialize only with very similar workmates, neighbors, and relatives, the worker's inherited political views are reinforced by contact with like-minded others. He is likely to expose himself primarily to the propaganda of the party he already identifies with, and prefers political discussions that consist most often of the exchange of mutually agreeable remarks rather than real differences of opinion. In the first instance, then, much of the political behavior of blue-collarites can be explained as both socially inherited and habitual.

2. Blue-collar religion is clearly a most significant variable. Large numbers of Roman Catholics in blue-collar ranks, for

example, have long employed the Democratic party as the principal vehicle for Catholic expression and recognition in politics. Similarly, the religious zeal of many blue-collarites, particularly as expressed in the more fundamentalist branches of Protestantism, has served as an alternative to the development of working-class political radicalism.

3. Blue-collar ethnicity ranks as a variable of considerable explanatory power. Ethnic minority-group members, particularly blue-collarites who retain old-country ties and look backward, vote "flag ties" with impressive regularity. In addition to seeking the election of a Polish, Italian, or otherwise ethnically identified "neighborhood boy" to city government, blue-collar voters may follow the advice of foreign-language newspapers, radio shows, and fraternal organizations in choosing among state and national candidates and issues.

Americans, in short, blue-collarites and others, bring to the polls their special backgrounds and vote for those candidates congenial to their religious ties and national origins. Indeed, one investigator concludes: "The proposition that the ethnic factor is second only to the economic factor in influencing an American's vote is unlikely to be overthrown in the near future." [19]

4. Finally, blue-collar "parapsychology" plays a generally overlooked role. Personality analysis, rather than program analysis, has special appeal to the blue-collar voter. Few appear to decide their vote on the basis of a candidate's stand on issues of a programmatic kind or on such factual standards as past performance, known associates, or professional repute. Rather, blue-collarites have a propensity to personalize this matter like so many others: Visceral responses, "gut reactions," or emotional and instinctual feelings are heavily relied upon.

Here, even more than in religious or ethnic matters, working-class clannishness and hostility toward outsiders come into play. In a magical, mystical, and parapsychological manner the vote-seeking candidate is appraised in terms of his "inner" character, his private stance.

Suspicion permeates the process: It is assumed that the vote seeker is out for personal gain, accepts payoffs (to obstruct social gains), and profits handsomely from his dealings. It is also assumed that politics is intrinsically and inevitably corrupt and that few politicians can resist temptation. The burden of proving otherwise rests with the prejudged candidate: "Something about his eyes," "looks icky and talks funny," "too polished," or "smug—looks crooked" will often explain a manual worker's vote, even as will such rarer positive judgments as "looks like he will try," "always had a smile and handshake," and "spoke with his heart and not his mouth."

Parapsychology and guesswork of this sort help to explain what little volatility there remains in blue-collar politics.

AUTHORITARIANISM AND RACE PREJUDICE: POLITICAL PREDISPOSITION

Coursing through blue-collar politics are two critical value constellations that interplay with the worker's Democratic voting habit and his background, religious, ethnic, and parapsychological affinities. These two value complexes, authoritarianism and race prejudice, are by no means confined to blue-collarites. Nevertheless, few other tendencies are as revealing of blue-collar ballot-box behavior.

Authoritarianism. "Working-class authoritarianism" goes far to explain the rigid and intolerant approach many blue-collarites take to American political affairs.[20]

Unable to understand how politics works, and contemptuous of conciliation and compromise, working-class authoritarians seek to impose on society some sort of "fundamental truth" that will liberate America from its soft-headed illusions. Championed is the tough-minded, old-fashioned "horse sense" of people who might know little of political complexities, but can "smell a Commie a mile away." America must and will be protected from conspiracy; patriotism, virtue, and morality must again take their rightful place as cardinal American values.

Important here is recognition of the fact that many blue-collarites are frightened today both by the vagueness of what is being allowed, and by the inadequacies they note in the control systems of family life, police justice, and the like. Many fear that the simple virtues are being threatened, that Americans are being administered and manipulated out of their common-sense, conventional, and time-honored way of life. These blue-collarites would trade off particular rights and freedoms for the chance to rebuild America in the conservative workingman's image.

Blue-collarites of this persuasion believe that democracy begins and ends with one's freedom to do what the majority thinks is right. Understandably, these workingmen are less than enthusiastic about the application of the ideals of freedom and equality to all men. These blue-collarites, by virtue of a different training and a different organization of interests, and not for any lack of personal virtue, have little affection for grand libertarian ideals in their universal forms (all men may be equal, but advocates of antimilitarism, draft avoidance, Black Power, Student Power, and Woman Power are clearly less equal).

Not surprisingly, working-class authoritarianism has a wide impact on the political scene. It is evident, for example, in blue-collar ballot-box opposition to legislation advancing civil rights and civil liberties. It is also apparent in opposition to the fluoridation of public water systems and to the modernization of local school systems. It has had a part in public opposition to the lifting of censorship on "smutty" books and movies and, at the national level, to maintenance of foreign aid programs and to continued United States membership in the U.N.[21] Indeed, in foreign policy, many blue-collar authoritarians call for preemptive first strikes, bombing Communist China, and so forth.

In the 1950s a blue-collar intolerance was starkly apparent in the fervid, evangelical anticommunism that underwrote Congressional investigations, security dismissals, and the creation of the Attorney General's list of politically deviant organizations. In the mid-1960s it played a part in national reluctance to reward the "lazy and immoral" poor, particularly the black poor, with an adequate antipoverty program. It has also been prominent in the fears of some that a subversive Warren-Fortas Supreme Court was "coddling criminals" and undermining the nation. More recently it has played a significant role in the defeat of local referendums against the war in Vietnam, in the defeat of peace-and-welfare candidates to the political party conventions, and in the violence directed at peace paraders by longshoremen, seamen, teamsters, and other unionists in New York, San Francisco, and elsewhere.[22]

S. M. Lipset traces the source of blue-collar intolerance both to structural and to related personality matters.[23] Workers are thought to be more authoritarian than members of the middle classes because they come from more authoritarian family backgrounds and have less education and more economic insecurity. Many are likely as impressionable children to have been exposed to a lack of love, to punishment, and to a general atmosphere of tension and aggression since early childhood. Experiences that follow from such conditions often produce deep-rooted hostilities that can and do find expression in political intolerance (and racial prejudice). The worker's general lack of sophistication and his psychic insecurity are viewed as significant intervening variables between personality and politics:

> The less sophisticated and stable an individual, the more likely he is to favor a simplified and demonological view of politics, to fail to understand the rationale underlying the tolerance of those with whom he disagrees, and to find difficulty in grasping or tolerating a gradualist image of political change.[24]

Acceptance of the norms of democracy, Lipset contends, requires a high level of sophistication and ego security—both qualities conspicuous by their relative absence from the blue-collar community.

Considerable controversy marks the "working-class authoritarianism" thesis. Critics insist it is a distortion of the grossest form to explain political behavior by pointing to psychological origins or to individual symptoms. Instead, they seek to reestablish the independence of political behavior by demonstrating that rationality is a factor in voting behavior independent of the psychological and sociological.[25] Other critics take still a different tack, claiming that workers are simply being maligned and misjudged. Their punitiveness and concreteness allegedly offend ethnocentric middle-class social scientists who move in turn to punish the working class with pejorative labels.[26] Certain critics turn the Lipset thesis on its head, and contend that there are overlooked elements of blue-collar life that actually encourage a democratic, rather than an authoritarian, personality. Workers, it is argued, do not constitute a solidary body. Like every social group, the blue-collar bloc has members at its center (democratic types), and members at its periphery (authoritarians). The central tendency here is allegedly democratic, and, in its internal variation, the blue-collar bloc differs little from any white-collar bloc.[27] Finally, aroused by the far-reaching ideological implications of the material, one critic locates authoritarianism in Lipset himself, rather than in the blue-collar worker.[28]

Recently, much of blue-collar authoritarianism has been traced to the impact that conservative rural origins have on certain workers.[29] If this is the case, a steady decline in an influx of rural migrants to the ranks of white blue-collarites might significantly reduce authoritarianism. Similarly, blue-collar/white-collar differences in the matter have been traced primarily to differences in educational attainment.[30] If this be so, a slow and steady increase in blue-collar schooling might help scale back authoritarianism even as it further reduces the gap that may now separate the classes in this matter.

Somewhat more likely, however, is the steady persistence of components of blue-collar authoritarianism into the foreseeable future.

In the first place, support for this political style is available in growing resentment over loss in status by men whose self-esteem depends in large part on a sense of superiority. For example, certain blue-collarites fear that "lower-class" Negroes are catching up with them. Others resent the stress now placed on attaining a college education, a lure that tempts a growing number of their sons to draw away from them. And still others, displaced by new methods and machinery, find it hard to keep their self-regard from wavering. All three kinds of experience leave blue-collarites ever more open to authoritarian appeals, with their promise of emotional identity and support.[31]

In the second place, the structural sources of this political predisposition are substantial and they are unlikely soon to change.[32] Government will long seem distant and impersonal to some, the decision makers "foreign" and out of touch to others, and various social and cultural "happenings" immoral and threatening (and tempting). Accordingly, a reaction of distrust, intolerance, and hostility probably will long characterize the blue-collar political scene. To hate what one does not understand—and fears—can be a deep-rooted and most persistent matter.

Race Prejudice. Much of the blue-collar record in political matters reflects the apparent race prejudice of many Caucasian workers. Blue-collarites, for example, are disproportionately represented among the so-called white-backlash voters. Many are responsive to the political advice of the various Klan organizations and are heavily numbered among the racist backers of George Wallace and other segregationist politicians. Blue-collar votes have played a prominent part in the local defeat of various Northern Fair Housing referendums. Indeed, passing beyond the boundaries of law and order, blue-collarites have dominated the lists of men indicted for the beatings and political murders of civil rights advocates in the South.[33]

Some social scientists argue that the idea of pure racism is an oversimplification, and thereby an inadequate explanation of the blue-collar record.[34] More salient in the matter may be the status quo bias, the economic anxieties, and the element of envy characteristic of race relations where blue-collarites are involved.

As first suggested in Chapter 7, "Blue-Collar Neighborhoods," some of the seemingly racist behavior of blue-collarites may primarily revolve about a defense of the familiar, the secure, and the comfortable. For example, blue-collarites helped defeat New York City's Police Civilian Review Board in 1968, and were bitterly criticized thereafter for anti-Negro bigotry. Some observers have pointed out, however, that workers in this instance were not especially opposed to the Negro or his goals. Rather, many blue-collarites voted against a perceived attack on the community status quo and in favor of the established way of doing things. Race relations and civil rights became involved only insofar as they represented a threat of unsettling change.[35]

There is also reason to believe that some of the seemingly racist behavior of blue-collarites may actually disguise forms of social competition. For example, psychiatrist Robert Coles links white hostility in this matter to economic uncertainties and political envy. These in turn he traces to structural forces that victimize the blue-collar bigot—and make him as much a victim as the Negro. Many of the Caucasian blue-collarites in Coles' study are not only afraid of the Negro. Barely making a go of it themselves, these working-class whites live in constant fear of a depression they or their parents remember all too well. The Negro, Coles suggests, reminds such anxious whites of their own marginal and precarious social and economic condition.[36]

Perhaps even more significant, many of the small number of whites that Coles has studied intensively have come to envy the Negro's recent political successes. While these same whites vaguely seek answers to their own political and economic problems, they differ from many Negroes in not feeling driven to do so. They are also unwilling to act in a concerted and dramatic way—as they imagine the Negroes they envy are doing (Herbert Gans suggests that particular elements of blue-collar culture militate against joint activities and "this, perhaps, is the peer group society's most serious weakness").[37] Harboring an old-world or ethnic suspicion of authority, blue-collarites hesitate to bring government into their lives and resent the successes that such action seems to bring to Negroes.

Finally, blue-collarites have an additional propensity in this matter: Many are racists in reaction to their own envy of a hedonistic, idyllic, and sexually exhilarating life that they fantasize as characteristic of "devil-may-care" naturalistic Negroes.

Given this complex of motives and meanings it is not difficult to understand why the so-called white backlash continues to command disproportionate blue-collar support. Speculation even includes the possibility of white blue-collarites soon judging the Republican party the whiter of the two, and urging the G.O.P. to move against the blacks. Without doubt there is much antagonism and some political volatility: More likely, however, is public grumbling to this effect, but private voting in the thirty-six-year tradition of blue-collar support for the Democratic party (as with vast blue-collar switching in 1968 from Wallace to Humphrey). The welfare state is the creation of the Democratic party, and the bane of the Republicans. Workers know this, respect the difference, and generally vote accordingly rather than in terms of racial issues.

There *is* reason to fear that the gulf between white blue-collarites and Negro Americans is widening. But there is nothing inevitable about this. Coles, for one, points out that "there is nothing in the minds of *any* group of Americans that necessarily compels our present [race] problems to continue." [38] The possibility always remains that substantial alterations in the structural foundations of race prejudice could stem blue-collar antagonism, bolster the positive aspects of contemporary blue-collar race relations, and significantly alter the character of blue-collar politics. While presently only a small possibility, it should not be overlooked.

LABOR AND CLASS IDENTIFICATION

Organized labor is far less successful in guiding the votes of 16 million unionists and their 24 million dependents than is often alleged by business and conservative critics. As pointed out in Chapter 6, "Blue-Collar Unionists," labor does not seem to command strong political allegiance from its increasingly youthful post-New Deal membership.

Labor can get more workers out to vote for their own Democratic party favorites than would otherwise be true without the unions. Labor can reinforce party appeals and activate what little role social class plays in blue-collar politics. But labor cannot meet the stern test of independent leadership: It cannot effectively swing this same bloc of union voters to the Republican party, or to a third party. Blue-collarites remain headstrong and independent in this matter.

Labor is particularly limited in the kinds of issues for which it can rouse support. Thus a congressional aide comments: "The average union member doesn't give a damn about 14B [the controversial right-to-work section of the Taft-Hartley Act]. He's concerned about taxes, and neighborhood schools, and grocery prices, and the size of his paycheck." [39] Only in those rare cases in which labor can link its political efforts to "wages, hours, and working conditions," rather than to espousal of "reform" or "liberal government" or "friends of labor," is there clear-cut rank-and-file response. Accordingly, there appears to be little or no broad political movement within the labor movement. There has always been more myth than truth in talk of labor's monolithic political power; this is becoming ever more apparent.

A similar conclusion holds with respect to the controversial matter of class identification and blue-collar voting. Analysis of this relationship poses three questions: Do workers vote as they do because they identify themselves as members of the working class and seek through political action to enhance their economic interests? Are workers competing with other social classes for political control of the allocation process? And is there a united "working class," that is, a self-conscious group striving toward recognized goals? A qualified no appears to be in order in response to all three questions, to judge at least from the contemporary political attitudes and behavior of white male blue-collarites.

Manual workers are discouraged from class-conscious politics by self-satisfaction, acceptance of the status quo, and substitution of consumption rivalry for class conflict. More specifically, large numbers of workers take pride in being mark-

edly better off than their fathers and in faring well economically with respect to their own expectations. These men remain
positively oriented toward the society, its government, and its
class system. Where fault-finding becomes necessary, blue-
collarites are as likely as not to employ an individualistic
ideology to deflect blame from society to themselves or to fate:
Few, outside of working-class authoritarians, project blame
upon the government or the other social classes. Exposed endlessly to pressures to consume, many blue-collarites also channel whatever social dissatisfaction they feel into intraclass consumption rivalry rather than interclass resentment and conflict:
"The Great American Medicine Show creates consumer unrest,
working wives, and dual jobholding, not antagonism toward
the owning-classes." [40]

Moreover, blue-collarites are further discouraged from class-
conscious politics by the underrecognized presence in their
ranks of two types of mobile individuals, those "displaced"
workers skidding down from above, and those Horatio Alger
types aspiring up and out. Perhaps 10 percent of all urban
workers are "skidders," blue-collarites who either were raised
in white-collar families or were once possessors of white-collar
work. These men often remain optimistic about their chances
to recoup status losses; as such they function to reduce working-class solidarity and social criticism from below.[41] Similarly,
as several studies have brought out, upward mobility results
in political conservatism for the majority of achievers.[42] Blue-
collarites who are busy making their way up and out of the
ranks attenuate ties among blue-collar peers, and in other ways
undermine class cohesiveness.

There is good reason, then, to doubt the existence of a blue-
collar bloc vote, a conscious product of class identity and
solidarity. As S. M. Miller and Frank Riessman comment:

> . . . an awareness of class differences exists but it is not tradi-
> tional class-consciousness. The recognition of class differences is
> not tied to any specific political ideology or platform and most
> often is implicit (bring a group of college students to an auto
> plant, and the awareness of class differences on both sides will

electrify the air). Workers with a strong "class-awareness" can be quite conservative or uninterested in politics. . . .[43]

In short, America's creed of classlessness, if not an altogether objective sociological fact, nevertheless effectively diminishes the impetus to class conflict and politics: "There is no class struggle here. Instead, we find a much more complicated fluid accommodation among shifting coalitions of interest groups." [44]

This is not to embrace the theory of a classless America; it is rather to challenge the notion that ascribes self-consciousness and related militancy to a bloc of Americans nowhere so constituted. "Class" in America undoubtedly continues to apportion "a man's share of justice, health, culture, education, and ordinary respect—as any visit to a jail, an emergency room, a theatre, a college or a municipal bureau will illustrate. And class perpetuates itself." [45] But class does not dominate blue-collar politics. It is far less salient than often alleged and is far more subtle than often imagined. To project by inference a "political class" from an occupational category is finally to assume a continuity and correspondence simply not warranted by the facts.

SUMMARY

If historians still exist fifty years from now, muses sociologist Barrington Moore, Jr., one of them might conceivably select as a dominant feature of our times this political trend: "By the 1960's advanced capitalist society had succeeded, with the help of a prolonged war boom, in absorbing and neutralizing its own industrial proletariat, never in any case a really serious revolutionary threat." [46] Much of the analysis in this chapter runs in a similar vein: Whatever volatility may have once marked blue-collar politics has long since left it. As stressed above, the white male worker is early influenced to choose a style of political accommodation, and with the small exception of a few extremists, he grips it very tightly thereafter.

Notes to Chapter Twelve

1. John Ciardi, "Manner of Speaking: Aphorisms and Doodles," *Saturday Review* (May 21, 1966), p. 8.

2. The first quote is from Anon., "Johnson Pleased by a Philosopher," *The New York Times,* October 7, 1967, p. 32; the second quote is from Eric Hoffer, *The Temper of Our Time* (New York: Harper & Row, 1966), p. 91. See also Eve Hoffer, *Working and Thinking on the Waterfront* (New York: Harper & Row, 1969).

3. As quoted in Jim Hampton, "The Odds Say Eric Hoffer Cannot Be: An Uncommon Spokesman," *National Observer,* December 11, 1967, p. 12. See in this connection, James M. Perry, *The New Politics: The Expanding Technology of Political Manipulation* (New York: Potter, 1968).

4. Jack Newfield, "Idealist Without Illusions," *The New York Times Book Review,* February 26, 1967, p. 3. See also Lloyd A. Free and Hadley Cantril, *The Political Beliefs of Americans* (New Brunswick, N.J.: Rutgers University Press, 1968).

5. Hampton, *op. cit.*

6. *Ibid.* See also Peter Collier, "Eric Hoffer: The Wizard of Was," *Ramparts* (December 1967), pp. 65–68. ". . . he is like a ghost come from another time, a time of Mail Pouch signs lettered on red barns, of early *Saturday Evening Post* covers and WPA art murals" (p. 68). Cf. Calvin Tompkins, *Eric Hoffer: An American Odyssey* (New York: Dutton, 1968).

7. See in this connection, V. O. Key, Jr., *The Responsible Electorate: Rationality in Presidential Voting, 1936–1960* (Cambridge, Mass.: Harvard University Press, 1966). See also Heinz Eulan, *Class and Party in the Eisenhower Years: Class Roles and Perspectives in the 1952 and 1956 Elections* (New York: Free Press, 1962).

8. Bernard R. Berelson, *et al.*, *Voting* (Chicago: University of Chicago Press, 1954), p. 333; Paul F. Lazarsfeld, *et al.*, *The People's Choice* (New York: Columbia University Press, 1948), p. 20.

9. Gallup Poll, "Poll Finds G.O.P. Stays at 27% Despite Sharp Attacks on Administration in Last 6 Months," *The New York Times,* June 30, 1968, p. 39. See also Robert R. Alford, "The Role of Social Class in American Voting Behavior," *The Western Political Quarterly* (March 1963), pp. 180–194.

10. Harold L. Wilensky and Hugh Edwards, "The Skidder:

Ideological Adjustments of Downward Mobile Workers," *American Sociological Review* (April 1959), pp. 215–231; Robert Blauner, *Alienation and Freedom: The Factory Worker and His Industry* (Chicago: University of Chicago Press, 1964); Raymond J. Murphy and Richard T. Morris, "Occupational Situs, Subjective Class Identification, and Political Affiliation," *American Sociological Review* (June 1961), pp. 383–392.

11. Norval D. Glenn and Jon P. Olston, "Rural-Urban Differences in Reported Attitudes and Behavior," *The Southwestern Social Science Quarterly* (March 1967), pp. 381–400; Gerhard Lenski, *The Religious Factor* (Garden City, N.Y.: Doubleday, 1961).

12. Fred I. Greenstein, *Children and Politics* (New Haven: Yale University Press, 1965), pp. 85–106, 162. See also Robert D. Hess and Judith V. Torney, *The Development of Political Attitudes in Children* (Chicago: Aldine, 1968).

13. Edgar Litt, "Civic Education, Community Norms, and Political Indoctrination," *American Sociological Review* (February 1963), pp. 69–75.

14. Dorothy L. Meier and Wendell Bell, "Anomie and the Achievement of Life Goals," *American Sociological Review* (April 1959), pp. 189–202; Richard L. Simpson and H. Max Miller, "Social Status and Anomie," *Social Problems* (Winter 1963), pp. 256–264.

15. See in this connection, Robert Coles, "Is Prejudice Against Negroes Overrated?" *Trans-Action* (October 1966), p. 45; Lester W. Milbrath, *Political Participation: How and Why Do People Get Involved in Politics?* (Chicago: Rand McNally, 1965).

16. President's Commission on Registration and Voting Participation, *Report on Registration and Voting Participation* (Washington, D.C.: Government Printing Office, 1963); Richard M. Scammon, "Why One Third of Us Don't Vote," *The New York Times Magazine,* November 17, 1963.

17. See in this connection, James Q. Wilson, *The Amateur Democrat: Club Politics in Three Cities* (Chicago: University of Chicago Press, 1962), p. 271, *passim.*

18. Seymour Martin Lipset, *et al., Union Democracy: The Inside Politics of the International Typographical Union* (Glencoe, Ill.: Free Press, 1956), p. 330. See also in this connection Robert H. Salisbury, "The Urban Party Organization Member," *Public Opinion Quarterly* (Winter 1965–1966), pp. 563–564, *passim.*

19. Moses Rischin, *"Our Own Kind:" Voting by Race, Creed, or*

National Origin (Santa Barbara: Center for the Study of Democratic Institutions, 1960), p. 38. See also Juris Veidemanis, "Sociological Deficiencies and Opportunities in the Study of Hyphenated Americans," unpublished paper read at the 1965 Meeting of the American Sociological Association, Chicago, Illinois; Robert A. Skedgell, "How Computers Pick an Election Winner," *Trans-Action* (November 1966), pp. 41–46.

20. Not at issue here, it cannot be stressed early enough, is the interest of certain blue-collarites, often better-educated craft and service workers, in conservative political philosophy. Rather, working-class authoritarianism entails a distinct core of ideas and attitudes whose central meaning and purpose is subversive of the major tenets of true conservatism: A distinction must be made between William Buckley and Robert Welch. See in this connection Tom Buckley, "When Good Birchers Get Together," *The New York Times Magazine,* June 5, 1966.

21. William A. Gamson, "The Fluoridation Dialogue: Is It an Ideological Conflict?" *Public Opinion Quarterly* (Winter 1961), pp. 526–537; Dwight G. Dean, "Alienation and Negative Voting on a School Levy," unpublished paper read at the 1966 Meeting of the American Sociological Association, Miami Beach, Florida; John E. Horton and Wayne E. Thompson, "Powerlessness and Political Negativism: A Study of Defeated Local Referendums," *American Journal of Sociology* (March 1962), pp. 485–495.

22. Victoria Bonnell and Chester Hartman, "Cambridge Votes on the Vietnam War," *Dissent* (March–April 1968), pp. 103–106; Joe Flaherty, "The Hawks in May: A Day to Remember," *The Village Voice,* May 18, 1967.

23. Seymour Martin Lipset, "Democracy and Working-Class Authoritarianism," *American Sociological Review* (August 1959), pp. 482–501. See also "Isolated Workers," in William Kornhauser, *The Politics of Mass Society* (New York: The Free Press, 1959), pp. 212–223, *passim;* Pete Hamill, "The Revolt of the White Lower Middle Class," *New York* (April 14, 1969), pp. 24–29.

24. Lipset, "Democracy and Working-Class Authoritarianism," *op. cit.,* p. 492.

25. John H. Bunzel, *Anti-Politics in America: Reflections on the Anti-Political Temper and Its Distortions of the Democratic Process* (New York: Knopf, 1967), p. 217, *passim.* See also Michael P. Rogin, *The Intellectuals and McCarthy: The Radical Specter* (Boston: Massachusetts Institute of Technology Press, 1968).

26. Lewis Lipsitz, "Working-Class Authoritarianism: A Re-Evaluation," *American Sociological Review* (February 1965), pp. 103–109.

27. S. M. Miller and Frank Riessman, " 'Working-Class Authoritarianism': A Critique of Lipset," *British Journal of Sociology* (Fall 1961), pp. 263–276. See also Robert Wenkert, "Reply," *Berkeley Journal of Sociology* (Spring 1961), pp. 109–112.

28. On Lipset's "errors," see Sidney M. Peck, "Ideology and 'Political Sociology': The Conservative Bias of Lipset's 'Political Man,'" *The American Catholic Sociological Review* (Summer 1962), pp. 128–155.

29. John C. Leggett, "Uprootedness and Working-Class Consciousness," *American Journal of Sociology* (May 1963), pp. 682–692; Glenn and Olston, *op. cit.*

30. Lipsitz, *op. cit.* See also Robert Sokol, "Power Orientation and McCarthyism," *American Journal of Sociology* (January 1968), pp. 443–452.

31. Ira S. Rohter, "The Righteous Rightists," *Trans-Action* (May 1968), pp. 27–35. See also B. R. Epstein and A. Foster, *The Radical Right: Report on the John Birch Society and Its Allies* (New York: Random House, 1967); Gabriel Fackre, "The Blue Collar White and the Far Right," *The Christian Century* (May 7, 1969), pp. 645–648. See also A. Shostak, "The 'Forgotten Man' and the Institutions of Government" in *Report to the President of the National Commission on the Causes of Crime and Violence* (Washington, D.C.: Government Printing Office, 1969).

32. See in this connection, John H. Redekop, *The American Far Right* (Grand Rapids: Eerdmans, 1968); George C. Thayer, *The Farther Shores of Politics: The American Political Fringe Today* (New York: Simon and Schuster, 1968); Murray B. Levin, *The Alienated Voter: Politics in Boston* (New York: Holt, Rinehart and Winston, 1962); Robert E. Lane, *Political Ideology* (New York: The Free Press, 1962).

33. Jeffrey K. Hadden, *et al.*, "The Making of the Negro Mayors, 1967," *Trans-Action* (January/February 1968), pp. 21–30; Alex Garber, "The Matter with California," *Dissent* (March–April 1968), pp. 106–109; J. Michael Ross, *et al.*, "Negro Neighbors—Banned in Boston," *Trans-Action* (September/October 1966), pp. 13–16; Reverend Andrew Greeley, *Why Can't They Be Like Us?* (New York: American Jewish Committee, 1969). All four of the men indicted for the murder of Viola Liuzzo, and eleven of the

eighteen men indicted in the murders of Goodman, Schwerner, and Chaney, were blue-collar manual or service workers.

34. Bruno Bettelheim and Morris Janowitz, *Social Change and Prejudice* (New York: Free Press, 1964 ed.), p. 21, *passim*.

35. A provocative analysis is available in Milton Himmelfarb, "Are Jews Still Liberals?," *Commentary* (April 1967), pp. 67–72. See also William Cook, "Policemen in Society: Which Side Are They On?," *Berkeley Journal of Sociology* (Summer 1967), pp. 117–129; William M. Turner, *The Police Establishment* (New York: Putnam's Sons, 1968).

36. See, for example, a case study of Paul, a radio repairman, in Robert Coles, *Children of Crisis: A Study of Courage and Fear* (Boston: Atlantic-Little, Brown, 1967). See also John C. Leggett, *Class, Race, and Labor: Working-Class Consciousness in Detroit* (New York: Oxford University Press, 1968).

37. Herbert J. Gans, *The Urban Villagers: Group and Class in the Life of Italian-Americans* (New York: Free Press, 1962), p. 89.

38. Coles, "Is Prejudice Against Negroes Overrated?" *op. cit.* On complexities in the "White Backlash," and for a plan for less "reconstructionist righteousness," see William Lee Miller, "Analysis of the 'White Backlash,'" *The New York Times Magazine*, August 23, 1964.

39. Jim Hampton, "No Such Thing as a Deliverable Union Vote," *National Observer*, June 3, 1968, p. 6. See also J. Michael Eisner, "Implications for 1968: An Analysis of Labor's Recent Disaster at the Polls," *Business and Society* (Spring 1967), p. 8.

40. Lane, *op. cit.*, p. 80, *passim*.

41. Harold Wilensky and Hugh Edwards, "The Skidder: Ideological Adjustments of Downward Mobile Workers," *American Sociological Review* (April 1959), pp. 215–231.

42. See, for example, Joseph Lopreato, "Upward Social Mobility and Political Orientation," *American Sociological Review* (August 1967), p. 587.

43. S. M. Miller and Frank Riessman, "Are Workers Middle Class?" *Dissent* (Autumn 1961), p. 516.

44. Harold L. Wilensky, "Class, Class Consciousness, and American Workers," in William Haber (ed.), *Labor in a Changing America* (New York: Basic Books, 1966), p. 44. See also Norbert Wiley, "America's Unique Class Politics: The Interplay of the Labor, Credit, and Commodity Markets," *American Sociological Review* (August 1967), pp. 529–540.

45. Todd Gitlin, "Power and the Myth of Progress," *New Republic* (December 25, 1965), p. 20.

46. Barrington Moore, Jr., "In the Life," *The New York Review of Books* (June 15, 1967), p. 3.

13

BLUE-COLLAR HEALTH
AND ILLNESS

We are involved in nothing less than distributing the chances for physical and mental well-being on the morally invidious basis of economic class.

—RICHARD LICHTMAN

Fundamental issues with which this volume is concerned are covered by the questions, Is our working class as well off as the envious believe? By what standards? And what sort of problems and disappointments are especially its own? The subject of the physical and mental health and illness of the nation's blue-collarites and their dependents especially lends itself to these questions. Accordingly, discussion below focuses on the prevention of illness, coverage of the ill, treatment of illness, and the value direction of the entire treatment process.

PHYSICAL HEALTH

The nation's 21 million Caucasian male blue-collarites and their dependents have a very poor health record, one that has its source both in characteristic blue-collar ways and in conventional medical practices.

Research across social classes regularly finds blue-collarites handicapped by a lower degree of knowledge about disease, higher skepticism toward medical care, and greater dependency when ill than is true of white-collarites. Blue-collarites are much less likely than better-off Americans to engage in preventive medical behavior (inoculations, checkups), seek dental care, or have eye examinations. Thus two sociologists have commented:

> It is as though the white-collar class thinks of the body as a machine to be preserved and kept in perfect functioning condition . . . whereas blue-collar groups think of the body as having a limited span of utility: to be enjoyed in youth and then to suffer with and to endure stoically with age and decrepitude. It may be that a more damaged self-image makes more acceptable a more damaged physical adjustment.[1]

Whatever the mechanism, blue-collarites stand out as more likely than white-collarites to practice poor health habits (inadequate diet, excessive smoking, and the like).

Hardly surprising is the 1963 report that found chronic ailments highest among service workers, followed closely by blue-collar skilled and semiskilled workers, and, finally, at a distance, by white-collarites. Running a high risk of injury at work, blue-collarites experience longer hospital stays and higher-than-average rates of both short- and long-term disability.[2] Workers in 1963 spent an average of 4.4 days in bed because of illness conditions and underwent an additional 12.4 days of "restricted activity." [3] Provocative in this connection are data on health expenditures per person that reveal that in 1962 white-collar workers spent $169 apiece on the average for health costs; service workers (other than private household), $134; and blue-collar workers, $123 (skilled workers, $125; semiskilled, $107; unskilled, $104). Ironically, the greater the apparent need, the smaller the expenditure.[4]

ILLNESS AND ETHNICITY

More of the explanation for blue-collar illness behavior is available in the fact of old-country or ethnic impact on such behavior. Sociologist Irving K. Zola reports, for example, that blue-collar Irish patients in a large Boston study tended to abdicate responsibility for going to a doctor, and waited until they were "told" to go. Contrariwise, Italian-American blue-collarites did not wait to be told, but sought aid only after their illness symptoms had been linked by them to a new interpersonal crisis or had come to threaten valued social activities (for example, when bursitis interferes with bocce or bowling scores). The Irish-American "delayers" or "nonparticipators" had not been taught specifically to ask others for medical advice before seeing a physician, but their old-country culture had taught them a general deference of judgment to elders in important (and particularly anxiety-provoking) decisions.

Ethnicity not only affects the vital matter of the timing of medical aid-seeking, but it also influences what illnesses are spotlighted and from whom aid is sought. According to Zola, the stiff-lipped Irish blue-collarites in his study expressed their symptoms in terms of a specific location or malfunction, while the more emotional Italian-American workers emphasized complaints of a more diffuse and general malfunctioning.[5] Other related research suggests that the greater the membership in a blue-collar ethnic subculture (closely knit, dependent, traditionalistic groups), the greater the reluctance to seek early medical aid and the greater the suspicion of medical aid sources.[6]

In tracing the health-shaping implications of Irish and Italian ethnic attitudes toward seeking aid and reporting symptoms, Zola suggests that Italian overinvolvement with physical symptoms might lead in a costly way to their complaints being "overdiagnosed" as psychological problems. The nature of the Irish blue-collarite's delayed decision to seek aid is linked by Zola to the worker's great fear of doctors and to his hazardous propensity prematurely to terminate medical treatment. Ethnicity, in short, has considerable influence inside the current blue-collar medical scene.

DOCTORS AND CHIROPRACTORS

Generally speaking, blue-collar attitudes toward physicians are a mixture of antagonism and respect. Gossip on the workshop floor frequently turns to angry review of conventional or "breakthrough" treatment that proved "unsuccessful" or of operations that are suspected of having been unnecessary. Anecdotes from personal experience, hearsay, or the mass media (such as television dramas) are employed to make the point that doctors are profit-seeking businessmen, quite capable of error, but more successful than most in disguising greed and culpability. Labor press coverage of Medicare problems blamed on "greedy physicians" also fans worker resentment, as do union warnings that the government seems more inclined to pass Medicare cost increases on to patients than to adopt a control system aimed at profiteering doctors.

Respect, however, coexists with antagonism and serves to mitigate the latter. Blue-collarites remain impressed with the long and arduous years of schooling involved, the extraordinary work hours entailed, the life-and-death responsibilities undertaken, and the considerable affluence thought to be the province of most successful physicians. Blue-collarites, for all of their uneven gains in lay sophistication in medical matters, remain passive and pliable as patients, and trusting and appreciative in treatment. They are antagonistic as they see doctors as only human and are respectful as they perceive them as superhuman.

Indeed, of major concern to many blue-collarites is the decline in number of the "old family doctors" (down from 72 percent of all doctors in 1931 to 36 percent in 1961).[7] While there was more myth than reality in the notion of the steadfast old gentleman who healed in your home by his understanding more than his skill, a man who somehow intuited when (if ever) to send his modest bill, the family physician nevertheless offered much that complemented the worker's high valuation of personableness, pragmatism, and professionalism. Blue-collarites are impressed, but also confused, by the impersonal team of specialists now steadily replacing the solo general practitioner who in turn replaced the old family doctor. Medical practice seems ever to draw the (group-insured) blue-collarite into the "cold" and "foreign" hospital—with its factory-like procedures and its omnipresent encroachment on the patient's individuality. At least some members of the older generation among the blue-collarites think on occasion with nostalgia of an earlier era in doctor-patient relations and the locus of treatment.

A growing number of manual workers and their families are seeking a substitute for the disappearing medical doctor in a new and unusually personable medical type, the chiropractor. Treatment by a chiropractor is generally less expensive than that available from the few remaining family doctors, and it is often more readily available in blue-collar neighborhoods. Chiropractic medicine, moreover, has the appeal of appearing clean-cut and certain in diagnosis (all illness is traced to irritation of a spinal nerve root), simple and direct in treatment (no drugs or surgery are employed), and speedy and sure in results (the patient may return to work quickly). Healing is by manual "adjustment" of the spine, supplemented by massage, and by advice as to diet and rest, the latter defined as proper amounts of sleep, not as taking to one's bed. In background, education, and social class origins, successful chiropractors tend to resemble their blue-collar patients and therefore may achieve much empathy with them.[8]

Chiropractic medicine, in short, provides an especially good fit with several aspects of the general blue-collar style. Consuming less money, time, incapacitation, and thought than do the ministrations of a medical doctor, chiropractic medicine will likely grow ever more significant on the blue-collar scene.

QUALITY AND COST

Blue-collar attitudes toward American medical services mix begrudging admiration for innovative technical advances with exasperation or worse over uneven care and rising costs.

Uneven care, of course, is not confined to blue-collar ranks, but is a national scandal. Every review of the quality of medical care, one authority writes, "has found a high rate of unnecessary and incompetent surgery, of faulty and delayed diagnosis, of sins not only against medical science but against common sense." [9] Although the problem is commonplace, there is nevertheless little doubt that blue-collarites share disproportionately in poor medical treatment, laborers reliant as they are on overworked and underskilled clinic personnel, while more affluent blue-collarites are dependent on often fee-hungry private practitioners.

An especially disturbing report is the finding that the introduction in the early 1950s of union-management health insurance protection for coal miners resulted in "unnecessary" appendicitis operations in 75 percent of the insurance-paid cases.[10] More recently a 1962 union-sponsored study of the medical care experienced by New York City teamsters and dependents found that

45 percent of all cases hospitalized under union insurance plans received substandard care

18 percent of the cases did not warrant hospitalization at all

60 percent of the children hospitalized received less-than-optimal care

67 percent of nonsurgical cases received less-than-optimal care.

In an earlier 1959 study of a similar sample of 300 Teamster union families, 43 percent of the hysterectomies performed and 50 percent of the Caesarean sections were judged by medical reviewers to be "unnecessary." Overall, some 40 percent of the 1959 Teamster cases were thought to have received less-than-optimal care, the figure actually rising slightly in the 1962 study.[11]

Blue-collarites especially find rising medical costs a hardship. Medical costs nationally averaged about $104 per person in 1960, rose to $162 in 1966, and reached above $170 in 1967. While the cost of living rose 3½ percent in 1966, total medical care costs rose 8 percent. Hospital costs rose 17 percent to an average charge of about $45 a day in 1966, and up another 15 percent to $58 in 1967. Fees charged by doctors in 1966 rose nearly 8 percent, more than double the 1965 increase, and the biggest one-year rise in forty years; in 1967, the increase was 7 percent.[12]

Many workers are angered by the fact that their medical insurance never catches up with rising medical costs. A 1965 union-sponsored study found matching increases in surgeons' fees largely draining off union-negotiated insurance improvements, most bills for operations coming to nearly twice what the patient received from his union-management insurance policy. "When a covered employee was reimbursed $50 for a tonsillectomy and adenoidectomy, the average surgical charge was $74; and when the benefit went to $65, the average physician's charge rose to $85." [13] Ominous here is the prediction of a 1967 Presidential Study Group: If current medical practices continue, the average yearly medical expenses of an individual are likely to rise by more than 140 percent by 1975, hospital costs going up 250 percent, dental care 100 percent, drug prices 65 percent, and doctors' fees 160 percent, while the general cost of living is expected to increase only about 20 percent.[14]

UNION RESPONSE

As might be expected in view of these facts, blue-collarites as unionists have stood out in the general population in demanding more adequate health insurance protection. Vulnerability is thought to be the explanation here, blue-collarites perceiving a greater-than-average likelihood of incurring, and lesser likelihood of meeting, medical expense for and by themselves and others.

Accordingly, the latest government survey found in 1963 that 76 percent of all workers hospitalized during the year had hospital insurance, and 71 percent had surgical insurance.[15] Both figures probably are significantly higher at present, although one authority in the matter insists that "of the 70-odd percent [of our population which has health insurance] only about eight percent has really comprehensive coverage." [16] A second critic points out that while the plans cover about 70 percent of hospital costs they cover only 30 percent of a family's regular medical bills.[17]

Labor unions continue to press for additional blue-collar medical coverage gains. A government review of labor contract changes in health benefits between 1962 and 1966 located the following:

1. the gradual elimination of employee contributions as health plans become completely employer-financed

2. the addition of supplemental major medical insurance, prenatal and postnatal maternity benefits, dental and vision care, and coverage for out-of-hospital psychiatric treatment and posthospital care in nursing and convalescent homes

3. liberalization of the recuperation period covered by accident and sickness benefits, along with the schedule of allowances payable for hospital costs

Labor Department specialists in the matter suggest "the most striking change in existing benefits was the shift in a few plans from a schedule of cash allowances to payment of all 'reasonable and customary' charges for surgical procedures—the standard for payment under Medicare." [18] Through 1968 health benefits for employees have grown steadily more liberal under union prodding (the Rubber Workers, for example, pushed hospitalization benefit coverage up from one year to two, while the Steelworkers Union won provision of a year's stay in a nursing home beginning in 1970). [19]

Blue-collar unions have also been in the forefront of the effort to liberalize the terms of disability benefit laws, Workmen's Compensation laws, and relevant public health measures. [20] The 1965 Medicare Act, in particular, owes much to labor's lobbying efforts. It is safe to assume that the union press, in combination with the personal efforts of union officials, has ensured a high labor representation among the 4 millon elderly Americans who received Medicare help in meeting medical bills in the first year of the Act's operation. Many such retired unionists and their dependents were spared from receiving care as ward patients or as a matter of charity. Instead, in a fashion most vital to status-insecure blue-collarites, the new Medicare beneficiaries presumably enjoyed the dignity and freedom of choice that comes with the ability to pay (union specialists helped such retirees live with the various frustrations and delays that accompanied the Act's first-year complexities). Labor's twenty-year fight to win enactment of a Medicare program appears now as one of the signal labor political successes of the post-World War II era.

MENTAL HEALTH

Mounting research continues to suggest that blue-collarites suffer from poorer mental health than most other (nonfarm) segments of society. [21] Research findings also underline the fact that mental health differs among the skill blocs and declines perceptibly as one moves from the skilled to the semiskilled to the unskilled bloc. [22]

Mental illness among blue-collarites takes the general form

of some major behavioral anomaly, psychophysical difficulty, or community dislocation, such as a conflict with the law. In contrast, mental illness among the middle class manifests itself more often as a subjective malaise, such as a pervasive sense of depression. One social psychiatrist describes this class differential:

> . . . the Class V [lower-class] neurotic behaves badly, the Class IV [blue-collar] neurotic aches physically, the Class III [middle-class] patient defends fearfully, and the [well-off] patients in Classes I and II are dissatisfied with themselves. Thus, we have a motor pattern of community dislocation, a "body language" of pain and malfunction, social anxiety, and verbal symbolic dislocation, all called *neurotic*.[23]

Blue-collarites are more often diagnosed as suffering from forms of psychoses, rather than less-severe neuroses. As explained above, however, this is probably linked to the worker's practice of "acting-out" his disturbance, delaying the seeking of treatment, and attracting punitive police attention—rather than being caused by any inherent difference in class-linked ills.

Several features of blue-collar home life and marriage contribute heavily to the poor mental health record of the working class. These features include sex role stereotypes and rigidities, the isolation of family members from one another and from members of the opposite sex, the lack of self-understanding and emotional sophistication of family members, and the general stringency of life in the personal setting of most blue-collar homes. Blue-collar men have difficulty expressing their feelings and identify emotional self-expression with weakness and femininity. Sometimes they withdraw in the face of conflict into silence, drunkenness, and violence. The high divorce, separation, and marital instability rates in blue-collar marriages, as cited in Chapter 8, are relevant here, as is the discussion of the psychic costs to blue-collar youngsters of the narrow role choices generally available to them (rebel, accommodator, and achiever, as analyzed in Chapters 9 and 10).[24]

Many blue-collar men pay a high price in mental health for

their type of work. For example, a substantial number of male auto workers surveyed in 1954 indicated reduced ambition and lowered desire both for personal achievement and for the satisfactions of workmanship. Social psychologist Arthur Kornhauser found two major patterns among the auto workers:

> . . . large numbers of industrial workers are troubled by negative self-feelings, personal anxieties, inner tensions, and defensive emotional reactions. In other workers, deficient self-esteem and lack of confidence take the form of resigned acceptance of life, neither happy nor unhappy, but passive, inert, disengaged from the concerns of the world. Factory workers, especially those at low-skill levels, are somewhat worse than [white-collar, small town, and nonfactory blue-collar] groups in these respects.[25]

Factory work is singled out as the variable with particular responsibility for the comparatively poorer mental health of these blue-collarites. It is also thought to be related to the inadequacy of blue-collar techniques of tension management and stoicism.

Factory work, especially in routine production tasks, can help to extinguish ambition, initiative, and purposeful direction toward life goals.[26] There is a clear positive correlation of overall purposefulness with mental health—and blue-collarites in particular show up poorly on both scores. This in turn may help to explain the sharp rise in mental hospital admissions that accompanies a recession and intensified unemployment.[27] It is probably also linked to the disproportionate representation among known suicides of male Caucasian blue-collarites.[28]

To be sure, blue-collarites subscribe to a host of common defense mechanisms designed to cushion their discomforts, frustrations, and anxieties. Many of the men seek to protect themselves against the lack of ego gratifications on the job by coming to their jobs originally with low expectations and desires for fulfillment or by quickly adjusting to the lack of meaningful opportunities for such fulfillment. Also, like most Americans, many seek to protect themselves from the challenge of discovering any larger meaning in their lives, any touch of idealism or imaginative purpose beyond "happiness" and material well-being. To this end, and in the cultural mainstream, blue-collarites "focus their desires overwhelmingly on security and material gratifications, on passive, comfortable satisfactions of family life and pleasures of consumption, with little emphasis on intangible goals of personal achievement and self-expression and almost total neglect of altruistic devotion to social causes and participation in collective efforts for human betterment." [29]

TREATMENT RATES

The comparison of occupations only according to the frequency of psychiatric treatment among those members of their ranks who are sufficiently ill to receive treatment is misleading. Two groups, the poorest-educated and the well-educated, or the lowest and the highest occupational ranks, have received proportionately the majority of mental health treatment services. The former have been eligible to receive free or low-cost public care, with its emphasis on medicinal and nonverbal treatments. The latter have been able to afford expensive private care, with its attendant psychotherapeutic benefit.[30] Blue-collarites have fallen in between, and therefore may constitute the least well-cared-for segment of the entire population—from a mental health service point of view.

Low treatment rates for blue-collarites have additional sources in circumstances blue-collarites either share with the general population or have as special characteristics of their own. With the bulk of adult Americans, large numbers of blue-collarites decline to seek help for mental illness out of fear of public scorn. Blue-collarites also share a general fear of admitting the existence of mental illness, and a general pessimism regarding the prospects for the patient's full recovery. In greater degree than the general public, blue-collarites have little personal knowledge of the forms and functions of available mental help. They also have a greater tolerance for aberrant behavior by (never-yet-institutionalized) disturbed members of their own close-knit communities (such as Little Italy's "crazy man"—nonviolent, but delusional). Finally, they have a special uneasiness about the costs of treatment and a special hostility toward induced forms of personality change. It is little surprise, in short, that blue-collar treatment rates are as low as they are; more surprising is the fact that any workers seek or accept treatment at all.

Relevant here is the research finding on people who might have profited from treatment but sought successfully instead to evade it: Such people do not seem to meet their problems unusually well through their own resources. They are not spared distress and are not especially successful in substituting internal coping resources (such as prayer and faith) or informal social ties (such as the family circle or the camaraderie of workmates) for the more formal aid they are not using. The equilibrium of treatment evaders is not grounded in improved mental health, but rather in the stabilization and "socialization" of their mental illness. Their absence from a serious treatment routine is not a sign of more successful informal handling of their own problems. Instead, it appears to reflect mental health needs that have been met less adequately than they might have been.[31]

PROBLEMS IN TREATMENT

When treatment is sought, voluntarily or otherwise, the record is hardly encouraging. Blue-collarites turn especially for mental relief and counselling to their parish priest and their family doctor, neither of whom is as well-prepared for this responsibility as many workers and their wives believe. Even when clinical psychologists, psychiatric social workers, and psychiatrists are relied upon, various blue-collar practices handicap the establishment of an effective therapeutic relationship.

To examine only one such practice, it is characteristic of blue-collarites to fall silent for long periods during initial interviews of psychotherapy. Such behavior on the part of a middle-class patient is thought indicative of a reluctance to talk about something, a fear of taking the next step. When encountered in blue-collar patients, prolonged silence often leads overworked psychiatrists hastily to conclude that the patient is a poor treatment prospect—a conclusion that correlates highly with later withdrawals of disappointed blue-collar patients from stillborn treatment processes.

In fact, however, the "poor risk" conclusion is premature, class-biased, and unsuited to the blue-collarite. What looks like suppression or resistance may actually be a combination of blue-collar awe of the therapist and blue-collar ignorance of what is expected of a patient in psychotherapy. The blue-collarite, familiar only with the model of the questioning family or clinic physician, sits in silence waiting for the psychiatrist to ask questions. A misunderstanding rooted in educational differences divides the two and sabotages the healing process from the very start.[32]

Treatment also flounders on the shoals of blue-collar expectations, which are especially at odds with the middle-class character of psychotherapy. Blue-collarites often expect to find the roots of their problem in present-day external matters, while therapists more often focus on past internal matters. Blue-collarites may expect change to come primarily from outside, and may underestimate the amount of self-correction that treatment may require. Like many other Americans, large numbers of blue-collarites are too divorced from their own fearfully perceived emotional feelings and, at the same time, too emotionally entangled in their own family relations to recognize that one can openly criticize but still love and respect family members. Many often expect specific gains, such as marital happiness or equilibrium, while therapists may focus instead on more general matters like self-realization and the expansion of consciousness.[33]

Blue-collarites who are finally institutionalized are often so far along in their illness as to make their recovery from advanced psychoses an uncertain prospect. A follow-up study made in 1960 of 1,900 persons receiving psychiatric treatment in 1950 found more than 1,400 hospitalized in 1950, and more than half of these still hospitalized in 1960 (31 percent had died, and 16 percent had been discharged). The higher the social class, the greater the percentage of discharged patients, ranging from 30 percent of classes I and II (the well-off) to only 18 percent of class V (the poor).[34] Blue-collar patients also decrease their chances of ever returning to the community with every year they remained hospitalized, a grim finding given the paucity of out-patient resources necessary if hospital stays are to be kept short.

Hospitalization can be a mixed blessing. On the one hand it does relieve the family and community of the presence of a seriously ill individual, and it can also provide a respite or moratorium for the harassed patient himself. Blue-collarites, however, are disproportionately found at inexpensive or free state institutions, rather than at expensive private sanitariums. While many of these state hospitals are no longer "snake-pit"-like horror chambers, most still suffer from grossly inadequate funding, staffing, and servicing, as suggested by the following comment by a social worker:

> . . . the usual state hospital physician does not even know the name of the patients on his ward, and most patients do not have such simple amenities as a toothbrush and the use of a toilet seat. Life in a federal prison is infinitely superior to that in the state mental hospital.[35]

Anthropologist Jules Henry adds:

> State hospitals today seem still to exhale from their antique bricks and dark labyrinths the miasmas of misunderstanding, prejudice, callousness, and hate whose origins lie deep in our history. Who knows what happens in the pit, for their voices do not come up to us? [36]

While conditions vary somewhat from state to state, the general picture remains discouraging in the extreme.

Blue-collar state hospital patients are particularly poorly treated where their critical work-perceptions are concerned. In slave-labor fashion many are put to work at maintenance tasks that may be important to the hospital, but that contribute little or nothing to the gains in status the confused and deprived patient may desperately seek. Along with other patients the blue-collarites receive little work therapy of any relevance and little prerelease job counselling of any use. Many find the limited therapy available in most state hospitals superficial and easily ignored or manipulated. Game-playing often substitutes for the rigors of genuine recovery and personal growth; here, as elsewhere, the blue-collarite may turn "accommodator" and seek "the easy way." [37]

Limited data suggest that posthospital rates of recovery are related significantly to the skill-level identification of the ex-patient. Skilled craftsmen apparently have the least amount of trouble regaining their former employ, unskilled, the most. Overall, blue-collar families and after-care specialists have a propensity to treat the ex-patient as a sick man rather than as a recovered worker. As blue-collarites in particular look to work as the area within which to validate themselves, this failure of "significant others" to expect recovery through work from the blue-collar ex-patient costs society dearly. Sensing the lack of confidence others have in them, many ex-patient blue-collarites adjust themselves permanently to failure.[38]

UNION RESPONSE

A small, but influential and growing number of international unions have for years been interested in the various problems considered above.

On the neighborhood level the more progressive locals of the more progressive unions have placed labor representatives on the boards of all the important community organizations working in the field of mental health. The locals have also lobbied for improved legislation in the mental health field and have participated in campaigns to raise financial contributions for nonprofit mental health programs.

A growing number of local unions are slowly but steadily adding a demand for mental treatment insurance coverage to their list of new bargaining demands. Pioneered in 1961 in Los Angeles by a local of the Retail Clerks International Union, the operational feasibility and financial savings to subscribers have both been clearly established. (The Los Angeles facility now treats over 3,000 workers a year, twice its 1961 volume).[39] Progress, however, is slowed in large part by the unwillingness of certain rank-and-filers to admit their illness. Many decline to agree to help share the costs of another man's mental illness treatment through support of a mutual health insurance plan. Large numbers are still reluctant to accept a trade by union negotiators of a familiar wage or hour demand for a new employer concession in the comparatively unknown area of voluntary mental health insurance protection.

While developments in this area wait on the uncertain prospect of alterations in rank-and-file attitudes, certain local unions experiment anew with a custom-tailored answer to the related question—Where might treatment be located? Blue-collarites by and large do not seek psychiatric help for their mental problems, but they do rely heavily upon union health centers for early diagnosis and treatment of their physiological ills. Aware that workers are likely to resist the treatment of their psychiatric disorders even where special facilities are available, several local unions have carefully integrated into their well-established physical health centers a new "guidance" unit that serves both as a source of referral and as a place of treatment for mental ills.[40]

The challenge to organized labor goes beyond even that of evolving cost-saving insurance plans and enlarging the services of union health clinics. Labor is especially looked to by the rank and file to provide the personal touch, the human touch, in time of mental, even as in time of physical, illness. In small but steadily growing numbers local unions around the country are rising to this challenge.

Strategic here is the use being made by various locals of volunteer, nonpaid, specially-trained lay counsellors drawn from the rank and file. These volunteers engage both the ex-patient and his family in a living-room dialogue designed to replace ignorance with constructive knowledge of mental illness and recovery. The volunteers receive special schooling themselves in an extension course of a university labor education service, and then translate their new insights and facts into the colloquial language of their blue-collar peers. In the relaxed informality of a home visit much prejudice and fear can be uncovered, examined, and often dispelled, or at the very least, challenged and mitigated. Only a characteristic blue-collar reluctance to undertake volunteer work, to presume themselves unequal to counselling work, and to fail to differentiate between "meddling" and aiding restricts the size and impact of this unique labor effort.

Finally, organized labor is steadily confronting the question of how it might turn its considerable influence in the labor market to the advantage of former patients among its membership. Local unions across the country are seeking cooperation from employers in guaranteeing recovered patients their old employ, or in providing the equivalent of "sheltered workshop" employ for ex-patients who desire it. Unionists are often visited while still hospitalized by local representatives and business agents who work out a job-reentry plan with the patient and his doctors. The security possible in knowing that the local union stands squarely behind one's vocational rehabilitation is especially important to blue-collarites who characteristically associate human merit with marketplace employment.[41]

SUMMARY

The world the blue-collarite lives in—and helps to make —shapes the development, manifestation, prevalence, treatment, and consequences of his own physical and mental health. Limited progress is currently being made in the blue-collarite's health record, thanks in large part to union-negotiated health plans, employer-sponsored Blue Cross coverage, and the government's Medicare, Public Health, and Community Mental Health programs. Overall, however, the record remains one of inadequate preventive medicine, inefficient treatment procedures, and underdeveloped after-care programs. The worker's tradition-bound, fatalistic style of life is a factor here, as is also the class bias of health personnel and institutions. Despite wonder drugs, reductions in hospital stays, and heart transplants—where the worker is concerned—there remains too little that protects and restores health, and even less that enhances it.

Notes to Chapter Thirteen

1. Daniel Rosenblatt and Edward A. Suchman, "The Underutilization of Medical-Care Services by Blue-Collarites," in A. Shostak and W. Gomberg (eds.), *Blue-Collar World* (Englewood Cliffs, N.J.: Prentice-Hall, 1964), p. 344. See also Saxon Graham, "Sociological Aspects of Health and Illness," in Robert E. L. Faris (ed.), *Handbook of Modern Sociology* (Chicago: Rand McNally, 1968), pp. 319–322.

2. National Center for Health Statistics, *Selected Health Characteristics by Occupation, United States: July 1961–June 1963* (Washington, D.C.: Government Printing Office, 1965).

3. National Center for Health Statistics, *ibid.,* pp. 11, 38.

4. *Ibid.,* pp. 59, 20. See also National Center for Health Statistics, *Personal Health Expenses: Per Capita Annual Expenses, United States: July–December 1962* (Washington, D.C.: Government Printing Office, 1966), Table E., p. 16.

5. Irving Kenneth Zola, "Illness Behavior of the Working Class: Implications and Recommendations," in Shostak and Gomberg (eds.), *op. cit.,* pp. 350–361.

6. Daniel Rosenblatt and Edward A. Suchman, "Blue-Collar Attitudes and Information Toward Health and Illness," in Shostak and Gomberg (eds.), *op. cit.,* pp. 324–333. See also Robert Lane, *Political Ideology* (New York: Free Press, 1965), pp. 36–38.

7. Harold M. Schmeck, Jr., "Broad Changes in Medical Care Urged for Nation," *The New York Times,* November 20, 1967, p. 37.

8. Thomas McCorkle, "Chiropractic: A Deviant Theory of Disease and Treatment in Contemporary Western Culture," *Human Organization* (Spring 1961), pp. 20–23. See also Walter I. Wardwell, "Limited, Marginal, and Quasi-Practitioners," in Howard E. Freeman, *et al.* (eds.), *Handbook of Medical Sociology* (Englewood Cliffs, N.J.: Prentice-Hall, 1963), pp. 213–239.

9. Elinor Langer, "The Shame of American Medicine," *The New*

York Review of Books (May 26, 1966), p, 8. See also Anselm L. Strauss, "Medical Ghettos," Trans-Action (May 1967), pp. 7–15.

10. Fred J. Cook, The Plot Against the Patient (Englewood Cliffs, N.J.: Prentice-Hall, 1967), p. 115.

11. Ibid., pp. 40–47. See also Raymond S. Duff and August B. Hollingshead, Sickness and Society (New York: Harper & Row, 1968); Charles Kramer, The Negligent Doctor (New York: Crown, 1968).

12. Joe Western, "Prepayment for Group Practice: What's Behind Credit-Card Medicine," National Observer, August 28, 1967, p. 1. Between 1946 and 1968 all medical costs rose an average of 125 percent, while all other costs rose only 71 percent. Anon., "Medical Costs Up 125% Since 1946," The New York Times, October 30, 1968, p. 39.

13. Anon., "Surgery Fees Drain Increases in Benefits," AFL-CIO News, November 20, 1965, p. 10. See also, Anon., "The Doctor Gouge," AFL-CIO News, October 14, 1967, p. 4 (editorial).

14. Anon., "Federal Study Hits High Medical Costs: 'Severe Hardships' Found," AFL-CIO News, March 11, 1967.

15. National Center for Health Statistics, op. cit., p. 20.

16. Raul Tunley, The American Health Scandal (New York: Harper & Row, 1966), p. 51.

17. Elinor Langer, op. cit., p. 8.

18. Robert C. Joiner, "Changes in Negotiated Health and Insurance Plans, 1962–66," Monthly Labor Review (November 1966), p. 1246.

19. Anon., "Labor Letter," Wall Street Journal, April 9, 1968, p. 1.

20. See in this connection, Raymond Munts, Bargaining for Health: Labor Unions, Health Insurance, and Medical Care (Madison: The University of Wisconsin Press, 1968). See also Howard A. Rush, "Labor and Health," The New York Times, April 23, 1967, p. 51; Hyman J. Weiner, et al., Demand for Rehabilitation in a Labor Union Population: Part One—Research Report (New York: Sidney Hillman Health Center, 1964); Hyman J. Weiner, et. al., Demand for Rehabilitation in a Labor Union Population: Part Two—Action Program (New York: Sidney Hillman Health Center, 1964).

21. For a review of the literature suggesting mental health is positively related to socioeconomic status, see James A. Davis, Education for Positive Mental Health (Chicago: Aldine, 1965), pp. 68–77. See also Arthur Kornhauser, Mental Health of the Industrial Worker: A Detroit Study (New York: Wiley, 1965), p. 262; Claude

C. Bowman, "Mental Health in the Worker's World," in Shostak and Gomberg, *op. cit.*, pp. 371–380; Leo Srole, *et al.*, *Mental Health in the Metropolis: The Midtown Manhattan Study, Volume 1* (New York: McGraw-Hill, 1962), p. 240; Gerald Gurin, *et al.*, *Americans View Their Mental Health: A Nation-wide Interview Survey* (New York: Basic Books, 1960), pp. 226–227. Cf. H. Warren Dunham, *et al.*, "A Research Note on Diagnosed Mental Illness and Social Class," *American Sociological Review* (April 1966), pp. 223–227.

22. Kornhauser cites as "the outstanding finding" of his 1954 research on auto workers the observation that mental health varies consistently with the level of jobs the men hold. This variation occurs almost independent of the amount of education or the personal characteristics of the job-holder. It is especially related to the opportunity a man has to use his abilities, to perform a worthwhile function, to fulfill his role as a competent human being, and to find interest in his work and a sense of accomplishment and self-respect. The discussion in Chapter 5, it may be recalled, made plain how rare such a chance is for the majority of blue-collarites who are not skilled craftsmen—and increasingly for some of the craftsmen in newly automated work settings as well. Arthur Kornhauser, *Mental Health of the Industrial Worker: A Detroit Study* (New York: Wiley, 1965), p. 262. See also Gurin, *et al.*, *op. cit.*, p. 225.

23. Lawrence Zelic Freedman, "Psychopathology and Poverty," in Shostak and Gomberg (eds.), *op. cit.*, p. 369. ". . . there is an apparent difference in concept of self as patient in the social classes if one is (1) uncomfortable or unhappy, (2) if his body hurts or functions poorly, (3) if he is unable to be effective at his work, (4) if he is in trouble with his social community, or (5) if he is in difficulty with the law." *Ibid.* See also Charles Kadushin, *Why People Go to Psychiatrists* (New York: Atherton, 1968); Jerome K. Myers and Bertram H. Roberts, *Family and Class Dynamics in Mental Illness* (New York: Wiley, 1968), pp. 204–205; S. M. Miller and Elliot G. Mishler, "Social Class, Mental Illness and American Psychiatry," *Millbank Memorial Fund Quarterly* (1959), pp. 189–191.

24. See, for example, John F. McDermott, *et al.*, "Social Class and Mental Illness in Children: Observations of Children of Blue-Collar Families," *American Journal of Orthopsychiatry* (April 1965), pp. 500–508; Daniel R. Miller and Guy E. Swanson, *Inner Conflict and Defense* (New York: Holt, 1960); Lee Rainwater and Karol Kane Weinstein, *And the Poor Get Children: Sex, Contra-*

ception, and Family Planning in the Working Class (Chicago, Ill.: Quadrangle, 1960).

25. Kornhauser, *op. cit.*, p. 259. Note however the position developed in this volume's chapters on work and blue-collar workers, namely, the "instinct of workmanship" continues to animate much blue-collar behavior, albeit in variously disguised ways.

26. For a contrary thesis, see William R. H. McWhinney and Sidney R. Adelman, "Mental Health of the Industrial Worker: An Analysis and Review," *Human Organization* (Summer 1966), pp. 180–182; Arthur Kornhauser, "Rejoinder," *Human Organization* (Summer 1966), pp. 182–184.

27. William Borders, "Professor Sees Mental Health Tied to Economy," *The New York Times*, November 23, 1967, p. 58.

28. On the disproportionate use by blue-collarites of suicide as a response to failure, see Ronald Maris, "Suicide, Status, and Mobility in Chicago" (unpublished paper, January 1967, Dartmouth College); Warren Breed, "Occupational Mobility and Suicide Among White Males," *American Sociological Review* (April 1963), pp. 179–188.

29. Kornhauser, *op. cit.*, p. 251. See also Murray Hausknecht, "The Blue-Collar Joiner," in Shostak and Gomberg (eds.), *op. cit.*, pp. 207–215.

30. J. G. Kelly, "The Mental Health Agent in the Urban Community," in Leonard J. Duhl (ed.), *Urban America and the Planning of Mental Health Services* (New York: Group for the Advancement of Psychiatry, 1964); Miller and Mishler, *op. cit.*, pp. 174–199.

31. Gurin, *et al.* (eds.), *op. cit.*, p. 6. See also C. Richard Fletcher, "Social Class Variations in Psychiatric Referral of Withdrawn and Aggressive Case Descriptions," *Social Problems* (Fall 1968), pp. 227–241.

32. Alice M. White, L. Fichtenbaum, and John Dellard, "Evaluation of Silence in Initial Interviews with Psychiatric Outpatients," *Journal of Nervous and Mental Disease* (1964), p. 6.

33. See in this connection, five essays in a section entitled "New Approaches to Intake and Diagnosis" in Frank Riessman, *et al.* (eds.), *Mental Health of the Poor: New Treatment Approaches for Low Income People* (New York: Free Press, 1964). See also Orville R. Gursslin, *et al.*, "Social Class and the Mental Health Movement," *Social Problems* (Winter 1959–1960), pp. 210–218; August B. Hollingshead and Frederick C. Redlich, *Social Class and Mental Illness* (New York: Wiley, 1958). On the "better fit" of one type of

non-medical "adviser," see Lee Sechrest and James H. Bryan, "Astrologers as Useful Marriage Counselors," *Trans-Action* (November 1968), pp. 34–36.

34. Lee L. Bean, *et al.*, "Social Class and Schizophrenia: A Ten-Year Follow-Up," in Shostak and Gomberg (eds.), *op. cit.*, pp. 381–390. See also Jerome K. Myers and Lee L. Bean, *A Decade Later: A Follow-Up of "Social Class and Mental Illness"* (New York: Wiley, 1968).

35. Harris Chaiklin, "The Inferno of Illness," *Trans-Action* (March 1967), pp. 53–54.

36. Jules Henry, "The Human Demons," *Trans-Action* (March /April 1966), p. 48.

37. For relevant discussion, see Ozzie G. Simmons, *Work and Mental Illness: Eight Case Studies* (New York: Wiley, 1965).

38. For relevant discussion, see Howard E. Freeman and Ozzie G. Simmons, *The Mental Patient Comes Home* (New York: Wiley, 1963).

39. Anon., "Labor Notes," *Wall Street Journal*, November 28, 1967, p. 1. Labor negotiations in 1968 saw increasing attention paid to mental-health fringes: Major meat packers, for example, now provide employees with up to 365 days of hospital treatment for mental or nervous disorders. The new steelworkers' pact with canmakers covers up to 400 in individual or group psychotherapy or "family counseling." Anon., "Labor Letter," *Wall Street Journal*, April 9, 1968, p. 1.

40. The Sidney Hillman Health Center in New York City, the St. Louis Labor Health Institute, and the Eleanor Roosevelt Union Health-Guidance Center in Chicago are leading union clinics in the mental health area. See in this connection, Antonio Blanco and Sheila H. Akabus, "The Factory: Site for Community Mental Practice," *American Journal of Orthopsychiatry* (April 1968), pp. 543–552; Hyman J. Weiner, "Labor-Management Relations and Mental Health," in Alan McLean (ed.), *To Work Is Human: Mental Health and the Business Community* (New York: Macmillan, 1967), pp. 193–203; Hyman J. Weiner, "A Group Approach to Link Community Mental Health with Labor in National Conference on Social Welfare," *Social Work Practice, 1967* (New York: Columbia University Press, 1967), pp. 178–188.

41. See in this connection, John J. Sommer, "Labor and Management: New Roles in Mental Health," *American Journal of Orthopsychiatry* (April 1965), pp. 558–563; Hyman J. Weiner and Morris

S. Brand, "Involving a Labor Union in the Rehabilitation of the Mentally Ill," *American Journal of Orthopsychiatry* (April 1965), pp. 598–600; Anon., "A Union Fights Mental Illness," *Industrial Bulletin* (New York State, October 1964), pp. 2–6.

14

BLUE-COLLAR RELIGION
AND RETIREMENT

Through want of enterprise and faith men are where they are, buying and selling, and spending their lives like serfs.
—THOREAU

Religious faith is the "glue" that finally holds together the various parts of the blue-collarite's culture. With striking effect such faith helps keep blue-collar behavior responsive to the central discipline of a religiously defined and internally supported conscience. In its turn retirement is the capstone state of life that finally magnifies the strengths and weaknesses of the entire style of life that has gone before. With striking effect retirement attitudes help blue-collarites adapt to the loss of their work roles and to the terminal character of their last stage of life.

RELIGION

Male Caucasian blue-collarites are aligned with two polar types of religious organization, sects and churches. While only a very small minority of manual workers, particularly those

from rural origins, are sect members, the majority of the nation's sect members are manual workers. The overwhelming
majority of all manual workers, in fact, are identified with the
Roman Catholic Church and with the major Protestant denominations, especially the Baptist and Lutheran churches.
Nevertheless, while a large portion of the total membership
of these churches consists of blue-collarites and their families,
the workers rarely dominate church affairs—and at present find
many religious developments around them little to their liking.
Even as material success leads many sect members to "graduate" into more formal churches or to convert the sect into a
more conventional denomination, so does the contemporary
modernization drive of the formal churches lead many blue-
collar members to look restlessly for alternative religious institutions. Elaboration on these related developments follows
below.

RELIGIOUS SECTS

Blue-collarites are drawn to the evangelical Protestant
sects for reasons closely associated with their material circumstances, social status, and life-style.[1] Critical in the matter is
the long history of failure and loss that some manual workers
have known, their nostalgic view of whatever comfort they
knew in olden days, and their longing for a time and place
where things will finally work out well for them.

In keeping with blue-collar predilections, religious sects are
the most exclusive, demanding, informal, and personal type of
religious organization extant in America. Spiritually qualified
lay members, who may otherwise live as poverty-stricken, unskilled Chicago "hillbillies," pass on the eligibility of candidates
for membership and continuously enforce religious sanctions.
Once accepted into the fold, the brethren relate to each other
in highly emotional, intimate, and trusting ways. Services
stress a cathartic emotional element, with dynamic and partici-
pating members seeking to recapture the thrill of conversion.
Audience participation is extensive, the Scriptures receiving a

very literal interpretation. Opposition to the central authority of the state or conventional church is unabashedly advanced.

In connection with such opposition, blue-collarites are also attracted to the sects by their "leftwing Protestantism," or their variation on class hostility and their unique resolution of class conflict. Economically deprived, low-status Americans, particularly poorly educated and undertrained blue-collarites, resent their fate and are often hostile to other more fortunate people. The religious teachings of various sects assure such believers that theirs is truly the better and happier life, apparently well-off nonbelievers actually suffering now and forevermore. In this way class hostility is legitimized and vented, but cast in religious terms. Class conflict is also recognized and celebrated, but side-tracked from an economic or political course of action. Instead, a new religious dialectic makes it plain that the good (all sect members) will effortlessly triumph and enjoy otherworldly rewards of every possible kind. ("The first shall be last, and the last shall be first.")

The expressive sect, whether Pentacostalist, Holy Roller, Snake-Handler, or Southern Baptist splinter-group, meets a blue-collar need for emotional, episodic, and action-oriented kinds of religious experience. Along with sect members from other social classes, blue-collarites seek and value religious informality—if also religious ethnocentrism and social passivity. In very small but persistent numbers blue-collarites choose the antiestablishment motif of the otherworldly expressive sects, and thereby both celebrate and blunt their own radical energies. Revealingly, in moderately large numbers sect members transfer "up" to more formal denominations when they begin to share in the general American prosperity. The clandestine, idiosyncratic, and emotional sect is left behind in favor of "high" church status, normalcy, and restraint. Or, to put it another way, the blue-collar (religious) rebel gives up his old expressive ways and joins the contained mainstream of blue-collar (religious) accommodators.

CHURCHES

Paradoxically, religious accommodation is challenged today as seldom before. To grasp the significance of the turmoil one must first understand the very heavy and thoroughgoing involvement of many blue-collarites with their religious faith.

A majority, though by no means all manual workers, and, most particularly, many of their wives, other female members of their families, and the older generation of their parents take their religion very seriously. A good many workers expect their faith to confirm that their present fate is somehow reasonable and bearable and that their future will be (mercifully) appropriate and also bearable. Because life is complex, and sin and temptation ubiquitous, a man's religious faith is also expected to provide a feasible way to expunge both his routine and his exceptional sins.

Religion, as understood by many blue-collarites, is not intended to foster humility or an uneasy conscience. Rather, to borrow from Will Herberg's more general comments, religion is something that reassures the worker about the essential rightness of everything American, his culture, and himself. Religion validates his goals and his ideals rather than calling them into question and enhances his self-esteem instead of challenging it. Religion offers him salvation on manageable terms instead of demanding blind faith.[2]

In everyday affairs religion is employed as a critical guide to communality (where to live, with whom to be friendly, and whom to date or marry). Blue-collar men often vote along religious lines and sometimes join religious fraternal organizations (such as the Knights of Columbus and various Masonic lodges). Their children are heavily represented among day and Sunday school pupils, even as their wives make up for the irregular attendance record of their husbands with a steadfast record of their own. Characteristically, the men are allowed to sleep through Sunday services, at home or in the church, so long as they trust the children's moral education to the faith, provide generously for the weekly donation, and rally to the faith at every challenge.

Given this incorporation of the church, particularly of the Catholic Church, into the worker's style of life, it becomes clear why blue-collarites value ritual, dogma, and tradition. All three are heavily relied on to protect the faithful against "godless modernism" and "middle-class immorality." All three are used to protect the ethos of a group on the defense: "Preserve the faith." "Stick together." "Listen to your elders." "Cause no scandal." "Learn to be prudent."

RELIGIOUS CONTROVERSIES

To the frequent astonishment of many workers certain of the major churches appear to have broken faith with the worker and with their own conservative past. These churches are suspected of having set off on a course of modernization that undermines the calm and complacency many blue-collarites rely on.

Recent Catholic liturgical reforms, for example, including especially a substitution of English for Latin or a local ethnic tongue in the services, are reportedly opposed and resisted in many staid blue-collar congregations. Similarly, the vast majority of Protestant blue-collarites probably do not have the foggiest notion of what agitates the young radical theologians who, in bitter doubt, insist that "God is dead." Jarring to old complacencies, the related tumult is most likely to create new doubts among blue-collarites about the adequacy of seminary instruction of young would-be theologians. Former Catholic priests, like James Kavanaugh, who criticize the "pharisees and high priests," probably frighten the few blue-collarites who might hear their criticisms; the call of such men for a community of love and meaning in life and for an end to childish rule-bound living finds little acceptance among conventionally devout blue-collarites.

Very confusing to many workers and their families is the ferment among younger ministers, priests, and nuns, a good many of whom are prominent in the ranks of civil rights marchers, antiwar protesters, and civil liberties demonstraters. The large majority of blue-collarites probably can be found among the plurality of Americans who, in April 1968, informed Gallup pollsters that they disapproved of the increasing involvement of organized religion in social and political issues.[3] Even as most blue-collar men seem to prefer that their women follow the ancient prescription of *"kirche, kinder und küche"* (church, children, and kitchen), so do they prefer to have churchmen and churchwomen stay close to *"kirche"* quite narrowly defined.

In this situation, perplexity and frustration is undoubtedly reciprocal. Boston's outspoken Cardinal Cushing probably speaks for many clergy in and outside of the Catholic faith when he comments on the average parishioner's sense of community:

> Sometimes I wonder about the value of our parochial-school system. I mean, the sort of product we're turning out. So many of our people never even pick up a book once they leave school. They never miss mass on Sunday, but you have to kick them in the shins to get them interested in things like the ecumenical movement or hunger in Latin America.[4]

Part of the explanation for the conservatism of the blue-collar parishioners may lie in the fact that as city dwellers these churchgoers worship in neighborhood parishes that draw parishioners of the same race and ethnic background (S. H. Lipset suggests that "to be a Catholic ordinarily means to live near Catholics, work with them, and associate with them").[5] Much like the "old shoe" or "safe port" feeling-tone of the old neighborhood, the parish church represents historic continuity, life-style reinforcement, and life space "purity." Blue-collarites prize their religious communality quite highly and do not apologize for maintaining separate communal lives based on the religious factor. Intermarriage and friendships across religious lines are discouraged, and the parish church is viewed as the most appropriate arena for the forging of all new relationships.

When the young reformers among the clergy support open-housing legislation (as does the controversial blue-collar priest, Father James Groppi of Minneapolis), they threaten the neighborhood's sense of insulation. When these same "agitators" and others press the church fathers to integrate the races in denominational schools and at church services, they are apt to bring down on themselves the wrath of anxiety-ridden blue-collarites. So strong is resentment against integrationist and similar social action agitation that sometimes rocks, bottles, firecrackers, and obscenities are reserved for nuns and priests as special targets when protest groups march through blue-collar neighborhoods.

Equally disturbing, though confined to the large Catholic sector of the blue-collar community, is the opposition of elements of the Catholic Church to birth control. Catholic blue-collarites are divided on the morality of birth control, and many priests report that conflict about this issue is the major reason for married couples' remaining away from the sacraments. Research suggests that perhaps two out of three married Catholics practice birth control, and as many as seven out of ten Catholics want the Church to lift its controversial ban on birth-control implements.[6]

Many workers are affected in this connection both by husband-wife differences of opinion and by the guilt that may accompany a joint decision to employ some method other than the Church-sanctioned rhythm method. There is much frustration in waiting for the adoption of a new Church standard compatible with the use of oral contraceptives. Some of this frustration works its way out in a pattern of contraception, confession, contrition, and contraception all over again. Particularly the younger blue-collar couples, those confronted with the possibility of adding a fourth or fifth child to a fast-growing family, find the birth-control predicament real and costly. Few things, including the Church's opposition to selected movies, to the godlessness of public schools, or even its refusal to sanction divorce, divide and tax the blue-collar Catholic community as does the birth-control issue.

SUMMARY

In an ironic and revealing way blue-collarites need and seek more but possibly get less than ever before from their religious faiths. Perplexed by the hurly-burly of endless change around them, blue-collarites cling to the old faiths for comfort and confirmation. To the dismay of many, however, they find the old faiths in ferment and the old rituals on trial. Having been taught to hold the faith in unexamined reverence, and thereby to assure themselves a hallowed life and blessed reward, blue-collarites watch at present while the verities dissolve. Pressed to make sense of a world of religion they never made, many blue-collar men and women stand by instead—anxious, confused, and not a little embittered.

RETIREMENT

As 40-year-old men of the generation focused on in this volume have another twenty-five years or so before reaching the customary age of retirement, it might be thought that the latter subject could be ignored. The present circumstances of retired blue-collarites, however, many of whom are the fathers of the subjects of this volume, tell us a good deal about the present generation's future. A good many forty-year-old median-aged blue-collarites are shaken even today by what they see or suspect in the retirement of their fathers. Furthermore it is unlikely that many will escape a similar fate—twenty-five years from now.

THE WORKING OLDSTERS

Fewer blue-collarites (30 percent) than any other occupational type elect to stay in the labor force after reaching sixty-five years of age.[7] Personal ill-health (discussed in the previous chapter) is a factor here, as is also employer discrimination, first against men over forty-five, and, decisively, against those over sixty-five. So thoroughgoing is this (often illegal) discrimination that older workers find it harder to get a job, to avoid layoffs, and to regain a post-unemployment job than do younger men of perhaps comparable training, but far less experience. For older men and women downward occupational mobility in blue-collar ranks appears a common fate.[8]

Why, then, do even a few blue-collarites struggle to retain wage-earner status? The most freely given answer is "money." Some men have an urgent need to earn more than either Social Security or private pension benefits provide. (In 1962, men over sixty-five with any work earned an average of $2,500; men who worked the full year averaged $4,260).[9] There is evidence, however, that earnings decrease steadily with advancing age— the more you try to "hang on," the less you get paid for your efforts.[10]

Less often given as a reason to seek work after sixty-five, but fully as significant, is fear. To be sure, some blue-collarites, particularly craftsmen and artisans, persist at careers for the sheer love of craft. Still larger numbers, however, or those who "stick around," do so out of fear of "going crazy" or disintegrating without the "glue" of gainful employment. (In the words of a hundred-year-old worker, "Doc" Swenson: "What would I do if I didn't have this job to keep me busy?")[11] These habituated workers explain that they just have to work, that they have never learned how to live unless they are working.

THE RETIRED OLDSTERS

Seventy percent of the nation's blue-collarites do not remain in the work force on reaching their sixty-fifth birthday. Indeed, a larger proportion of blue-collarites than of any other occupational type leave work at that age to wrestle with retirement, perhaps the most important crisis of all in the aging process (death, for example, is feared less). These men confront three alternative patterns of aging—accepting, denying, or resigning. For most Americans, research suggests considerable acceptance—and successful aging by any standard.[12] That the record appears otherwise in the case of many blue-collarites reveals significant disutilities of the blue-collar style.

Symptomatic of blue-collar difficulties in the matter is the fact that most workers are forced out of work; few leave voluntarily.[13] A 1963 national survey found that only 28 percent had retired to enjoy leisure, to help out at home, or to escape from job dissatisfaction. Another 72 percent retired because of poor health, a compulsory retirement age, or being laid off.[14] That loneliness, ill health, economic hardship, and disillusionment follow retirement is consistent with its inauspicious start. The following observations on each of these four problems may help to make this clear.

1. Loneliness can play a large and long-developing role in blue-collar retirement. For example, while frequency of social contact is considerable within working-class generations, it is not common across the generational divide. Although visits with parents are exchanged, the older generation is often not part of the continuing social life of the family circle. Possessing few special skills or traditional knowledge valued by the younger people, many blue-collar oldsters lose influence in the extended family, respect from "significant others," and personal self-esteem.

Coming out of the blue-collar tradition of distrust of "outsiders," group activities, and reliance on others, many blue-collarites shun the very activities other older Americans use to defend against loneliness (volunteer services, adult education, Golden Age or hobby clubs, and travel). As they age, many feel they cannot admit the need to lean more and more upon others, lest they be judged useless or obsolete, "children," or fools. So convinced, large numbers of proudly independent blue-collar oldsters "keep their peace, their social distance, their insularity, their inviolable selfhood—even at the cost of loneliness and isolation." [15]

2. Ill-health is a major characteristic of blue-collar retirement. More manual workers (80 percent) than the members

of any other occupational category cite their own poor physical health in explaining the termination of their work careers.[16] Illness here is thought to be related to physical strain and the relative absence of regular physical checkups. Folk medicine, or the practice of prescribing patent or homebrewed "medicines" for oneself, is probably relevant, as is also a class-linked reluctance to see a doctor ("why invite trouble") or enter a hospital ("the house of death").

After many years of neglect of the subject, social scientists are now studying the emotional wear and tear of lives spent at manual work and the trauma of the loss of employment status represented by retirement.[17] Whatever the causes, and almost regardless of the aid now finally available in Medicare for skyrocketing medical costs, the worker's considerable ill-health biases the entire course of the terminal phase of his life.

3. Economic want, often degenerating into poverty, is a grim accompaniment of much blue-collar retirement. The average retired city couple needed about $4,000 in 1968 to maintain a "moderate living standard," but newly increased Social Security benefits provided 16 million retired workers and their wives with only $1,980 per annum (or only about 42 percent of the median $6,600 preretirement earnings of a blue-collarite).[18]

While nearly 30 million employees are covered by 30,000 private pension plans, they actually receive very little (20 to 40 percent of preretirement pay is common; a thirty-year union steelworker gets only $2,100 to add to his Social Security payment). The number protected here in any case excludes slightly over half of the labor force.[19] Indeed, research by the government found "a relatively small proportion of the beneficiaries in each survey [1941–1963] were retired by their employers under company pension plans. . . . Most of the workers were simply laid off, although occasionally one reported receiving a gift, such as a rocking chair or a wristwatch." [20]

To be sure, oldsters have fewer and smaller debts than others. They pay smaller income taxes. And they may receive financial aid from their children. None of these benefits, however, adds very much: In 1962, for example, only 5 percent of all persons over sixty-five received cash contributions from relatives, and these contributions constituted less than 1 percent of their total income.[21] It is not surprising that two out of three elderly persons live below the poverty line, including an unknown, but probably large number who have slid downward from stable blue-collar origins.[22]

4. All of this contributes to the ultimate disillusionment that characterizes the blue-collar scene. As writer Midge Dechter explains, the older the worker the more he discovers that a life unlived cannot be recouped in one's sixties or seventies. Consistent with blue-collar tradition the oldsters have sacrificed great quantities of their human substance, their longings, and imaginings to their work and to their savings, only to find that "the spirit is a substance that turns rancid in storage." [23] Having been taught that by denying themselves what D. H. Lawrence called the "good, warm life" they would be earning some great reward at the end, they are living long enough to watch all the possibilities for love and reward in this life run out.

SUMMARY

Unless fundamental changes occur, the details of tomorrow's blue-collar retirement picture may alter but many more of its present features will remain the same. Blue-collar retirees two decades hence may know more people, but not very well. They may feel better, but not from a sense of any achievement of their own. They may have more, but not enough of the "good, warm life" they miss. In the cast of the bulk of median-age blue-collarites scheduled now to retire in the mid-1990s, many are likely to approach and to experience retirement as do their grim and disappointed fathers today.

Notes to Chapter Fourteen

1. See in this connection, Nathan L. Gerrard, "The Serpent-Handling Religions of West Virginia," *Trans-Action* (May 1968), pp. 22–28; Howard Elison, "The Implications of Pentacostal Reli-

gion for Intellectualism, Politics, and Race Relations," *American Journal of Sociology* (January 1965), pp. 403–415. On the religious distribution of blue-collarites, see Sidney Goldstein, "Socioeconomic Differentials Among Religious Groups in the United States," *American Journal of Sociology* (May 1969), pp. 612–631.

2. Will Herberg, *Protestant-Catholic-Jew: An Essay in American Religious Sociology* (Garden City, N.Y.: Doubleday, 1960 ed.), p. 269, *passim*.

3. Gallup Poll, "Churches Should Ignore Issues of Day, Most Say," *Philadelphia Evening Bulletin,* April 12, 1968.

4. Edward R. F. Sheehan, "Not Peace, But the Sword: The New Anguish of American Catholicism," *Saturday Evening Post* (November 28, 1964), p. 40.

5. Seymour Martin Lipset, *et al., Union Democracy: The Internal Politics of the International Typographical Union* (Glencoe, Ill.: Free Press, 1956), p. 314 f. See also Charles H. Anderson, "Religious Communality Among White Protestants, Catholics, and Mormons," *Social Forces* (June 1968), pp. 501–508; Milton M. Gordon, *Assimilation in American Life* (New York: Oxford University Press, 1964). On ethnic resonance, see Kenneth W. Underwood, *Protestant and Catholic: Religious and Social Interaction in an Industrial Community* (Boston: Beacon Press, 1957), pp. 207–221. On the underrepresentation of Jews in the blue-collar ranks, see Sidney Goldstein and Calvin Goldscheider, *Jewish Americans: Three Generations in a Jewish Community* (Englewood Cliffs, N.J.: Prentice-Hall, 1968), pp. 77–91.

6. "How U.S. Catholics View Their Church," *Newsweek* (March 20, 1967), p. 69. The Harris Pollsters also found that half the laity opposed the Church's stringent laws against divorce. Forty-eight percent were in favor of allowing priests to marry. On the other hand, 59 percent disapproved of the U.S. hierarchy's decision to drop Friday abstinence, and only 20 percent would feel morally bound to follow a priest's instructions to integrate their neighborhoods. More recently reported data are consistent in every way: See John Leo, "Catholics Found Easing Sex and Birth Curb Views," *The New York Times,* October 1, 1968, pp. 1, 53; John Leo, "Enforcing the Unenforceable," *The New York Times,* September 29, 1968, p. E–7. See also Michael Novak (ed.), *The Experience of Marriage: Thirteen Couples Report* (New York: Macmillan, 1966).

7. See in this connection, Lenore A. Epstein and Janet H. Murray (eds.), *The Aged Population of the United States: The 1963*

Social Security Survey of the Aged (Washington, D.C.: Government Printing Office, 1967).

8. B. V. H. Schneider, *The Older Worker* (Berkeley: Institute of Industrial Relations, University of California, 1962).

9. Epstein and Murray (eds.), *op. cit.*, p. 14.

10. *Ibid.*, p. 91.

11. Jack Star, "Age: 100; America's Oldest Worker Still Going Strong," *Look* (December, 1965), p. 4–5.

12. See R. H. Williams and C. G. Wirths, *Lives Through the Years: Styles of Life and Successful Aging* (New York: Atherton Press, 1965).

13. Richard H. Williams, "Changing Status, Roles, and Relationships," in Clark Tibbitts (ed.), *Handbook of Social Gerontology* (Chicago: University of Chicago Press, 1960), pp. 261–297.

14. Epstein and Murray, *op. cit.*, p. 13.

15. Margaret Clark and Barbara G. Anderson, *Culture and Aging: An Anthropological Study of Older Americans* (Springfield, Ill.: Thomas, 1967), p. 425, *passim*.

16. P. O. Steiner and R. Dorfman, *The Economic Status of the Aged* (Berkeley: University of California Press, 1957).

17. On the centrality of work, see Woodrow W. Morris, "The Meaning of Work to the Older Person," in John E. Muthard and W. W. Morris (eds.), *Counseling the Older Disabled Worker* (Iowa City: State University of Iowa, 1961), pp. 69–77; Herman J. Loether, "The Meaning of Work and Adjustment to Retirement," in A. Shostak and W. Gomberg (eds.), *Blue-Collar World: Studies of the American Worker* (Englewood Cliffs: Prentice-Hall, 1964), pp. 525–534.

18. John D. Morris, "Pensioner Checks Up by $250-Million," *The New York Times*, March 4, 1968, p. 23; Anon., "Social Security Hike to Aid 24 Million," *AFL-CIO News*, February 17, 1968, p. 7; Anon., " 'First-Rate Social Security' Termed Major Labor Goal," *AFL-CIO News*, April 20, 1968, p. 7.

19. Anon., "Getting an Early Start on Those Golden Years," *Business Week* (April 27, 1968), pp. 104–106.

20. Edna C. Wentworth, *Employment After Retirement: A Study of the Postentitlement Work Experience of Men Drawing Benefits Under Social Security* (Washington, D.C.: Government Printing Office, 1968), p. 5.

21. See in this connection, Chamber of Commerce, *Poverty: The Sick, Disabled, and Aged: Second Report* (Washington, D.C.: Chamber of Commerce, 1965), p. 65, *passim*.

22. Epstein and Murray, *op. cit.*, p. 16.

23. Midge Decter, "Growing Old in America," *Commentary* (January 1963). See also Suzanne Reichard, *et al.*, *Aging and Personality: A Study of 87 Older Men* (New York: Wiley, 1960).

15

BLUE-COLLAR
PROSPECTS

We are moving from an age in which we could afford just to state our ideals about human rights to an age when these ideals must become realities if the society is going to function at all.
—ROBERT THEOBALD, *The Challenge of Abundance*

To the late Carl Sandburg, writing in 1915, blue-collarites looked far too much "like men who had been somewhere." Old before they were young, their work (to paraphrase Sandburg) "tapped the blood of their wrists" the whole day long. By nightfall workingmen were left only "tired of wishes, [and] empty of dreams." [1] At present the AFL-CIO, the Chamber of Commerce, and the Department of Labor insist that the intervening fifty-four years have made a vast positive difference. Perhaps. And then again, perhaps not. My own judgment is offered in this concluding chapter.

Three final tasks are undertaken: The fundamental questions raised in the Preface and used to direct the entire volume's discussion are considered once again in the light of ideas developed in the preceding chapters. Thereafter, a selection of practical social reforms are discussed, which might direct the blue-collar odyssey in new and rewarding ways. Finally, a case for the reforms is championed.

POST-1915 AFFAIRS

The first of the four questions with which this book has been concerned asks, Is the working class as well off as others believe? Does it really merit admiration and envy?

On a first reading the record encourages admiration for the progress apparently made by blue-collarites. For example, from 1915 to date, or in a mere three generations, Italian manual workers have moved from the poverty of Mulberry Street on the Lower East Side to the comfort of Brooklyn brownstones, and thereafter, to the affluence of blue-collar suburbs on Long Island. Certain manual workers, particularly those better-educated men with developed skills who participate in modern marriages, have also freed themselves within their own lifetime from traditional blue-collar ways which have become increasingly less appropriate in today's dynamic cosmopolitan settings. Such men are apt to elicit our admiration and, perhaps, envy for their substitution of real choice for stultifying tradition and constraint.[2]

On a second and more careful reading, however, admiration for these gains gives way to concern for their durability. More specifically, blue-collar gains are threatened in the following ways: Blue-collar prosperity is precariously supported, maintained as it is largely by heavy installment debt and steadily declining purchasing power. The job of the man of the house is made uncertain by technological displacement and upgrading in the educational requirements of jobs. The situation of the woman of the house is uneven, for the "modern" goals she may adopt (including intimacy with her husband and sensitivity with her children) require personal ego-strength and ingenuity that can easily elude her. Finally, the advancement of blue-collar youngsters is unlikely, for the quality of schooling now being experienced is inadequate to the challenge of social opportunities. Blue-collar children may spend increasingly more years in school, but high-quality educational content and not time alone influences postschool achievement.

These observations, as noted above, refer only to the unique situation of the minority of better-off, modernistic, suburban-dwelling blue-collarites. The vast majority of Caucasian male blue-collarites and their dependents are still less well-off on all counts.

Many blue-collarites, particularly those in the median-age generation, remain haunted by nagging memories of the defeating Depression decade. More are unnerved by unending alterations in their own work. A vast majority of all manual workers are revealing in their persistent fantasies about escaping the factory, and in their hope that their sons will not follow them into blue-collar work. And large numbers are put off by bureaucratic developments in their own impersonal labor unions.

Blue-collarites live fearfully in the larger cities and uneasily in the suburbs. They pay dearly for the sharp differentiation of the world of their wives and the considerable emotional distance between husband and wife. They have a high separation and divorce rate, along with excess fertility. Their youngsters have both a high dropout and a high arrest record.

Blue-collarites contribute few leaders to the ranks of American politics. They have only enough ability to convert their leisure into a reinforcement of the cultural status quo. They stagger under the weight of an alarming incidence of little-treated physical and mental illness. They are put off by middle-class-directed efforts at modernizing religion, and the oldsters among them find it difficult to survive long days stripped of the mind-swaddling routine of factory work.

With respect to most blue-collarites, one comes finally to admire not so much accomplishment as endurance and to envy not so much achievement as persistence. Pathos and "affluence" to the contrary, blue-collarites today in America are *not* especially well off. Many know this and vaguely sense that somehow things ought to "feel" better. How to make things better eludes almost all of them.

The second major question with which this study has been concerned asks, Is the life style of stable blue-collarites an adequate answer to the plight of the nation's poor?

Hardly. There are many circumstances already shared by steadily employed workers and the poor that plague both groups. For example, with respect to the less-educated, less-well-off blue-collarites and to large numbers of the poor, estranged relations between the sexes and generations, pervasive alienation from the political process, and debilitating health attitudes and practices are typical of many shared characteristics.

Nor do the poor, contrary to popular impression, have many lessons to learn from blue-collarites in the assimilation of conventional social and material goals. A large majority of the poor already rival blue-collarites in their hunger for education, for consumer goods, and for gainful employment. Many of the poor want high school diplomas for their youngsters, want what the commercials tell them they should have, and want paychecks instead of welfare checks. They have these goals without any special reference to the stable working class immediately above them in the social scale, but because such goals are powerfully encouraged by the culture that includes them.

Indeed, it might be revealing to reverse the study's original question: What do the poor have for the more prosperous workers? It has been argued, persuasively, that there are elements of the life style of the poor, particularly that of the independent-minded, leisure-loving, preindustrial Hill poor, that effectively speak to the many-faceted plight of the nation's blue-collar class.[3]

The third question with which this book has been concerned asks, Is the American manual worker in fact disappearing as a separate and distinct social, psychological, and political entity?[4]

Probably not. At least with respect to the male Caucasian blue-collarite little support can be found for the notion of the "homogenization" of American life. The argument that most workers, especially better-educated, better-off skilled blue-collarites, are willfully disappearing into the lower echelons of the white-collar or middle-class mass is not borne out by the available evidence. Indeed, little support can be found for the "class-centric" notion that all or even most of such mobile people want to become middle-class or are eager to assume the signs of membership in that group.[5]

The life of many blue-collar suburbanites suggests just the opposite. Their families, and the families of many others still in the cities, retain their working-class mode of life. Raised in the blue-collar style, and reinforced in their class history and style by ethnic, religious, occupational, and social communalism, these adult blue-collarites remain a distinct and highly predictable working-class type. Impressed with a generally prevalent equalitarian ideology ("I'm just as good as anyone else"), these workers carry blue-collar values with them wherever they go, virtually intact, without any substantial modification or transformation.

The contemporary blue-collarite, conformist in the extreme, models himself carefully on his own class peers. He does not especially do the bidding of Hollywood, BBD&O, or CBS. Rather, he selectively screens and uses mass media fare to bolster his own inimical and intransigent style. And his new affluence has not lured him into a new overidentity as a zealous consumer, indistinguishable at a bargain counter from the lower middle-class white-collarite beside him. Outside of the marketplace there is little evidence that longstanding social barriers are being broken down, or that blue-collarites and their families are being accepted as equals into status groups from which they were previously excluded.[6] Workers remain workers in large part because better-off Americans will not let them be anything else—outside of the marketplace.

It may be that the most controversial and sensitive issues of public life are no longer associated with symbols of class status and position. Private lives are something else again, however. Class continues to count, and blue-collarites fully understand this. Rising over all the confusion and superficiality of mass culture and mass society developments is this well-grounded proposition: The worker is likely to persist, even as at present, in his own particular class style of life.

POST-1969 POSSIBILITIES

The last of the major questions with which this book has been concerned asks, Is there anything that social planning and deliberate social change can contribute to the blue-collar pursuit of the "good life"?

Although many ideas are advanced below, it should be clear from the start that space severely limits this discussion. Accordingly, excluded from consideration are reform notions widely discussed elsewhere: These include plans for income redistribution (tax law changes, price and wage regulation, and so on), plans for income supplementation (family allowances, guaranteed annual income, and so on), and conventional proposals for increased public ownership and management of industry.[7] Instead, the reforms discussed below are chosen for their comparative freshness and their potential for stimulating new interest in blue-collar reforms:

1. Reforms should soon be addressed to a wide range of blue-collar family ills. Excess fertility, for example, might be sharply reduced if hospitals and labor unions initiated dynamic educational programs in family planning and child-spacing. Blue-collar wives might especially appreciate the establishment of a nationwide chain of public or low-cost private child-care centers. Such agencies could free mothers for other interests outside the household and offer counselling as well in child-rearing.

Husbands and wives could profit from the establishment of a nationwide chain of public or low-cost private marriage and family counselling clinics. Changes in the states' divorce laws are a long-standing problem, and would greatly benefit blue-collar families as well as others. These might rationalize alimony, minimize adverse relationships, and enlighten conditions of child-sharing. Such reforms would help many blue-collar spouses correct a "mistake" and prepare more realistically for a new phase in life. Finally, blue-collar youngsters (and others, to be sure) would profit considerably from regularly offered and ably manned courses in "Meeting Life Issues" focused upon personal relations, health aids, home economics, home repairs, the "facts of life," and so on.

2. Reforms are in order with respect to the inadequacy of the blue-collar worker's educational attainment and the persistent inadequacy of schooling for his children.

Where blue-collar children are at issue, a relevant reform casts the problem in straightforward "capitalistic" terms: Thus educator Christopher Jencks recommends (as have other commentators) that all families receive federal subsidization of the tuition required at new public-turned-private schools. The ensuing quality competition among now-profit-making (and federally regulated) schools should finally make attainable the nation's best education for blue-collar offspring—which would be, of course, an unprecedented development.[8]

For blue-collar adolescents, sociologist Edgar Z. Friedenberg urges that the government sponsor a national network of boarding schools. Serving as an alternative to continued residence at home, these residential schools would maintain superior educational standards.[9] A more elastic proposal is Paul Goodman's recommendation of the subsidization of attractive alternatives to high-school, or to the lock-step advance from high school into college, or to college itself. These alternatives might take the form of an enlarged VISTA and Peace Corps program, national and world travel, time spent exclusively in the study of a favorite subject, or the like. Blue-collar youngsters, although they might be initially confused by such options, could especially profit from the moratorium involved.[10]

Blue-collar men could garner new strength from an expansion of the GI Bill. One of the most imaginative social investments ever made in the United States, this act could be revised so that in peacetime anyone with talent could be paid to develop it.[11] Even as many business executives now return periodically to Graduate Business Schools for "retooling," so might blue-collar men be publicly subsidized to seek refresher education of their own preference.[12]

3. Reforms should grapple with the workingman's sense of powerlessness in confrontation with anonymous and authoritarian bureaucracies. Pertinent here is Michael Harrington's call for a National Bureaucratic Relations Act similar to the National Labor Relations Act of the thirties.[13] Such an act could insure blue-collarites (and others) of independent appeals from bureaucratic decisions, both public and private. These could range from appeals concerning the cancellation of one's auto insurance without any stated reason to the tragedy of having a private security check destroy a defense-related factory career.

In a reform setting administrators could be required to make a clear, open statement of the reasons for any ruling. Taking off from the independent Review Boards initiated in the late 1950s by the Auto, Upholsterers, and other labor unions, the public review boards could significantly help to reduce blue-collar bewilderment and impotence induced by the giant bureaucracies.

4. Reforms should be addressed to the workingman's loss of the meaning of work. Increasingly technology undermines the conviction that it is through his labor that a man establishes his identity and his relationships both to his neighbor and to God. Large numbers of blue-collarites might profitably discover a new meaning in work as part of an unprecedented paraprofessional labor force. Reforms might usefully be directed to opening up several million new jobs for ex-blue-collarites as research assistants, teacher aides, social-work aides, and other service-oriented occupations.[14]

5. Reforms must soon be aimed at impediments to the professional care of blue-collarites. In mental health matters, for example, treatment as presently organized is not congenial to blue-collar clients, is not congruent with their traditions and expectations, and is poorly understood by them.

Reforms already underway merit considerable expansion: These include more use of walk-in clinics, day hospitals, and pills and needles. Reforms could profitably reach back even earlier in the treatment process and include special courses in professional training schools encouraging sensitivity and respect concerning different styles of life. Much as in the case of blue-collar relations to bureaucracies, the time is long past for restoration of humane and informed relationships between blue-collar clients and middle-class professionals.

6. Finally, reforms should boldly challenge institutional developments that have unexpected drawbacks for blue-collarites. Unexamined policy in physical medicine, for example, increasingly makes both doctors and patients dependent on hospitalization—the insured patient, in order to pay his bills, the doctor, in order to collect his fee. This unchallenged development frightens blue-collarites away from preventive care and checkups, even as it obstructs promotion of more economical, rational, and humane outpatient, home, and nursing services.[15]

Unexamined policy in work location is costly—and readily reformed. Sociologist Daniel Bell, for example, recommends that factories be redesigned so that mammoth plants could be broken into smaller units and moved closer to workers who would thereby commute less. Employers, Bell points out, now disregard the cost of travel time of the worker and the costs of roads and other transport to the factory site, which are paid for by the employee or by the community as a whole from taxes. But the time of life of men is irretrievably consumed in commutation, while the time of life of a piece of metal in transit between small production plants is not. Processed materials could be brought from several different small plants to a special plant for assembly. It might be less expensive to transport materials and mechanical parts twice a week than to cause large masses to commute twice daily to and from a common place of work. Less expensive, that is, when the calculation is carried beyond the narrow matter of strict market costs to include freeway costs, mass transit system costs, air pollution costs, and, above all, human time and effort.[16]

Unexamined policy in technological developments may increasingly result in reduced numbers of workers confronting ever-less-demanding tasks. This little-challenged alteration in job content erases valuable skill distinctions among blue-collarites. It may yet shape its own bland, craft-less, and inter-changeable mass of white-jacketed manual workers. Such men will not simply adjust or fail to adjust to their work, but like blue-collarites everywhere they will ingest the world to which they direct themselves: They will be deeply and continuously changed by their work.

Daniel Bell advises in this connection that "no question about satisfaction is meaningful unless the worker is aware of alternative possibilities of work." [17] Accordingly, labor unions might begin to examine the work process on behalf of their constituency in an entirely new light: Paul Jacobs asks—

> Does the auto workers' union have to accept, as an absolute truth, that the best way to build cars is with the assembly line? Are the new, highly automated, packinghouse plants the only way meat should be brought to the consumer? Obviously it's the best way yet devised for the employers, but why shouldn't unions make the work process itself a subject for study and bargaining in a far more intensive way than they do now, even to the point of proposing and insisting on radical changes? [18]

Reforms in this area might also revolve about the effort to restore more of the entire job to single workers. Field tests suggest that the significant return possible in such programs in terms of morale, efficiency, and safety make up for loss experienced in unit turnout.[19] In any case, reforms should soon assay the breadth and depth of automation and do more than at present to help men prepare for challenges to craft.

Finally, unexamined institutional drift creates a similar situation for organized labor. The progressive vision in union affairs is a corporate one, a response to institutional inefficiency and waste, not to personal inhumanity and demoralization. Unions are affluent but anomic, powerful but poor in spirit, prestigious but taken for granted.

Union reforms might be modeled on the many "demonstration projects" already proven out by the more progressive locals in the more progressive unions. The related use of militant personal unionism in the ranks of teachers, agricultural field hands, and state and municipal employees also are promising.[20] Professionals have a reform agenda of their own:

> Let every liberal lawyer who makes his living out of the labor movement devote his services free to one (only one) insurgent group fighting against corruption. Let every civil-liberties institution seriously and publicly take up one (just one) important case of union democracy. Let every labor writer compose one article (paid or unpaid) out of every dozen to tell the story of union reformers. Let the idea man, the public-relations expert assume the duty of aiding and advising (incognito, perhaps) just one democratic opposition movement. How quickly the inner mood of unionism would change! If they will not do it out of idealism, let it be out of simple charity. If the liberal intellectual cannot share a genuine solidarity with the rank-and-file reformer, let there be *noblesse oblige.* "Not Marxism but philanthropy" could be the watchword of our day.[21]

Rank-and-filers who recently dethroned David McDonald in Steel, James Carey in Electronics, and O. A. Knight in Chemicals called with their election ballots for a "new unionism"; their call should be heeded.

THE CASE FOR REFORM

It remains now to reflect on these matters: Is there any evidence of blue-collar interest in reform? Do the six kinds of reforms proposed really meet the problems exposed? And, if happiness and maturity everywhere elude vast numbers of men, is there really anything with which to encourage curious blue-collarites?

1. To begin with, there is evidence of considerable blue-collar unrest with the status quo. (Contract rejection rates, job quit rates, and days idle due to strikes are now all far above previously top 1959 levels.) Workplace unrest may be associated with a revealing preference for particular workplace reforms: Men appear to want their dignity enhanced, and pursue

nonfinancial humanistic job changes with earnest conviction. Some blue-collarites also participate in novel humanistic ventures previously outside the blue-collar experience—these include weekend college retreats for shop stewards, sabbatical vacations for plant workers, and residence in blue-collar retirement villages.[22] Overall, then, there appears to be limited, but undeniable—and possibly even growing—evidence of blue-collar reform venturesomeness.

2. The argument that the reforms advocated are insufficient rests on a set of assumptions about means and ends. It may be contended that the six kinds of reforms advocated are only superficial means, gimmicks likely to produce only momentary results, shortcuts that fail to reach deep-seated sociological and psychological roots. In response, however, one can point to the need to consider multifactor models and probabilities. No one reform will solve all the workers' problems, but each additional reform may lead in that direction. Also relevant is the fact that Americans are unlikely soon to transform the basic conditions that underlie blue-collar problems. As Amitai Etzioni points out: "Often our society seems to be 'choosing' not between symptomatic (superficial) treatment and 'cause' (full treatment), but between treatment of symptoms and no treatment at all." [23]

It may also be contended that the reforms serve unworthy ends. Put in overly simplistic terms, when advanced from the conventional or Marxist political left this argument assumes the primacy of replacing the capitalist order with the dictatorship of the proletariat, the eventual withering away of the state, and beyond that, the achievement of humanistic communism. When advanced from the conventional political right the argument assumes the primacy of replacing the capitalist order with the dictatorship of the individual, the cooptation of the state, and eventually, the achievement of autonomous individualism. When advanced from the extreme new left the argument assumes the primacy of built-in contradictions in industrial societies (capitalistic *or* socialist), the utter hopelessness of liberal reform efforts, and the inevitable betrayal of revolution and the rout of reason.

In contrast, the six kinds of reforms previously advocated rest on very different assumptions: The working class is considered to be a class like any other. If it is hardly predestined to dominate the future, its members are also unlikely to soon lose their predilection to share common life experiences and hold similar attitudes and values. The political state is expected to grow ever more influential. If it is unlikely to soon wither away, it is likely to continue to reward disproportionately blue-collarites (as with welfare legislation), and may even soon provide all citizens with a greater sense of participation in and control of the political process. Class conflict will persist, but it will be increasingly institutionalized and muted. "Revolutions," if unlikely to meet contemporary social needs in meaningful and substantial ways, will nevertheless build on one another and encourage the peculiarly American faith that still better solutions will be forthcoming for our dislocations and discontents.[24]

3. Finally, some people may be persuaded that since happiness seems to elude all or most Americans there is no reason to assist any special reform effort by workers as such. That is, since "alienation," "anomie," and "disenchantment" are alleged to characterize the more affluent areas, there is nothing to hold out to reform-curious blue-collarites. This, however, is to beg the question: Even widespread social disorganization would not reduce by a unit the independent case that can be made for the relief of blue-collar anguish. Establishment of a state of general anxiety makes the case for response all the stronger; it is symptomatic of the insidiousness of such anxiety that reformers might think otherwise.[25]

In other words, there very well may be, for example, considerable "hidden" alcoholism in affluent suburbs, and it may be linked to general social ills that lie in wait to trap the blue-collar climber. All the more reason to better equip him for the climb—or help him choose another destination, help him join with sometimes-sober suburbanites in redoing the entire scene. There *are* dreams other than nightmares.[26]

SUMMARY

An overview is advanced in this final chapter of a particular theory, or interpretation of evidence: This theory maintains that more than wrists may be tapped today at work, and more than wishes and dreams may elude the blue-collarite after work. Linked to this is a conception of reform that suggests that the larger social context determines which aspects of blue-collar culture come to the fore. This larger context should be the major target of our reform efforts.

Notes to Chapter Fifteen

---

1. See in this connection, "The Mayor of Gary," in Carl Sandburg, *Smoke and Steel* (New York: Harcourt, Brace, 1921), p. 25; and "Mill Doors" and "Halsted Street Car," in Carl Sandburg, *Chicago Poems* (New York: Holt, 1916), pp. 10–11. Reprinted by permission of Harcourt, Brace & World and Holt, Rinehart and Winston, Inc.

2. On the progress blue-collarites have made over the situation of their parents, see Herbert J. Gans, *The Levittowners: Ways of Life and Politics in a New Suburban Community* (New York: Pantheon Books, 1967), p. 195, *passim*. See also Herbert J. Gans, "Diversity Is Not Dead: A Report on Our Widening Range of Choice," *New Republic* (April 3, 1961), pp. 11–15.

3. For related discussion of the idea that "perhaps the mountaineer will be more ready to enter the cybernetic age (in one leap from the agrarian age) than those who are deeply enmeshed in the industrial age," see Jack E. Weller, *Yesterday's People: Life in Contemporary Appalachia* (Lexington: University of Kentucky Press, 1965), pp. 134–160, *passim*.

4. The homogenization thesis is most carefully developed in Kurt Mayer, *Class and Society* (New York: Random House, 1955), pp. 41–42, *passim*. See also Harold L. Wilensky, "Class, Class Consciousness, and American Workers," in William Haber (ed.), *Labor in a Changing America* (New York: Basic Books, 1966), pp. 12–44; John Brooks, "Mr. White and Mr. Blue: Notes on the New Middle Class," *Harper's* (June 1966), pp. 88–97; *How American*

Buying Habits Change, Department of Labor (Washington, D.C.: Government Printing Office, 1955), p. 6, *passim.*

5. The homogenization thesis is sharply criticized in Norval D. Glenn and Jon P. Alston, "The Cultural Distance Among Occupational Categories," *American Sociological Review* (forthcoming); Richard Hamilton, "The Behavior and Values of Skilled Workers," in A. Shostak and W. Gomberg (eds.), *Blue-Collar World* (Englewood Cliffs, N.J.: Prentice-Hall, 1964), pp. 42–57; W. Lloyd Warner, *American Life: Dream and Reality* (Chicago: University of Chicago Press, 1962); S. M. Miller and Frank Riessman, "Are Workers Middle Class?," *Dissent* (Autumn 1961), pp. 507–513, 516.

6. See in this connection, John H. Goldthorpe and David Lockwood, "Affluence and the British Class Structure," *The Sociological Review* (July 1963), pp. 133–156; see also Mark Lefton, "The Blue Collar Worker and the Middle Class Ethic," *Sociology and Social Research* (January 1967), pp. 158–169; Ralf Dahrendorf, *Class and Class Conflict in an Industrial Society* (London: Routledge, 1959).

7. For accounts of efforts by social scientists to affect public affairs, see A. Shostak (ed.), *Sociology in Action* (Homewood, Ill.: Dorsey, 1966). Cf. Lewis A. Coser, "Social Involvement or Scientific Detachment—the Sociologist's Dilemma," *Antioch Review* (Spring 1968), pp. 108–116.

8. Christopher Jencks, "The Future of American Education," in Irving Howe (ed.), *The Radical Papers* (Garden City, N.Y.: Doubleday, 1966), pp. 282–285.

9. Edgar Z. Friedenberg, *Coming of Age in America* (New York: Random House, 1965), pp. 244–266, *passim.* See also Theodore Sizer and Philip Whitten, "A Proposal for a Poor Children's Bill of Rights," *Psychology Today* (August 1968), pp. 59–63.

10. Paul Goodman, *Growing Up Absurd: Problems of Youth in the Organized System* (New York: Random House, 1960).

11. Michael Harrington, *Toward a Democratic Left: A Radical Program for a New Majority* (New York: Macmillan, 1968), pp. 160–162.

12. Jack London and Robert Wenkert, "Obstacles to Blue-Collar Participation in Adult Education," in A. Shostak and W. Gomberg (eds.), *Blue-Collar World* (Englewood Cliffs, N.J.: Prentice-Hall, 1964), pp. 445–458.

13. Michael Harrington, *op. cit.,* p. 147, *passim.* See also Alex Carey, "The Hawthorne Studies: A Radical Criticism," *American Sociological Review* (June 1967), pp. 403–416.

14. Useful in this connection is Frank Riessman and Hermine I. Popper, *Up from Poverty* (New York: Harper & Row, 1968); Arthur Pearl and Frank Riessman (eds.), *New Careers for the Poor: The Non-Professional in Human Service* (New York: Free Press, 1965).

15. For discussion, see Elinor Langer, "The Shame of American Medicine," *The New York Review of Books* (May 26, 1966), pp. 6–12.

16. Daniel Bell, *Work and Its Discontents: The Cult of Efficiency in America* (Boston: Beacon, 1965).

17. Daniel Bell, *The End of Ideology* (New York: Collier, 1960), p. 249. See also Dennis Clark, *Work and the Human Spirit* (New York: Sheed and Ward, 1967).

18. Paul Jacobs, "What Can We Expect from the Unions?" in Howe (ed.), *op. cit.*, p. 259. See also Anon., "Motorola Scrubs the Hourly Worker," *Business Week* (October 26, 1968), pp. 58–59.

19. Chris Agyris, *Integrating the Individual and the Organization* (New York: Wiley, 1964), p. 205, *passim*. See also Abraham H. Maslow, *Eupsychian Management* (Homewood, Ill.: Dorsey, 1965); Paul Goodman, *People or Personnel: Decentralizing and the Mixed System* (New York: Random House, 1965); Lee Berton, "Permissive Plants," *Wall Street Journal*, March 14, 1966, pp. 1, 10.

20. On potential union reforms see André Gorz, *Strategy for Labor: A Radical Proposal* (Boston: Beacon, 1968); Eugene Nelson, Jr., "Huelga: New Goals for Labor," *The Nation* (June 5, 1967), pp. 724–725; Bernard Rosenberg, "The UAW: An Aura of Hope," *Dissent* (July–August 1967), pp. 390–397; Ben B. Seligman, *Most Notorious Victory: Man in an Age of Automation* (New York: Free Press, 1966); Alice Cook, *Union Democracy: Practice and Ideal* (Ithaca: Cornell University Press, 1963); cf. Lewis A. Coser, "Labor Pains," *Commentary* (June 1967), pp. 91–92; Harvey Swados, "The UAW—Over the Top or Over the Hill," *Dissent* (Autumn 1963), pp. 320–343.

21. H. W. Benson, "Intellectuals and the Lonely Union Reformer," *Union Democracy in Action* (New York: H. W. Benson, newsletter, May 1960), p. 3. See also Eleanor Leacock, "Distortions of Working Class Reality in American Social Science," unpublished paper read at the First Annual Socialist Scholars Conference, Columbia University, September 11, 1965 (Brooklyn Polytechnic Institute); Alan Adelson, "Student Radicals Seek Workers' Cooperation in Fighting the System," *Wall Street Journal*, July 16, 1969, pp. 1, 13.

22. For an exciting account of a unique effort in workers' education, see Austin J. Staley, *et al.*, "Exploration and Conjecture," *Human Potential* (1967), pp. 31–34. See also Anon., "Where Workers Help Make Top Decisions," *Business Week* (July 27, 1968), pp. 78–80; Anon., "Steel Men Thrive on Sabbaticals," *Business Week* (November 26, 1966), pp. 166–168.

23. Amitai Etzioni, " 'Shortcuts' to Social Change," *The Public Interest* (Summer 1968), p. 48, *passim*.

24. Of relevance here is John Kenneth Galbraith, *The New Industrial State* (Boston: Houghton Mifflin, 1967); David T. Bazelon, *Power in America: The Politics of the New Class* (New York: New American Library, 1967). For a critique of some of this writer's assumptions, see Dusky Lee Smith, "The Sunshine Boys: Toward a Sociology of Happiness," *The Activist* (Spring 1964), pp. 166–177, 200.

25. On the case for reform, see Lewis Mumford, *The Myth of the Machine* (New York: Harcourt, Brace & World, 1968); Robert L. Heilbroner, *The Limits of American Capitalism* (New York: Harper & Row, 1967); Richard Lichtman, *Toward Community: A Criticism of Contemporary Capitalism* (Santa Barbara, Calif.: Center for the Study of Democratic Institutions, 1966); Paul A. Baran and Paul M. Sweezy, *Monopoly Capital* (New York: Monthly Review Press, 1966); Herbert Marcuse, *One-Dimensional Man* (Boston: Beacon Press, 1964); Alex Inkeles, "Industrial Man: The Relation of Status to Experience, Perception, and Value," *American Journal of Sociology* (July 1960), pp. 1–31. Cf. Seymour M. Lipset, *Political Man* (Garden City, N.Y.: Doubleday, 1960), pp. 404–406.

26. On possible blue-collar contributions to a New Society, see Raymond Williams, *Culture and Society* (New York: Columbia University Press, 1958). Cf. Irving Howe, "A Bit Too Wholesome," *The Nation* (February 9, 1959), pp. 23–24; Mark R. Arnold, "Why the Workingman Is Bewildered: Taxes, Inflation, Negroes," *National Observer* (May 12, 1969), pp. 1, 10. On specific blue-collar reforms see Dennis Duggan, "Still Forgotten: The Working Poor," *The Nation* (June 9, 1969), pp. 724–726; Louise Kapp, (ed.), "The Other Other America: The White Working Class," *New Generation* (Spring 1969).

EPILOGUE

Understanding the plight and prospects of the American working class may help us get along with the too-long-deferred business of finding out just where we are in America. In the case of the working class the very techniques and structures of affluence and "progress" that men have created to control the environment seem to have themselves shaped an environment we now inadequately control.

As I see it, America's working class is one that fears to dare, figures small angles incompetently, and makes the least-best of its life-enhancing possibilities. Blue-collarites, or the Americans whose voices Walt Whitman heard singing, the sons of the Oakies that John Steinbeck and Woody Guthrie wrote of, the descendants of John Dos Passos' *U.S.A.*, and the masses exalted by intellectuals in the 1930s (and forgotten since), are very much in trouble. Their plight, however, is hardly unique, and resembles nothing so much as a national epidemic or fate: Too much at present has too many members of the working class making too little of their lives.

We can help change this situation—if we dare. Or we can continue to run the very real risk of soon sharing all the more in it. The price of procrastination, and thereby of increasing participation, comes exceedingly high: The greatest anomaly in nature, as the book's opening epigram suggests, is probably a human spirit that cannot soar.

Here, as in so many related matters, the hour grows late.

INDEX